AF473746

Las Vegas Studio

Images from the Archives of Robert Venturi and Denise Scott Brown

Edited by Hilar Stadler and Martino Stierli
in collaboration with Peter Fischli

Museum im Bellpark, Kriens
Scheidegger & Spiess

A project of the Museum im Bellpark, Kriens
www.bellpark.ch

Published by Verlag Scheidegger & Spiess AG, Zurich
www.scheidegger-spiess.ch

Editors	Hilar Stadler, Martino Stierli
Project idea	Gerold Kunz, Hilar Stadler
Photo selection	Peter Fischli, Hilar Stadler, Martino Stierli
Editing	Thomas Kramer, Hilar Stadler, Martino Stierli
Authors	Martino Stierli, Stanislaus von Moos
Conversation	Peter Fischli, Rem Koolhaas, Hans Ulrich Obrist
Copy editing	Nadine Olonetzky, Thomas Kramer, Lisa Rosenblatt
Transcription conversation	Daniela Janser
Design	Norm, Zurich
Typeface	Replica-Regular, www.lineto.com
Image editing and lithography	Tricolor, Zurich DZA Druckerei zu Altenburg GmbH, Thüringen
Printed and bound by	DZA Druckerei zu Altenburg GmbH, Thüringen

The original German and English editions were published by Verlag Scheidegger & Spiess AG, Zurich, in 2008.

For further information, see the photo credits on p. 190

English edition ISBN 978-3-85881-764-8
French edition ISBN 978-3-85881-765-5

The project has been supported by
Stanley Thomas Johnson Foundation
Stiftung Otto Pfeifer
Ernst and Olga Gubler-Hablützel Foundation
Grand Casino Luzern AG
Gemeinde Kriens

Thanks to:
Robert Venturi and Denise Scott Brown, Philadelphia
John Izenour, Mount Desert, ME
Jim Venturi, New York
Bret Taboada, New York
William Whitaker, Architectural Archives, University of Pennsylvania
Stanislaus von Moos, Zurich
Peter Fischli, Zurich
Rem Koolhaas, Rotterdam
Hans Ulrich Obrist, London
Pietro Mattioli, Zurich
Oliver Elser, Deutsches Architekturmuseum, Frankfurt a. M.
Gerold Kunz, Ebikon
Thomas Kramer, Verlag Scheidegger & Spiess, Zurich
Nadine Olonetzky, Verlag Scheidegger & Spiess, Zurich
Ronny Ochsner, Tricolor, Zurich

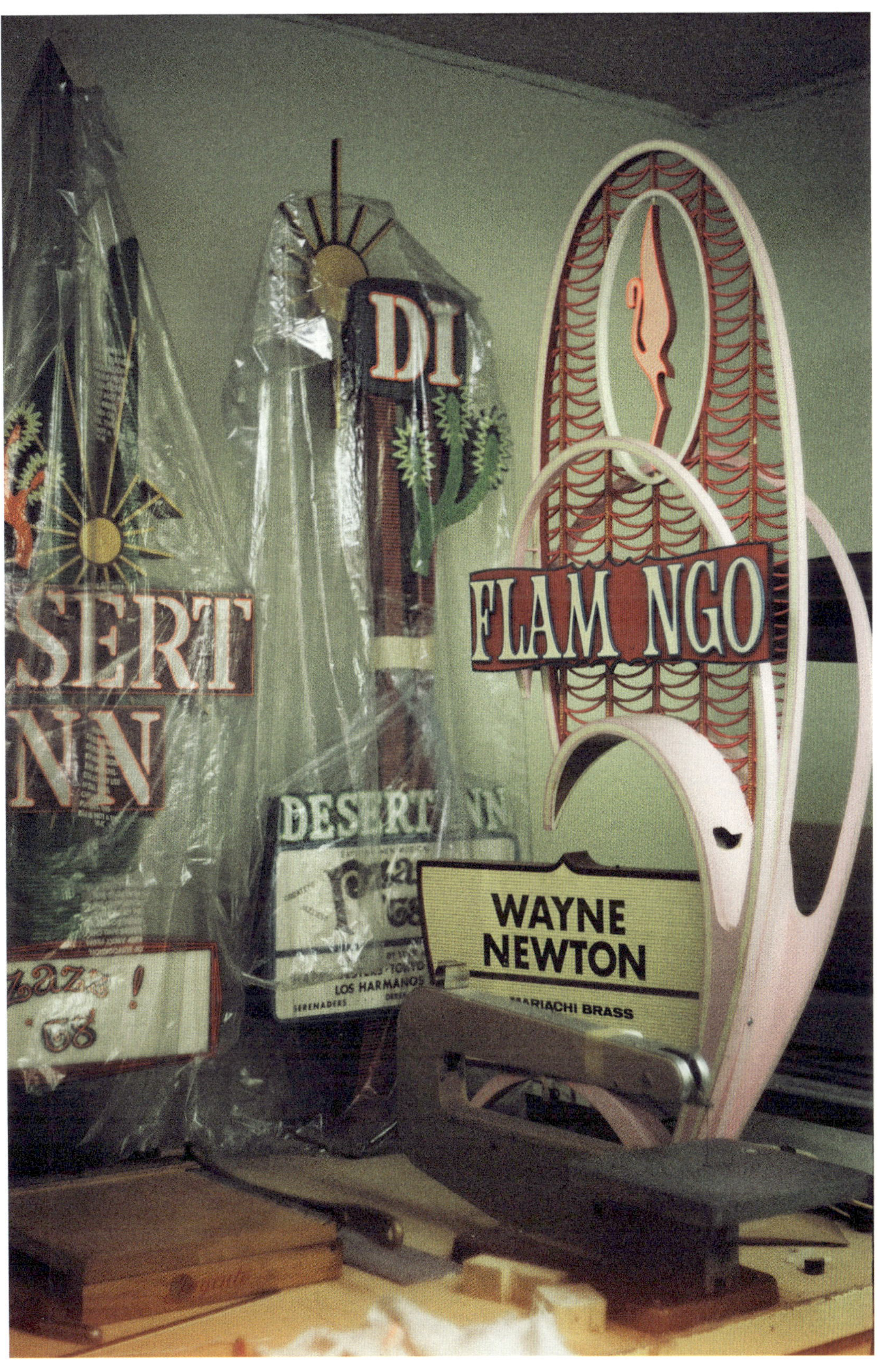
DI
SERT
NN
DESERT INN
FLAM NGO
WAYNE
NEWTON
MARIACHI BRASS
LOS HARMANOS
SERENADERS

Table of Contents

Second Reading

Learning from Las Vegas, a treatise on architectural theory published in 1972, captivates primarily through its engaging visual discourse. For Robert Venturi, Denise Scott Brown, and Steven Izenour, the photographic trace is both the means of argumentation and representation of their research object. If the breaking of taboos is repeatedly mentioned in connection with *Learning from Las Vegas,* the use of photography, borrowed from anthropology and art, can be seen as part of this provocation. Colleagues who understood architecture as a task developed out of structure reacted with surprise and disapproval when the protagonists of the Las Vegas research studio picked up cameras and treated architecture from the perspective of appearance and phenomenon.

The editors' overriding interest in the images from the Las Vegas studio is founded on this reading. We have taken on the task of rereading and reappraising these photographs. Our focus is therefore directed at the instrument that demonstrates Venturi's and Scott Brown's intentions picture for picture, namely to arrive at a theory of architectural communication. However, by being instrumentalized in such terms, these images increasingly lost their original, pictorial significance. For Venturi and Scott Brown, the photographs were primarily a means to an end. Our project returns to a point before theory formation, and refers directly to the photographic material, which impresses with an enchanting, careless beauty.

The photographs from the Las Vegas research are part of the archives of Venturi, Scott Brown & Associates in Philadelphia. Robert Venturi and Denise Scott Brown opened up their archives for our project and gave us comprehensive access. The opportunity to gain insight into this collection of slides was a particularly memorable event. Based on an overview, we arrived at a selection—in collaboration with Peter Fischli—presented for the first time in this book.

Our approach to the material is motivated primarily by an interest in the image. The genuinely pictorial, the photographic quality, provided a decisive guide in our reading. We removed the pictures from their original analytical context and present them as photographic sensations. The photographs were taken by various participants in the Las Vegas Studio. The pictures from 1966 can be attributed, for the most part, to Denise Scott Brown, but current knowledge of the authorship of the later images is fragmentary. However, Robert Venturi, Denise Scott Brown, and Steven Izenour gave the instructions and guidelines for taking the photographs. For this reason, we would like to attribute conceptual authorship to those responsible at the Las Vegas Studio.

Our selection focuses largely on secondary aspects and side products of the research project, without losing sight of the iconic images. It thereby shifts to the forefront previously unknown images that settled on the fringes of the Las Vegas research. We believe that the true interest in Venturi's and Scott Brown's approach to Las Vegas becomes clear precisely in these "unconscious" moments. These photographs thereby make their authors, in the sense of Rem Koolhaas, the ghost writers of Las Vegas whom we know and appreciate today.

We sincerely thank Robert Venturi and Denise Scott Brown for their trust and support. It is only due to them that we could make this project possible. We also thank Stanislaus von Moos for generously offering his guidance to the project from the start. We had the pleasure of selecting the images together with Peter Fischli whom we thank for the fascinating and stimulating collaboration. Our thanks also go to Rem Koolhaas and Hans Ulrich Obrist who carried out a highly personal reading of several of the photographs in the context of a conversation with Peter Fischli. Through this, some aspects that had not been thought of before have opened up. In addition, we thank John Izenour for handling the project as well as William Whitaker from the Architectural Archives of the University of Pennsylvania for loaning crucial original objects.

The project was organized and managed by the Museum im Bellpark. Verlag Scheidegger & Spiess, Zurich is responsible for the publication. We thank Thomas Kramer, Publishing Director, for his dedicated cooperation. We are very grateful to Dimitri Bruni, Manuel Krebs, and Ludovic Varone from Norm in Zurich for their inspired visual translation of our ideas. Various institutions and committees kindly supported the project with generous contributions.

Hilar Stadler, Museum im Bellpark, Kriens
Martino Stierli

Las Vegas Studio

Martino Stierli

1) The present essay is based on Martino Stierli's book *Las Vegas im Rückspiegel. Die Stadt in Theorie, Fotografie und Film,* Zurich, gta Verlag, 2010 (American edition: *Las Vegas in the Rearview Mirror. The City in Theory, Photography, and Film,* Los Angeles, Getty Research Institute, 2013).

2) Denise Scott Brown, "Learning from Pop" (1971), in Robert Venturi and Denise Scott Brown, *The View from the Campidoglio: Selected Essays, 1953–1984* (New York: Harper & Row, 1984), pp. 26–33, here pp. 28–31.

3) Cf. Diane L. Minnite, "Chronology," in David B. Brownlee, David G. De Long, and Kathryn B. Hiesinger, *Out of the Ordinary: Robert Venturi, Denise Scott Brown and Associates. Architecture, Urbanism, Design* (Philadelphia: Philadelphia Museum of Art, 2001), pp. 244–51, here p. 247.

4) See Robert Venturi and Denise Scott Brown, "A Significance for A&P Parking Lots or Learning from Las Vegas," *Architectural Forum* 128 (March 1968), no. 2, pp. 36–43, 89, 91; Robert Venturi, Denise Scott Brown and Steven Izenour, *Learning from Las Vegas* (Cambridge, MA: MIT Press, 1972).

5) The students involved were: Ralph Carlson, Tony Farmer, Ron Filson, Glen Hodges, Peter Hoyt, Charles Korn, John Kranz, Peter Schlaifer, Peter Schmitt, Dan Scully, Doug Southworth, Martha Wagner, and Tony Zunino.

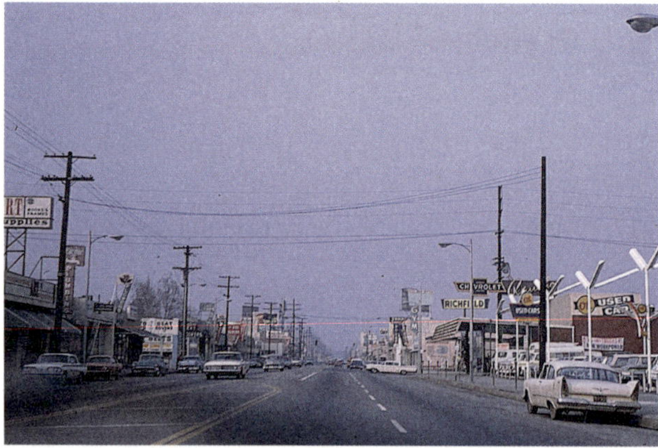

A)

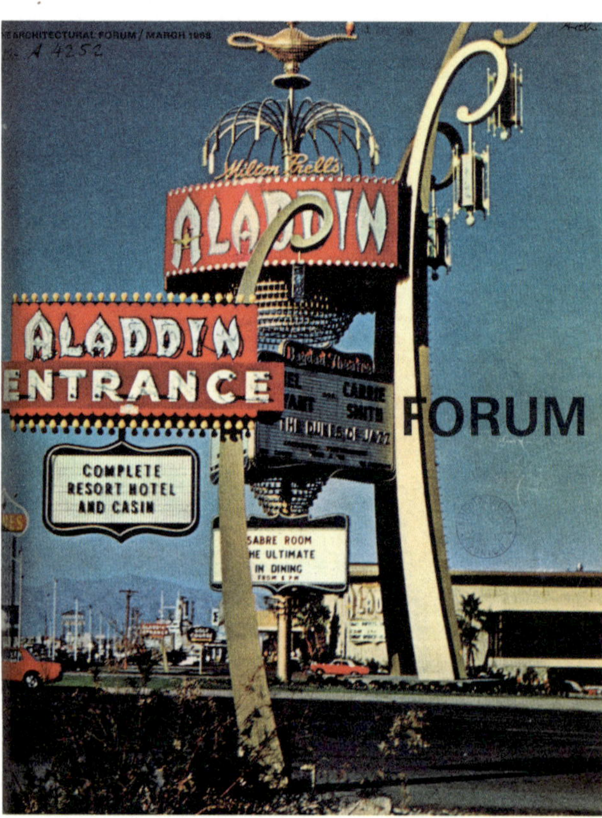

B)

A) Denise Scott Brown: Los Angeles roadscape, ca. 1966

B) Title page of the journal *Architectural Forum,* March 1968, with a photograph by Denise Scott Brown

Robert Venturi, Denise Scott Brown and the Image of the City

Learning from Las Vegas was both a serious urbanistic study and a rhetorical thunderbolt. The book presented its authors' unease with contemporary architectural discourse in a form that had both visual and verbal power.[1] Since its publication in 1972, hardly any other text has succeeded in monopolizing architectural discourse to the same extent—with the possible exception of *S, M, L, XL* by Rem Koolhaas and Bruce Mau (1995). The study tapped the nerve of the age in seeking answers to problems that had been preoccupying architecture and urbanism for a considerable time. What was at debate was the form and the aesthetics of the contemporary city. Architects and theoreticians regarded the increasing decentralization and suburbanization of the city with perplexity and disapproval. Such phenomena were seen not only as a crisis in the function, but also in the image of the city and were matters of controversy. A fundamental question in urbanistic discourse around 1960 was therefore, what was the image of the contemporary city? How could the sprawling cities still be conceived as coherent units and how could they be displayed visually? In their research on Las Vegas, which started in the mid-1960s and eventually led to the publication of their famous book, Robert Venturi and Denise Scott Brown attempted to find answers to these questions. Their interest focused on the commercial Las Vegas Strip, as they regarded it as representing the aesthetics of urban sprawl in its purest and most extreme form. They approached the object of their study in an ambivalent way—from both an analytical and an aesthetic point of view. On the one hand, they were concerned with documenting the specific visual characteristics of this urban form comprehensively and accurately. On the other, the spectacular aesthetics of the Strip's (sign) architecture unmistakably held an immense fascination for them. In their research project, Venturi and Scott Brown relied primarily on the popular visual media of photography and film. Even before the book, a number of publications had taken advantage of these relatively new media in order to represent cities. Venturi and Scott Brown for the first time used them consistently to achieve a comprehensive stocktaking of a city in the context of a study in architectural theory. "New analytic techniques," Denise Scott Brown wrote in this context, "must use film and videotape to convey the dynamism of sign architecture and the sequential experience of vast landscapes."[2]

Venturi and Scott Brown in Las Vegas: A chronology of events

The main impulse to carry out a detailed analysis of Las Vegas came from Denise Scott Brown. Born and raised in southern Africa, this architect and urban planner studied at the Architectural Association's School of Architecture in London. She moved to Philadelphia with her first husband, Robert Scott Brown, initially in order to study with the American architect Louis Kahn. Soon, however, she was teaching at the University of Philadelphia herself. It was there, as a young widow, that she met Robert Venturi during a faculty meeting in 1960.[3] In 1965, Scott Brown left for the West Coast to teach at the University of California and to study the automobile cities of the American Southwest [A].

In addition to the function and aesthetics of the Los Angeles roadscape, her interest turned to Las Vegas, to the Strip in particular, where a large number of casinos, hotels, and other places of entertainment had been developing since the early 1940s. While residing in Los Angeles, Scott Brown could easily visit the nearby entertainment city. The earliest documents on Las Vegas preserved in her personal slide archive date from April 1965. During the following year, she invited her colleague Venturi to take part in their first joint exploration of the desert city, which took place in November 1966. The journey proved to be seminal in two ways. On the one hand, it led to an essay that was published in the March 1968 issue of the journal *Architectural Forum,* which for the first time included the title of the later book: "A Significance for A&P Parking Lots, or Learning from Las Vegas."[B] The essay was illustrated with numerous photographs that Scott Brown had taken on site, and it anticipated much of the text of the book published in 1972.[4]

On the other hand, Venturi and Scott Brown's idea of elevating the Las Vegas Strip to an object of study in the framework of contemporary architectural education ultimately also originated during this trip, even though Scott Brown had previously considered teaching such a course during her tenure at the University of California at Los Angeles. They implemented their idea in a course given at Yale University in 1968. In this research studio, which was explicitly directed at architects, they were concerned with linking scientific and scholarly research with architectural design.[5] Scott Brown had adopted the idea of linking design to research from planning school and had already experimented informally with this format while teaching at the University of Pennsylvania in the early 1960s. In the context of the times, this was a highly innovative

6) Ralph Carlson, personal communication, May 2005.

7) Letter from Robert Venturi to Bruno Alfieri, 18 April 1969, VSB 505, "Out LLV," Architectural Archives, University of Pennsylvania and Pennsylvania Historical and Museum Commission.

8) See Robert Venturi, Denise Scott Brown, and Steven Izenour, "Studio LLV: Research Topics. Phase I, Tooling Up. Phase II, Library Research and Preparation," in Venturi et al., *Studio LLV: Learning from Las Vegas, or Form Analysis as Design Research, Third Year Studio* (New Haven: Yale University, Department of Architecture, 1968).

9) Ibid.

10) See note 7.

11) The films had the titles: *Fremont Electro-orgasmic* (by Peter Schlaifer), *Three Projector Dead Pan*, *Impulse Vision*, *Selected Vision*, *Sign Cycles*, and *Image* (by Peter Schlaifer), *Time Lapse* and *Three Projector Deadpan II*. See Robert Venturi, Denise Scott Brown, and Steven Izenour: "Final Presentation: Schedule," in Venturi et al. 1968 (see note 8).

12) Denise Scott Brown has pointed out that the specific use of imagery must also be seen in the context of advocacy planning, which was at its heyday at the time. According to her, this exhibition concept "too came from planning school and the stress on the need to produce graphic communication that could be seen and understood at a public meeting, and especially one attended by low-income people ... A major aim of the [Las Vegas] study was to understand and work with the diverse cultural values of those planned for in cities." Denise Scott Brown, personal communication, September 2008.

13) Letter from Robert Venturi to Vincent Scully, 16 January 1969, VSB 284, "Letters Jan–April 69," Architectural Archives, University of Pennsylvania and Pennsylvania Historical and Museum Commission.

14) See [Robert Venturi]: "A Significance for A and P Parking Lots or Learning from Las Vegas," in "Manuscript LV," Box VSB 27, Architectural Archives, University of Pennsylvania and Pennsylvania Historical and Museum Commission.

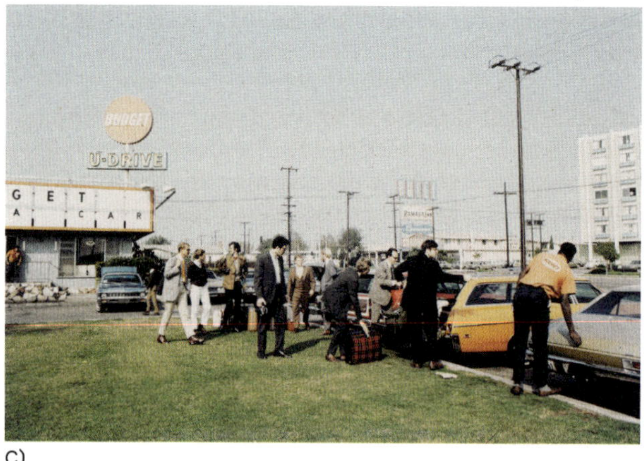

C)

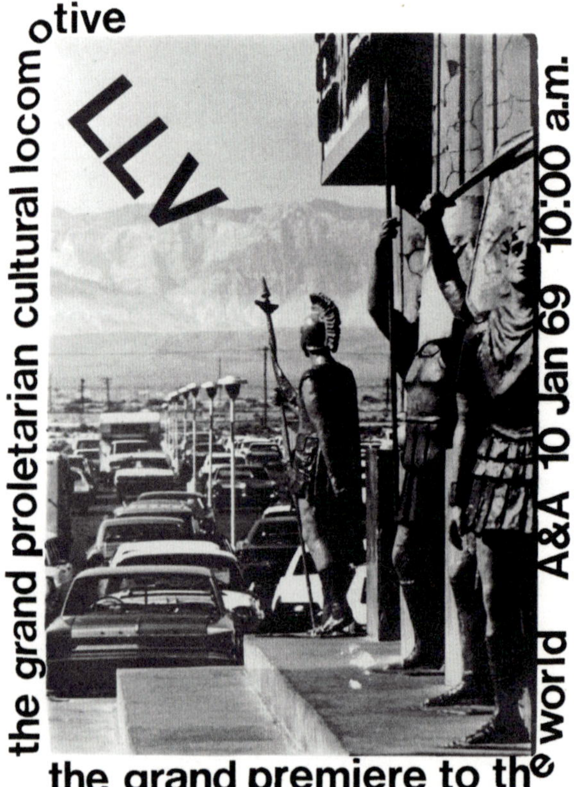

D)

C) Students of the "Learning from Las Vegas Research Studio" arriving in Las Vegas, 1968

D) "The Grand Proletarian Culture Locomotive": Invitation poster to the final presentation of the "Learning from Las Vegas Research Studio," Yale University, 10 January 1969 and—in view of its unusual topic—also subversive approach to architectural education. At the level of methodology, the students were to be taught to see research as an important foundation for their own design work. At the level of content, they were expected to concern themselves with visual phenomena of the everyday and of American popular culture, which were generally disregarded by the architectural establishment. Following a preparatory period of several weeks, a two-week excursion to Los Angeles and Las Vegas in October 1968 formed the highlight of the research studio. [C] While the four days spent in Los Angeles were used for visits to Disneyland and to the studio of the artist Ed Ruscha, [6] the subsequent ten days in Las Vegas were focused on collecting empirical data. The central goal was to document the specific aesthetics and form of the Strip and of suburban sprawl by means of photography and film. In addition to some five thousand color slides and three thousand meters of film, the group compiled a large number of documents with statistical, economic, and planning data. [7] A large number of the photographic documents and all of the films were produced by the students, although with detailed conceptual instructions from Venturi and Scott Brown, who were responsible for the overall project. They were supported by their studio assistant Steven Izenour, who became the head of production and eventually featured as the third author of the book.

In their research studio at Yale University, Venturi and Scott Brown identified a series of thematic emphases that were to be worked on by the students in various groups. The central goal was to obtain an understanding of the automobile-oriented city and to find an adequate image for it. For example, the topic "User behavior" was intended to analyze the behavioral patterns of the (mobilized) users of a "commercial strip" in New Haven. This involved investigating which representational means would be particularly suitable for the purpose, with films being considered in addition to maps and diagrams. In "Las Vegas image," the task was to find out how an appropriate "image" of Las Vegas might be established. Venturi and Scott Brown pointed out that literature and art had already constructed and conveyed a very powerful image of the city. Elsewhere, the students were encouraged to experiment with representational forms, such as "mapping, movies, collages, multi-media, multi-slide projection." Finally, "Graphic and other techniques of representation" explicitly addressed the topic of the image and representation of the city. The module was based on the hypothesis that due to their static quality, traditional representational techniques were an obstacle to understanding the form of the contemporary city and that alternative modes of presentation were therefore needed. [8] The primary goal of the research studio was restated by Venturi and Scott Brown in an interim report after their return from Las Vegas: "Our problem is to find the graphic means to distinguish our hard knowledge from the [t]remendous [*sic*] variety of subjective, but no less meaningful, knowledge we all brought back from Las Vegas." [9] The image material compiled in accordance with the research program developed into some eighty maps, tables, and diagrams, as well as film and slide sequences. [10]

The study was completed with a final presentation of the studio on 10 January 1969 at the Yale School of Art and Architecture. [D] This was an opportunity to show the films that the students had made during their visit to Las Vegas. [11] Furthermore, an exhibition showing the various tables, plates, maps, and collages was held. The scale and organization of these media were specifically tailored for exhibition presentation—i.e., in a large format and intended to be considered in an associative rather than in a linear and discursive context. [12] When the book was published, the same illustrative material was re-used, which proved problematic in some cases. The final presentation of the studio also encountered some severe criticism. In a letter of 16 January 1969 in which Venturi thanked several notable visitors for attending—such as the art historian Vincent Scully, the architect Morris Lapidus, and the writer Tom Wolfe—he noted, "We think it went well in general, but I am still a little unbelieving that some people can't understand we just wanted to look at Las Vegas in a dead-pan way which is also a poetic way of long standing." [13]

The sometimes vehement rejection of the project by fellow architects anticipated a debate that was to have a lasting influence on architectural discussions following the publication of *Learning from Las Vegas*. Publication was quickly undertaken after the Yale University studio. An early handwritten manuscript that already served as the basis for the first publication in *Architectural Forum* in 1968 suggests that Venturi was the first author, even though the preoccupation with the everyday American landscape and city as well as its image had first been triggered by Scott Brown. Joint authorship can be assumed during the revision phase at the latest. [14] Certainly, some of the characteristic style of the text would have been familiar to a reader of Venturi's first book, *Complexity and Contradiction in Architecture* from 1966. His witty use of language and evident penchant for alliteration and memorable formulations are found in *Learning from Las Vegas* as well, and are expressed in pairs of

15) See, for example, the letter from Robert Venturi to Michael Connelly, 11 February 1972, "LLV Book Current Notes Things to Do," Box 47626827, Architectural Archives, University of Pennsylvania and Pennsylvania Historical and Museum Commission.

16) On the popular image of Las Vegas in American perceptions that was widespread in literature and the media, see the unpublished dissertation by Edward E. Baldwin, *Las Vegas in Popular Culture* (Ph.D. thesis, University of Nevada, Las Vegas, 1997). Cf. also Mike Tronnes (ed.), *Literary Las Vegas: The Best Writing About America's Most Fabulous City* (New York: Henry Holt, 1995). On the architectural history of Las Vegas in general, see in particular Eugene P. Moehring, *Resort City in the Sunbelt: Las Vegas, 1930–1970* (Reno and Las Vegas: University of Nevada Press, 1989), Alan Hess, *Viva Las Vegas: After-Hours Architecture* (San Francisco: Chronicle Books, 1993); Mark Gottdiener, Claudia C. Collins, and David R. Dickens, *Las Vegas: the Social Production of an All-American City* (Malden, MA: Blackwell, 1999).

17) See Julian Halevy, "Disneyland and Las Vegas," *The Nation* 186 (7 June 1958), no. 23, pp. 510–3; John Pastier, "The Architecture of Escapism," *AIA Journal* 67 (1978), no. 14, pp. 26–37. On the issue of Las Vegas between reality, representation, and simulation (in the present day), cf. Joy Ramirez, "The Desert of the Real: Las Vegas and the Production/Reproduction of the Postmodern City," *Yearbook of Comparative and General Literature* 49 (2001), pp. 177–91. See also the canonical text in this regard, Umberto Eco, *Travels in Hyperreality: Essays*, trans. William Weaver (San Diego: Harcourt, 1986).

18) Cf. Jay Robert Nash and Stanley Ralph Ross, *The Motion Picture Guide*, 12 vols. (Chicago: Cinebooks, 1985–1987), p. 1602.

19) Stanislaus von Moos, "Die Zukunft liegt in der Wüste," *NZZ am Sonntag*, 8 May 2005, p. 67.

20) Cf. Nash/Ross 1985–1987 (see note 18), p. 1603.

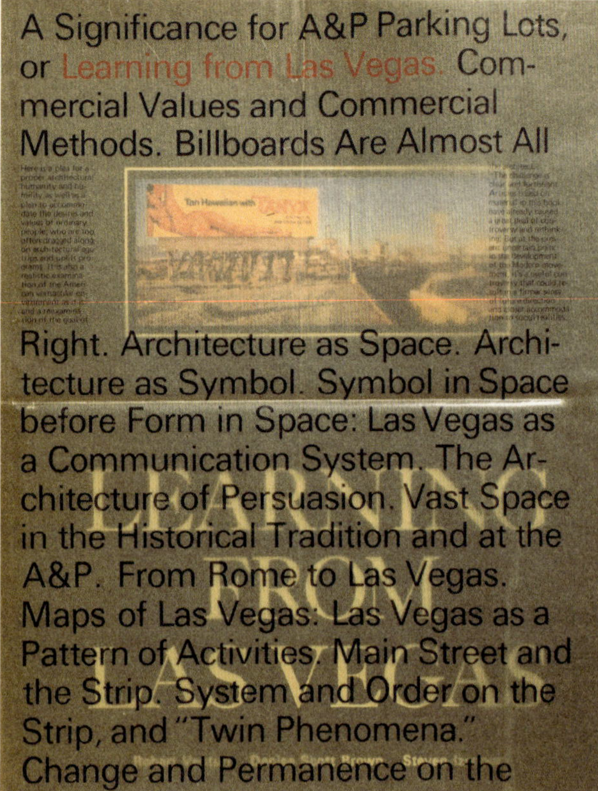

E1)

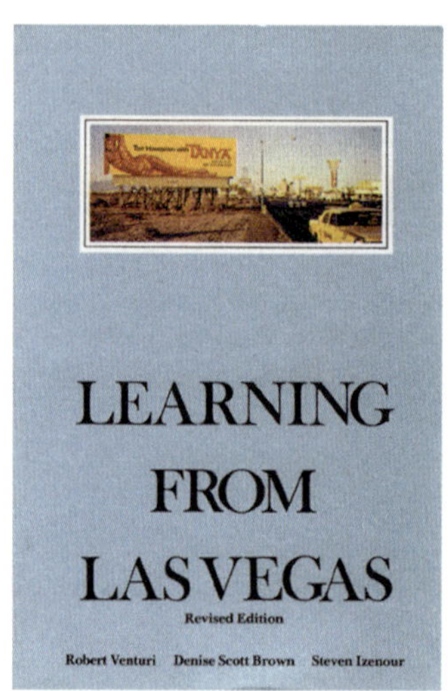

E2)

E) Cover of the first and second editions of *Learning from Las Vegas*, 1972 and 1977

terms, such as learning / Las Vegas, vitality / validity, and duck/decorated shed, as well as in phrases such as "(Billboards) Are Almost All (Right)."

Particularly from the authors' point of view, work with the book's publishers proved to be difficult. Venturi and Scott Brown had little taste for the elaborate modernistic design used by the book designer Muriel Cooper at MIT Press, and they made their displeasure known in numerous letters.[15] The graphic designer largely stuck to her principles; however the authors took full responsibility for the (radically different) design of the second edition. It appeared as a revised paperback edition in 1977, five years after the large-format, opulently designed first edition.[E] The differences are not limited to the severely reduced size of the volume, but also involve a substantial reduction in the number of illustrations. A coffee-table book for connoisseurs was turned into an academic treatise in which the textual part clearly predominates over the illustrative part. Ironically, it was not least the graphic design of the first edition, which was so disdained by Venturi and Scott Brown, that attracted attention and made a substantial contribution to the study's legendary reputation.

Las Vegas in popular perception

When Venturi and Scott Brown started to become interested in Las Vegas, the popular image of the city was markedly different from that of every other city in the country. Due to its founding in May 1905 as a small railroad town in the Mojave Desert, and even more so with its rapid rise starting in the 1930s to become the national mecca for entertainment and gambling, Las Vegas had a special place in America's collective imagination. On the one hand, in puritanical American society the city represented a kind of carnival-like counterpart to the predominant white Anglo-Saxon Protestant (WASP) culture. Much that was elsewhere regarded as taboo and was frowned upon or forbidden was permitted there, and the Dionysian, darker side of the American psyche was able to indulge itself in the city to the full. On the other hand, Las Vegas functioned as an outlet for postwar affluence, as a place where the newly wealthy middle class was able to satisfy its appetite for diversion. From the 1940s onward, descriptions of Las Vegas in literature repeatedly drew attention to the world of gambling and its (alleged) connections with organized crime.[16] Cultural critics and "prophets of doom" repeatedly compared Las Vegas with Disneyland, which opened in 1955, and condemned it as a repository for escapist dreams, where the average American was able to seek refuge from everyday life but in the process fell victim to the machinery of capitalist commercialization all the more.[17]

As a medium of popular imagery *par excellence,* film —more than print media—was an outstanding means of generating and communicating ideas about Las Vegas in the collective mind. The local tourist industry benefited from the city's exotic image and did everything it could to strengthen it, even when the results hardly corresponded to reality and often grotesquely distorted it. Hollywood willingly lent its assistance. The earliest movie centered on Las Vegas was Ralph Murphy's 1941 musical *Las Vegas Nights*.[18] The brief appearance made by Frank Sinatra and the Tommy Dorsey Band was of no little importance for the developing image of Las Vegas as an entertainment capital. This precedent was followed in 1960 by Lewis Milestone in the gangster comedy *Ocean's Eleven,* in which the main roles were played by Sinatra and the other jazz musicians who belonged to the "rat pack" that gave daily performances in Las Vegas at the time. The film conclusively established Las Vegas in America's collective memory as a serious mecca for entertainment. The alliance with show business was also expressed in the way in which Las Vegas provided the backdrop for more and more musical productions, as in Roy Rowland's 1956 movie *Meet Me in Las Vegas*. In contrast to earlier black-and-white movies, the scenery appeared in glowing Technicolor in this film, placing the city in the best light. In George Sidney's *Viva Las Vegas* of 1964, the city was finally "consecrated in pop culture,"[19] with Elvis Presley taking the principal role in a musical about a penniless race-car driver.[F] The film not only helped the rock star promote himself, but also presented the spectacular aesthetics of the night-time illuminations on the Strip and Fremont Street in glorious color. More than any other film, *Viva Las Vegas* dramatized the seductive power of Las Vegas's architecture of light and thus created the classic image of the city in the popular perception during the 1960s.

However, Hollywood sometimes also presented critical analyses of the city and its economy. The shadow of *film noir* was cast on the city in Robert Stevenson's *The Las Vegas Story* of 1952.[20] Sidney Salkow's *Las Vegas Shakedown* of 1955 was also set in the world of the casinos. The movie's plot is based on events involving (real) Senate hearings chaired by Senator Estes Kefauver, investigating and attempting to expose the links between the gambling industry and organized crime. Francis Ford Coppola took up the theme in 1972 in his crime epic *The Godfather,* in which he helped romanticize the world of the Mafia in America. These were all interpretations that shaped Las Vegas's

21) Venturi and Scott Brown quoted Wolfe's article in the first publication of their own Las Vegas text in the journal *Architectural Forum.* See Venturi and Scott Brown 1968 (see note 4), p. 42. The essay was also on the list of compulsory reading for their course on Las Vegas at Yale University. Cf. Robert Venturi, Denise Scott Brown, and Steven Izenour, "Introduction," in Venturi et al. 1968 (see note 8), p. 2.

22) Cf. Tom Wolfe, *The Kandy-Kolored Tangerine-Flake Streamline Baby* (New York: Bantam, 1977; 1st ed. New York: Farrar, Straus and Giroux, 1965).

23) Ibid., p. xvii.

24) "It is no accident that Las Vegas and Versailles are the only two architecturally uniform cities in Western history." Ibid., p. xvi.

25) Ibid., p. xvi.

26) Cf. Siegfried Kracauer, *Das Ornament der Masse* (Frankfurt am Main: Suhrkamp), 1977 / *The Mass Ornament: Weimar Essays*, trans. Thomas Y. Levin (Cambridge, MA: Harvard University Press, 1995).

27) On this topic, see in particular Herbert Gans, *The Levittowners: Ways of Life and Politics in a New Suburban Community* (New York: Pantheon, 1967); Gans, "Popular Culture in America: Social Problem in a Mass Society or Social Asset in a Pluralist Society?" in Howard S. Becker (ed.): *Social Problems: a Modern Approach* (New York: Wiley, 1966), pp. 549–620; Gans, *Popular Culture and High Culture: an Analysis and Evaluation of Taste* (New York: Basic Books, 1999); Denise Scott Brown, "Between Three Stools: a Personal View of Urban Design Pedagogy," in Scott Brown, *Urban Concepts* (London: Academy Editions / St. Martin's Press, 1990; Architectural Design Profile, 83), pp. 9–20, here p. 10.

28) See Reyner Banham, "The Missing Motel," *The Listener,* 5 August 1965, p. 6; Banham, "Toward a Million-Volt Light and Sound Culture," *The Architectural Review* 141 (May 1967), no. 843, pp. 331–5; Banham, "Mediated Environments or: You Can't Build That Here," in C.W.E. Bigsby (ed.), *Superculture: American Popular Culture and Europe* (Bowling Green: Bowling Green University Popular Press, 1975), pp. 69–82. Scott Brown knew Banham from when she studied in London and was very familiar with his writings. Cf. Denise Scott Brown, "Learning from Brutalism," in David Robbins (ed.), *The Independent Group: Postwar Britain and the Aesthetics of Plenty* (Cambridge, MA: MIT Press), 1990, pp. 203–6, here p. 203.

29) Banham 1967 (see note 28), p. 331.

30) Reyner Banham, *The Architecture of the Well-tempered Environment* (Chicago: University of Chicago Press, 1969), p. 269.

31) Reyner Banham, "Q: What Is the Main Drag of the American Fantasy? A: The Las Vegas Strip, in Case You Hadn't Noticed ...," *Los Angeles Times WEST Magazine,* 8 November 1970, pp. 36–41, here p. 39.

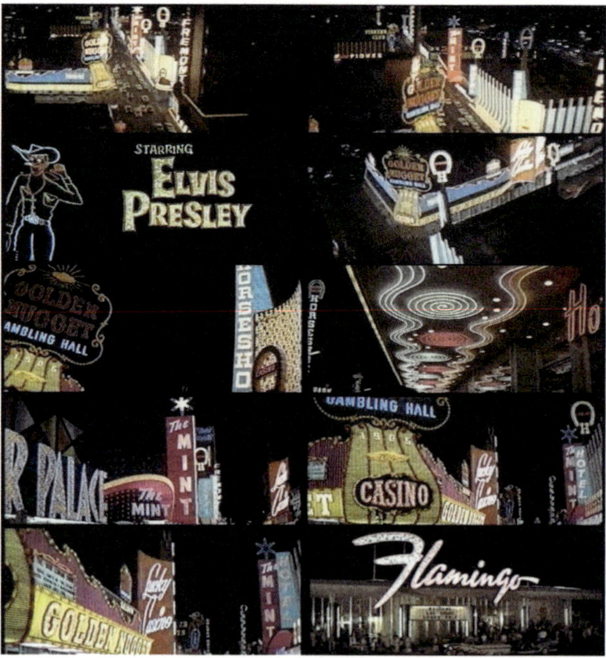

F)

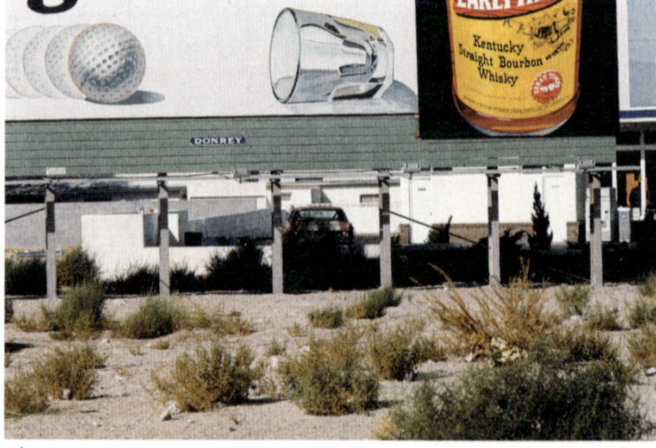

G)

F) George Sidney: *Viva Las Vegas,* 1964, stills from the opening sequence

G) Las Vegas as an emblem of pop culture? Billboard on the Strip

equivocal image and that conditioned the way in which Venturi and Scott Brown themselves "discovered" the city. Instead of contributing to further myth-making, however, their study was aimed at an unprejudiced image of the city and its architecture. Venturi and Scott Brown were well aware that an unprejudiced view was not possible, but that it was necessary to be aware of one's own prejudices.

Las Vegas as an emblem of popular culture

The equivocal image of Las Vegas conveyed by the media led to an intellectual analysis at an early stage. This focused on the question of what place the city had in contemporary American culture. An earlier key text on this issue was the essay "Las Vegas (What?) Las Vegas (Can't hear you! Too noisy) Las Vegas!!!!" by the American writer Tom Wolfe. The article was crucially important in drawing the attention of Venturi and Scott Brown to the city, and it decisively shaped their perception of Las Vegas as well.[21] The essay was first published in February 1964 in *Esquire* magazine. In 1965—well timed for the first trip made by Venturi and Scott Brown to Las Vegas together—it was reprinted in his anthology *The Kandy-Kolored Tangerine-Flake Streamline Baby*, in which Wolfe, who had studied English literature at Yale University, expressed his views on various topics of American popular culture.[22] Wolfe's approach was unusual in the context of the period since he did not treat mass cultural phenomena from an elitist point of view, but on the contrary recognized in them a vital and authentic form of new American folk culture. Wolfe saw a genuinely American style in the sometimes bizarre forms that this popular culture took, and even described it as "America's first unconscious avant-garde!"[23][G] For him, the Las Vegas Strip, along with the Versailles of the Sun King, was one of the only two "architecturally uniform cities in Western history."[24] For the first time in history, in his view, mass society had shaped a city in accordance with its own values and ideas: "The important thing about the building of Las Vegas is not that the builders were gangsters but that they were proles."[25] The aesthetics of the Las Vegas Strip was thus—freely adapting a phrase from Siegfried Kracauer—a "mass ornament" for the present day.[26] According to Wolfe, cultural development was not, or was no longer, taking place in the form of a top-down process in which the aesthetic preferences of the privileged social classes were imitated by the other classes, but instead as a bottom-up movement. As described by Wolfe, it was the socially peripheral and marginal that was aesthetically and culturally relevant. This hypothesis provided Venturi and Scott Brown, who belonged to the world of architectural high culture themselves, with further support for their preoccupation with Las Vegas. In addition to Wolfe, the writings of the sociologist Herbert Gans, to whom Venturi and Scott Brown made repeated reference, also played a decisive role.[27] In sociological terms, the cultural significance of *Learning from Las Vegas* thus lay in the way in which it oriented architecture toward the aesthetics of American popular culture, "from below." Venturi and Scott Brown drew decisive inspiration for this approach from Wolfe's writings, which in themselves reflected the interests of contemporary Pop Art.

Las Vegas in architectural discourse

Other important figures in the architectural discourse of the period had also taken note of Las Vegas, not least under the influence of Tom Wolfe's descriptions. In the developing debate, the primary question was the extent to which Las Vegas could be regarded as the model for a city of the future. Of particular significance in this context were comments made by British architectural historian Reyner Banham, who discussed Las Vegas in a series of texts following Wolfe.[28] As early as 1967, even before the first version of the Las Vegas text by Venturi and Scott Brown was published, he noted that "Las Vegas is now a mandatory stop-over in the English architectural student's grand tour of North America."[29] In his standard work, *The Architecture of the Well-Tempered Environment,* Banham discussed Las Vegas again in 1969. What primarily interested him in the desert city was its spectacular nocturnal architecture of light, while he regarded the daytime form and aesthetics of the city as being less important: "What defines the symbolic places and spaces of Las Vegas—the superhotels of The Strip, the casino-belt of Fremont Street—is pure environmental power, manifested as coloured light… [T]he effectiveness with which space is defined is… overwhelming, the creation of virtual volumes without apparent structure is endemic, the variety and ingenuity of the lighting techniques is encyclopaedic… And in a view of architectural education that embraced the complete art of environmental management, a visit to Las Vegas would be as mandatory as a visit to the Baths of Caracalla or La Sainte Chapelle."[30]

For Banham, Las Vegas was only "truly itself" at night; the nocturnally illuminated city even appeared to him, borrowing from Wolfe, as "one of the great works of collective art in the Western World."[31] Banham was following in the footsteps of German Expressionists such as Erich Mendelsohn here, who in the early 20th century had anticipated a sublimation of architectural form in light; or Paul Scheerbart, who had

32) Mendelsohn's fascination with the architecture of light was expressed in his book on America, for example, in which alongside a night-time photograph of New York, he writes, "During the day, the city fills itself with energy, while at night it sprays out the whole of life" (p. 25). Mendelsohn's comments on Broadway, which he classifies under the heading of "The Grotesque," are of interest. Here he draws a careful distinction between daytime and nocturnal architecture. On Broadway at night, he writes, "Uncanny. The contours of the buildings have been rubbed out. But in one's mind they still rise, chase each other, run each other down.... Still disordered, but with a fantastic beauty that will sometime reach perfection" (Plate 44). During the day, by contrast: "Loses the uncanny, rapturous, gleaming quality of the night. Is only untamed, wild, shouting itself down. Grandiose foolishness of the world fun-fair" (Plate 45). Cf. Erich Mendelsohn, *Amerika. Bilderbuch eines Architekten* (Berlin: Rudolf Mosse, 1926). On Scheerbart, see Paul Scheerbart, *Glasarchitektur* (Berlin: Gebr. Mann, 2000), pp. 99 and 71.

33) Banham 1969 (see note 30), pp. 269–70.

34) Ibid. p. 270. On this topic, cf. also another statement made by Banham in 1975: "Decades ago the great movie palaces transformed themselves by draping their structures in neon and lights. More recently the casinos of Las Vegas revealed that with enough light one could almost abandon structure. The spaces of that wild city tend to be defined by masses of light that often have no building around them or behind them. It may sound strange, almost blasphemous, to say so, but it is in Las Vegas that one comes nearest to seeing gross matter transformed into aetherial [*sic*] substance by the power of light." Reyner Banham, *Age of the Masters: a Personal View of Modern Architecture* (London: Architectural Press, 1975), p. 62.

35) On this topic, see Nigel Whiteley, *Reyner Banham: Historian of the Immediate Future* (Cambridge, MA: MIT Press, 2002), pp. 187–243.

36) Peter Cook, Dennis Crompton, and Ron Herron, "Instant City: First Stage," *Architectural Design* 39 (1969), no. 5, pp. 276–80.

37) Ibid., p. 280. This analysis anticipates the article by Tom Wolfe that was published in the same journal two issues later: "Electrographic Architecture," *Architectural Design* 39 (1969), no. 7, pp. 380–2.

38) In his travel diary, published as *America Revisited* in 1883, Sala condemned "the coarseness and indecency of the quicksalvers' announcements ... which alarm and disgust the eye at every turn ... The loveliest spots in the scenery of this vast continent are blighted with these loathsome stigmata—the portents of shameless imposture and rapacious greed for gold." Cited after Charles F. Floyd and Peter J. Shedd, *Highway Beautification: the Environmental Movement's Greatest Failure* (Boulder, CO: Westview, 1979), p. 16.

39) Cf. Paul Schultze-Naumburg, *Kulturarbeiten, Band IX. Die Gestaltung der Landschaft durch den Menschen, III. Teil,* ed. Kunstwart (Munich: Callwey, 1917), pp. 315 and 324.

40) Cf. *Architectural Review* 108 (December 1950), no. 648.

41) "Townscape," and also the "picturesque tradition" underlying it, had an immense influence on the way in which Venturi and Scott Brown conceived of architecture and the city. However, there is insufficient space to go into this issue in detail here.

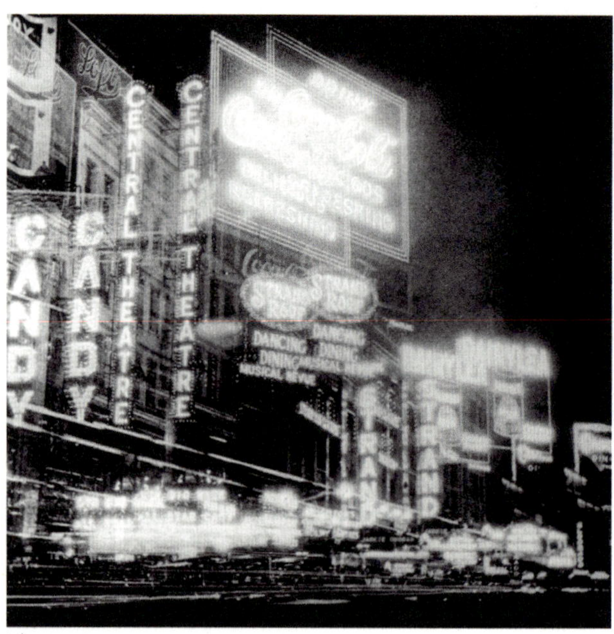

H)

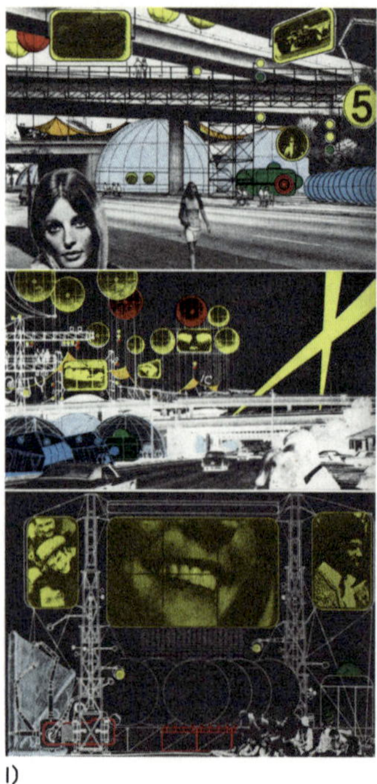

I)

H) New York's Broadway at night: Reproduction from Erich Mendelsohn's *Amerika. Bilderbuch eines Architekten,* 1926

I) Archigram (Peter Cook, Dennis Crompton, Ron Herron): "Instant City," 1969

dreamt of "indescribable" "nights of light" and of a "different"—i.e., "colored" light.[32)] [H)]

By repeatedly emphasizing the importance of a visit to the desert city for contemporary architectural education, Banham seemed to implicitly refer to Venturi and Scott Brown's Las Vegas studio. In contrast to Venturi and Scott Brown, however, he had no interest in either spatial organization, or in symbolic communication, or in the exchange between the aesthetics of popular and high cultures in architecture. For Banham, the emphasis was on the technological aspects "The point of studying Las Vegas, ultimately, would be to see an example of how far environmental technology can be driven beyond the confines of architectural practice by designers who (for worse or better) are not inhibited by the traditions of architectonic culture, training and taste."[33)]

According to Banham, Las Vegas deserved the architect's attention neither because it was the prototype for a form of the city as perceived from the automobile, nor because its form and aesthetics contained a treasure-trove of images for contemporary architectural production, as Venturi and Scott Brown suggested. Instead, the relevance of Las Vegas for Banham lay in the fact that it had converted built architectural substance into ethereal light. For Banham, Las Vegas thus marked a transition "from forms assembled in light to light assembled in forms."[34)] This expressed his fundamental conviction that architecture was increasingly losing its traditional role as a device of form and was instead mutating into a kind of amorphous software for the living environment. Architecture was apparently no longer of interest to him as a formal problem, but rather as a "fit environment for human activities" that had emancipated itself from rigid structure to become a changeable — and ultimately unarchitectural — container.[35)] In Banham's conception, Las Vegas was a test case for the extent to which architecture could be transformed into something ethereal.

Probably at Banham's suggestion, the British architectural group Archigram was also investigating Las Vegas during this period.[I)] In "Instant City," the architects Peter Cook, Dennis Crompton, and Ron Herron in 1969 presented a utopian design for an ephemeral city that was intended to tour through the English provinces as a kind of traveling circus.[36)] With its provisional quality, its use of gas balloons, its graphic symbols, and in particular its sound and light spectacles that were to be projected onto large-format screens, "Instant City" resembled festival or exhibition architecture. At the same time, however, it had absorbed the influence of the flat, symbolic billboard architecture of the Las Vegas Strip. At the end of their article, Archigram did in fact refer to Las Vegas as an actually existing model for "Instant City." Fully in agreement with Banham, the group emphasized the city's technological quality as representing a pure electric architecture of light that was not attached to architectural form "The use of electrics-as-place is important. Las Vegas suggests that a really powerful environment can be created simply by passing an electric current—in daytime the hardware is nothing. Lights combined with cinema projection can make the whole place a city where there is no city. It is suggested that the visitor himself could play with large areas of this lighting so that he makes it happen rather than gawp at it.[37)]"

The points emphasized by Venturi and Scott Brown in their exploration of Las Vegas were different. Although they were also fascinated by the nighttime architecture of light on the Strip and on Fremont Street in the city center, their interest focused more on the perspective of the automobile-based observer, which in their view explained the form and aesthetics of the contemporary city with its billboards and symbolic dimension.

Cityscape in dispute

The unprejudiced view of the form and aesthetics of the contemporary city that Venturi and Scott Brown were suggesting in *Learning from Las Vegas* had to prevail against the chorus of voices lamenting the collapse of the cityscape in the postwar period. These howls of complaint had a cultural tradition of their own, with the proliferation of large advertising billboards being particularly contentious in this respect. At the end of the 19th century, the English journalist George Sala was already expressing concern that the scenery of the American countryside was being threatened by the omnipresence of ugly advertising boards.[38)] In the German cultural sphere, it was Paul Schultze-Naumburg, in particular, who voiced such concerns, in his famous *Kulturarbeiten* [Cultural Studies].[39)] With the rapid spread of the automobile, the topic became even more explosive in the American context after 1945. A start in this process was made by a special issue of the British *Architectural Review,* under the title "Man Made America," published in December 1950.[40)] [J)] The issue represented an indictment of the image of the contemporary American city in the form of an illustrated broadsheet, and its content reflected the "townscape" philosophy supported by the *Architectural Review* at the time.[41)] The American *Architectural Forum* took aim at the same targets,

42) Cf. "What City Pattern?" *Architectural Forum* 105 (September 1956), no. 3, pp. 103–37.

43) Cf. Philip Morris, "Architect Casts Vote for BIGGER Billboards," *Oklahoma Journal,* 10 November 1967, in "Ed Bacon & Billboards," Box VSB 26, Architectural Archives, University of Pennsylvania and Pennsylvania Historical and Museum Commission; Rose DeWolf: "Billboard Fans and Lady Bird," *The Philadelphia Inquirer,* 14 November 1967, in "Ed Bacon & Billboards," Box VSB 26, Architectural Archives, University of Pennsylvania and Pennsylvania Historical and Museum Commission.

44) See note 14.

45) Peter Blake, *God's Own Junkyard: The Planned Deterioration of America's Landscape* (New York: Holt, Rinehart and Winston, 1964).

46) Robert Venturi, *Complexity and Contradiction in Architecture* (New York: The Museum of Modern Art, 1966; The Museum of Modern Art Papers on Architecture, 1), p. 102.

47) Denise Scott Brown, "Some Ideas and Their History," in Robert Venturi and Denise Scott Brown, *Architecture as Signs and Systems: for a Mannerist Time* (Cambridge, MA: Belknap Press of Harvard University Press, 2004), pp. 105–19, here pp. 105–8.

48) Ibid., p. 107.

49) Denise Scott Brown, interview, 23 August 2003, Petit Saconnex, Geneva.

50) Cf. Jonathan Green, *American Photography: a Critical History, 1945 to the Present* (New York: Abrams, 1984), p. 164.

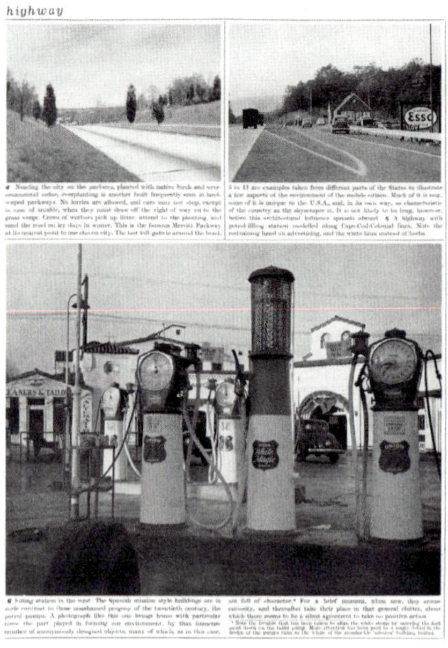

highway

J)

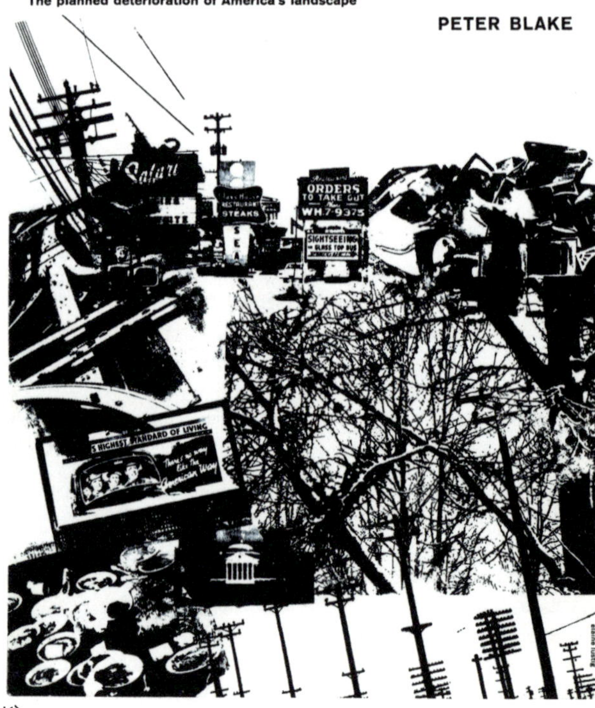

K)

J) Page from the special issue "Man Made America," *The Architectural Review,* December 1950

K) Peter Blake: *God's Own Junkyard,* 1964, cover

with similarly illustration-based argumentation, in a special issue published in September 1956 on the question "By 1976 What City Pattern?" [42] These publications reflected the predominant mood of the time, as increasingly vocal political demands arose during the course of the 1950s for regulation of outdoor advertising along the American highways and in the city centers—leading to what was called the Highway Beautification Act in 1965. *Learning from Las Vegas* thus undoubtedly represented a response to publications of this type.

These developments formed the background to Venturi's involvement in defending the billboard. In a campaign, he proposed (probably not in all seriousness) in several lectures that a "Committee to Preserve Our Billboards" [43] should be founded—a project directly connected with the writing of *Learning from Las Vegas*. [44] Further stimulus for this campaign was provided by another publication that set itself in judgment over the form and aesthetics of the American city —Peter Blake's *God's Own Junkyard* from 1964. [45] [K] In familiar fashion, the author complained in the book about the alleged cultural decline that he viewed as evident in the disfigurement of the countryside and the cities. Even in his first book publication, *Complexity and Contradiction in Architecture* of 1966, Venturi had reacted to this hypothesis by asking, "Is not Main Street almost all right?" [46] The question anticipated the analysis of the Las Vegas Strip, which he and Scott Brown had already started at the time when *Complexity and Contradiction* was published. The importance of Blake's book as a contrast to *Learning from Las Vegas* is also evident in the way that Venturi and Scott Brown adopted for their architectural theory the same "duck" that Blake had "discovered" at the roadside in Long Island and had used to illustrate his arguments in *God's Own Junkyard*. [L]

Scott Brown in particular had advocated an unprejudiced assessment of the city and the contemporary built environment. She was using photography for documentary purposes from an early stage. By her own account, her childhood in a colonial setting in southern Africa was a decisive influence on her later interest in phenomena of popular culture such as the Las Vegas Strip, the commercial aesthetics of which offended against the norms and values of the architectural high culture of the time: "Mine is an African view of Las Vegas." [47] Because "these early African experiences first raised the polarity of 'is' and 'ought' for me. Here it was the 'is' of the 'colony' and the 'ought' of the 'mother country,' and it could be translated artistically into a question: What environment lies around us, and how is this different from what the media of the dominant culture (mostly English) suggest should be there? [48]"

What was at stake here was thus not the city as it ought to be, but rather the city as it actually is. Moreover, Scott Brown's early experiences established a sensitivity for marginalized subcultures and respect for their aesthetic preferences. From Scott Brown's point of view, the imagery of popular culture in the American cities was one of these culturally marginalized phenomena. It was on the Las Vegas Strip where she saw them manifested in their purest form.

The background that shaped Scott Brown's thinking is clearly expressed in the numerous photographs that she had been taking since the early 1960s, and not least in her photos of Las Vegas. As an amateur photographer, she viewed her new urban and architectural environment with attentive and fresh eyes after she moved to the United States. Already evident in early photos dating from 1959 is the gaze of an (auto)-mobile observer that was to become a determining element in *Learning from Las Vegas*. [M] A number of photos taken in Tennessee in the summer of 1964 provide evidence of a decisive development in Scott Brown's image of the urbanized landscape. In addition to conventional motifs, there is increasing evidence of topics that are also the focus of attention in *Learning from Las Vegas:* billboards as part of the aesthetics of the contemporary urban landscape, a view of suburban settlements from the street, and, in general, the visual effects of the advent of the automobile on the built environment. Scott Brown's visual exploration of the American West dates back to 1965, when she was teaching at Berkeley during the spring semester. She traveled to California from Philadelphia by car, stopping off in cities such as Austin, Houston, Dallas, and Phoenix. [49] The photos she took show her interest in the aspects of the cityscape mentioned above, with which several professional photographers were also concerned at the same time.

Cityscapes in Pop photography

Starting in the 1950s, the aesthetics of the automobile-oriented American city increasingly became a focus for art, and for photography in particular. This was true of Dennis Hopper, for example, who photographed a Standard gas station from a moving car in 1961. An eye for everyday and banal items was also evident in the work of photographers such as Robert Adams, Lewis Baltz, Joe Deals, Frank Gohlke, and Stephen Shore, whose pictorial language became widely known as the "New Topographics" after an exhibition with that title held in 1979. [50] [N] In addition to Shore's

51) Cf. Venturi and Rauch, *Signs of Life: Symbols in the American City,* exhib. cat., Renwick Gallery of the National Collection of Fine Arts, Smithsonian Institution, Washington, DC (Washington, DC: Aperture, 1976). On Baeder, cf. John Baeders works: *Diners* (New York: Abrams, 1978); *Gas, Food, and Lodging* (New York: Abbeville Press, 1982); and *Sign Language: Street Signs as Folk Art* (New York: Abrams, 1996).

52) "I had a vision that I was being a great reporter when I did the gas stations.... It was just a simple, straightforward way of getting the news and bringing it back." Ed Ruscha, quoted in David Bourdon, "Ruscha as Publisher (or All Booked Up)," *Artnews* 71 (April 1972), no. 2, pp. 32–6, here p. 33.

53) Cf. Henri Man Barendse, "Ed Ruscha: an Interview," in Ed Ruscha, *Leave Any Information after the Signal: Writings, Interviews, Bits, Pages,* ed. Alexandra Schwartz (Cambridge, MA: MIT Press, 2002), pp. 210–19, here p. 215. Cf. also Katherine A. Smith, *Sign Language: Pop Art, Vernacular Architecture, and the American Landscape* (Ph.D. thesis, New York University, 2003), pp. 63–4.

54) Cf. Bourdon 1972 (see note 52), pp. 33–4.

55) Phyllis Rosenzweig has pointed out this connection; see Phyllis Rosenzweig, "Ed Ruschas Künstlerbücher," in Neal Benezra and Kerry Brougher (eds.), *Ed Ruscha* (Zurich: Scalo, 2002), pp. 178–88, here pp. 181–2. In contrast, Margit Rowell has recently queried the link with Conceptual Art: Margit Rowell, *Ed Ruscha, Photographer* (New York: Whitney Museum of American Art, 2006), p. 21.

56) On the connection between Ruscha and Conceptual Art, cf. Benjamin Buchloh, "Conceptual Art 1962–69: from the Aesthetic of Administration to the Critique of Institutions," *October* 55 (Winter 1990), pp. 105–43, here p. 119.

57) Cf. Robert Venturi in "The Summit," in Alex Farquharson (ed.), *The Magic Hour: the Convergence of Art and Las Vegas/ Die Konvergenz von Kunst und Las Vegas* (Graz, Austria: Neue Galerie Graz am Landesmuseum Joanneum, 2001), pp. 38–50, here p. 48.

58) Cf. letter from Robert Venturi to Ed Ruscha, 17 December 1968, "Correspondence," Box VSB 27, Architectural Archives, University of Pennsylvania and Pennsylvania Historical and Museum Commission.

59) Denise Scott Brown, "On Pop Art, Permissiveness, and Planning," *Journal of the American Institute of Planners* 35 (May 1969), pp. 184–6.

60) Ibid., pp. 185–6.

61) *Merriam-Webster's Collegiate Dictionary,* 11th ed. (Springfield, MA: Merriam-Webster, 2003).

62) "It was a subjectivity garbed as objectivity – a wolf in sheep's clothing. We were quite aware of it." Denise Scott Brown, personal communication, September 2008.

63) On "deadpanning," cf. also Michael Golec, " 'Doing it Deadpan': Venturi, Scott Brown and Izenour's *Learning from Las Vegas*," *Visible Language* 37 (2003), no. 3, pp. 266–87.

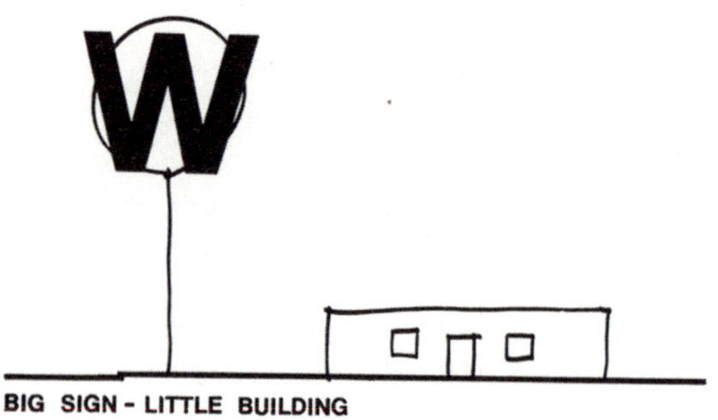

OR

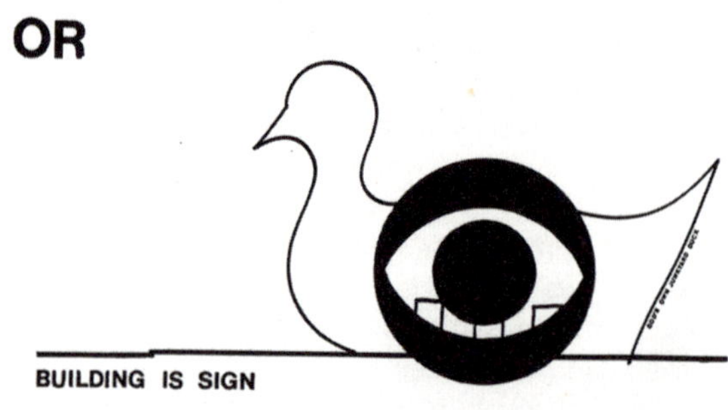

L)

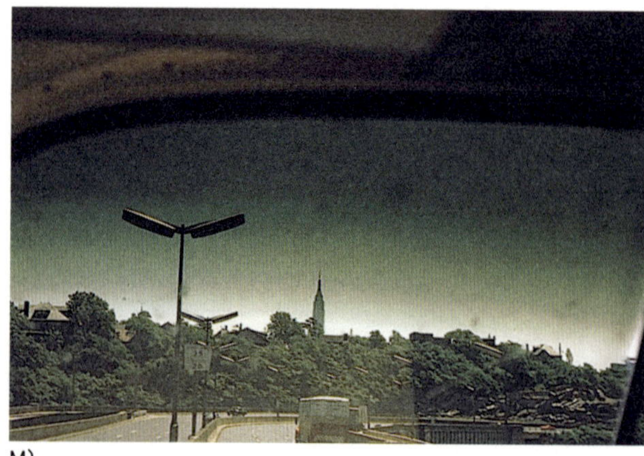

M)

L) "Decorated shed" vs. "Duck": The two modes of architectural communication according to *Learning from Las Vegas*

M) Denise Scott Brown: "Approaching New York," 1963

photographs, the work of John Baeder also proved to be influential in connection with Venturi and Scott Brown. Baeder made his reputation above all with colorful shots of everyday American commercial architecture. Neither of these photographers was mentioned in *Learning from Las Vegas,* but they were represented in Venturi's exhibition "Signs of Life: Symbols in the American City," held in Washington in 1976.[51)]

The work of Los Angeles-based artist Edward Ruscha was particularly influential during the 1960s for the way in which the American city and the car-oriented (urban) landscape were perceived through photography. His typologically arranged photo series, which documented the banal everyday reality of the urban landscapes of southern California, were particularly important in this context. Ruscha compiled his photographs into a series of artist's books, the first of which was his *Twenty-Six Gasoline Stations* of 1963. Five further publications were concerned with the aesthetics of the contemporary city: *Some Los Angeles Apartments* (1965), *Every Building on the Sunset Strip* (1966), *Thirty-Four Parking Lots in Los Angeles* (1967), *Nine Swimming Pools and a Broken Glass* (1968), and *Real Estate Opportunities* (1970).[O)] Various photos taken by Venturi and Scott Brown and their students in Las Vegas were clearly influenced by Ruscha's view of the city—both in their content and form. It is not only the motifs that are similar in the two projects; the view of vast, empty car parks from above is also obviously adapted from Ruscha.

Ruscha's photographs of the urban landscape are characterized by a decidedly cool, emotionless and documentary touch that apparently lacks any artistic pretensions. As he saw it, in his photography he was acting as a kind of journalistic reporter.[52)] The emphasis was on a search for factuality and accurate depiction of reality, rather than on artistic expression. Ruscha reinforced this (alleged) absence of any artistic claims by an (equally alleged) claim to have no interest in photography. His interest thus lay purely and exclusively in the object depicted, not in the artistic value of the depiction itself.[53)] Ruscha even denied giving any thought to the composition of the picture and claimed that he had taken the photos spontaneously, like amateur snapshots.[54)] The intended elimination of the artistic subject, his disappearance behind the factuality of the object found, presents a parallel to the way in which Venturi and Scott Brown treated the city in *Learning from Las Vegas:* as a found object that primarily had to be documented and described. The approach taken by Ruscha was related to Conceptual Art.[55)] It is not only the tendency to devalue craft in favor of the theoretical conception that links Ruscha's photography with Conceptual Art, but also the effort to extinguish artistic subjectivity and recognizable authorship, as is seen in characteristics such as the often-mentioned "coolness" or his affinity with documentary techniques.[56) P)]

Ruscha's image of the contemporary American city provided a central point of reference for Venturi and Scott Brown in the context of *Learning from Las Vegas.* The artist had come to Scott Brown's notice while she was teaching at the University of California at Los Angeles (UCLA) in 1965–1967.[57)] Her interest in the artist's photography coincided with her own project for a photographic documentation of the everyday urban landscape in the American city. In the fall of 1968, Denise Scott Brown and her students from Yale visited Ruscha in his studio before traveling on to Las Vegas to carry out their field studies.[58)] Venturi and Scott Brown also included Ruscha's work as a reference in several of their publications—for the first time in 1969 in Scott Brown's article "On Pop Art, Permissiveness, and Planning," which was illustrated with pictures from Ruscha's artist's books.[59)] Moreover, Scott Brown emphasized how important this artistic position was for the project of perceiving and representing the form and aesthetics of the contemporary city. A particularly important aspect in relation to *Learning from Las Vegas* was the fact that Scott Brown linked Ruscha's view of the city with the adjective "deadpan."[60)] According to the dictionary definition, the adjective signifies "marked by an impassive matter-of-fact manner, style, or expression."[61)] Beginning in the 1940s, the verb "to deadpan" also came to be used to mean "to speak, act or utter in a deadpan manner; to maintain a dead pan." The term thus means receiving external impressions without any visible emotional response. Hence, Scott Brown uses "deadpanning" to mean a specific way of viewing and documenting a visual environment. Through "deadpanning," the facts are (allegedly) reduced to their factuality while "creative" interventions are largely repressed. It goes without saying that this attitude represents a highly artificial artistic position. "Deadpanning" ought to be described not so much as a documentary or "objective" view of the world, but instead as a rhetoric of objectivity.[62)]

In *Learning from Las Vegas,* "deadpanning" became a specific method in connection with obtaining an image of the contemporary city.[63)] This applied particularly to an illustration which in the first edition of *Learning from Las Vegas* spread over four full pages.[Q)] The illustration forms a continuous photographic reproduction, in the photographic medium of collage,

64) Venturi et al. 1972 (see note 4), p. 26.

65) Cf. Bourdon 1972 (see note 52), pp. 35–6.

66) For a detailed discussion of this issue, see Martino Stierli, "Die 'Er-fahrung' der Stadt. Las Vegas, Film und der Blick aus dem Auto," in Andreas Beyer, Matteo Burioni, and Johannes Grave (eds.), *Das Auge der Architektur* (Munich: Fink, 2009) [forthcoming].

67) See note 2.

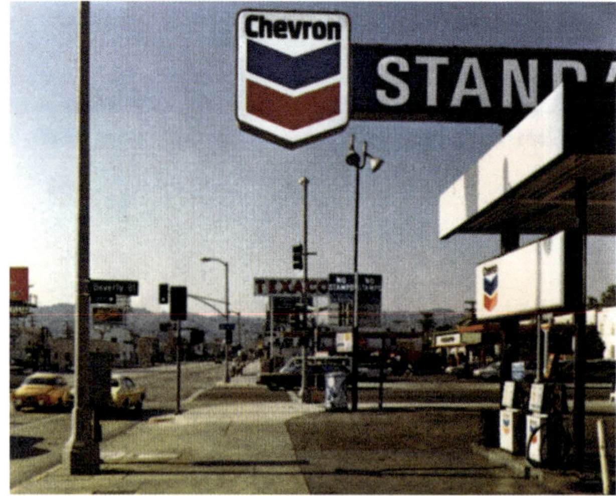

N)

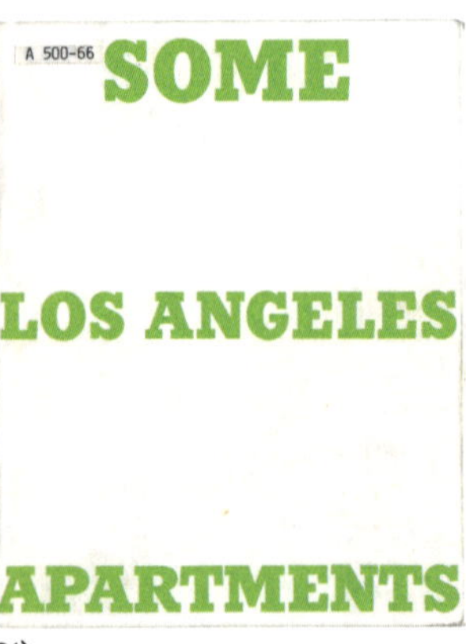

O[1])

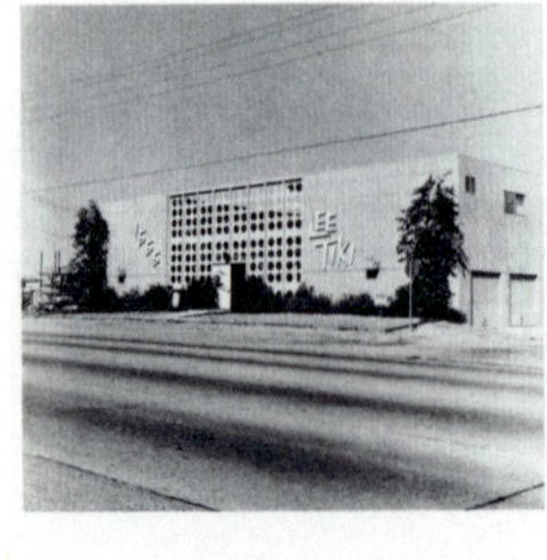

O[2])

N) Stephen Shore: *La Brea Ave.*, 1975, view onto Route 66

O) Edward Ruscha: *Some Los Angeles Apartments,* artist's book, 1965, cover and two-page spread

of the buildings on both sides of the street on the Las Vegas Strip between Tropicana Avenue and the Sahara Hotel. The illustration thus directly and conceptually relates to Ruscha's concertina fold-out *Every Building on the Sunset Strip*—a connection that Venturi and Scott Brown explicitly indicate in the caption " 'Edward Ruscha' elevation." [64] Not only conceptually, but even at the technical level, Venturi and Scott Brown followed Ruscha in developing an image of the city that aimed at factuality and an absence of emotion. Like the artist, they were replacing the human eye's selective perception with the camera's mechanical gaze. For the photograph of the Strip, a camera equipped with a motor was attached to the hood of a car. During the subsequent journey, the camera documented both sides of the street without interruption and without any human intervention. It was thus an attempt to obtain a "desubjectivized" version of the cityscape.

However, the way in which Venturi and Scott Brown viewed the city is not capable of being reduced to a purely documentary aspect. Many of their photographs show evidence of an aesthetically motivated gaze—departing from a purely documentary investigation of the city's image—that was described by various critical reviewers of the book as representing a form of glorification. Even in Edward Ruscha's work, two clearly different strategies for visualizing the contemporary city can be distinguished. The artist makes a point to differentiate between media and genres: While his photography is committed to a distinctly documentary gaze, in his prints and paintings he intensifies his motifs through interventions, such as shifting the point of view, using glowing colors, or increasing the scale, thereby contributing to an idealization of the motifs. Quite adequately, David Bourdon has spoken of a "dual aesthetic" in this connection. [65] It applies also to the visual approach to Las Vegas taken by Venturi and Scott Brown.

Experiencing the city in motion

According to Venturi and Scott Brown, the new automobile-oriented form of the city demanded a different, dynamic form of representation. On the premise that urban space was primarily perceived by an observer moving in an automobile - that is, space is experienced in motion, Venturi and Scott Brown based their analysis of the Strip on moving images, film techniques, and proto-filmic image sequences. They thus not only attached themselves to the modern topos of giving space a dynamic quality and to experiments carried out in and around the German *Werkbund*. Rather, they could also draw upon a number of contemporary research studies that described the perception of the city as a filmic experience. [66] Denise Scott Brown in particular made various references to the opportunities provided by film for analyzing and depicting the contemporary city, which were subsequently tested by the students during the Las Vegas studio. [67] This focus on movie techniques to represent the city is clearly evident in the book. This applies in particular to a sequence of black-and-white movie stills that covers two full pages of the book and shows a car journey on the Strip. The time sequence, which cannot be depicted in the static medium of the book, is translated here into a spatial and linear arrangement.

During their research trip to Las Vegas, the students from the Yale seminar made several movies that captured the way in which urban space is perceived from various different points of view by an observer in motion. The first of these films, entitled *Las Vegas Deadpan*, lasts around 21 minutes. The title indicates the mode of emotionless reporting that Venturi and Scott Brown had developed analogously to Ruscha's photography, but also as a reaction to those architects who were acting as visionaries. [R] It is a commentary-free recording of an automobile journey on the Strip. It implements the "deadpanning" aspect in that the camera, mounted on the car in a fixed position, documents the cityscape that passes in front of the lens without any horizontal or vertical movement. In contrast to this unanimated "city portrait," a second film is characterized by comparatively mobile camera work. It is labeled "Las Vegas Strip LfLV Studio (Day: Night)," is approximately 14 minutes long, and was made by the course participant Dan Scully. The strikingly different representational style results from the plan of the research program, according to which the intention was to experiment with different methods of visualization. In contrast to the "desubjectivizing" thrust of the "deadpan" movie, this one was primarily concerned with the symbolic aspect of the architecture along the Strip. The same also applied to another short movie that documents a helicopter flight over the Strip shot during daylight. The camera's focus here is mainly on the towering advertising signs for the hotel casinos along the street, which appear to represent the only architectural elements in this peculiar urban landscape.

The most spectacular of the movies that have been preserved is labeled "Las Vegas Electric," with a running time of only around four minutes. [R] Once again, it is essentially a journey through Las Vegas, although in contrast to the three movies mentioned above, the special emphasis here is on the night-time illuminations,

68) Kevin Lynch, *The Image of the City* (Cambridge, MA: The Technology Press/Harvard University Press, 1960), p. 113.

69) György Kepes and Kevin Lynch, "Summary of Accomplishments: Research Project on the Perceptual Form of the City," ca. 1959, 8, Box 4, Kepes Papers, AAA, cited after Reinhold Martin, *The Organizational Complex: Architecture, Media, and Corporate Space* (Cambridge, MA: MIT Press, 2003), p. 138.

70) Cf. Venturi et al. 1972 (see note 4), p. 9.

71) Donald Appleyard, Kevin Lynch, and John R. Myer, *The View from the Road* (Cambridge, MA: MIT Press, 1964), p. 4.

72) "We are ... tempted to go into motion pictures, which record sequences in a permanent form that can be shown to large groups of people. Movies may be taken of existing highway sequences, either at normal speed or at exaggerated speeds, to convey in brief the essentials of the major visual effects." Ibid., p. 20.

73) Cf. Martino Stierli, "Die Stadt ins Bild gerückt. Der 'Alameda Report' als Beispiel visueller Stadtanalyse bei Venturi und Scott Brown," in Vittorio Magnago Lampugnani and Matthias Noell (eds.), *Stadtformen. Die Architektur der Stadt zwischen Imagination und Konstruktion* (Zurich: gta, 2005), pp. 282–99.

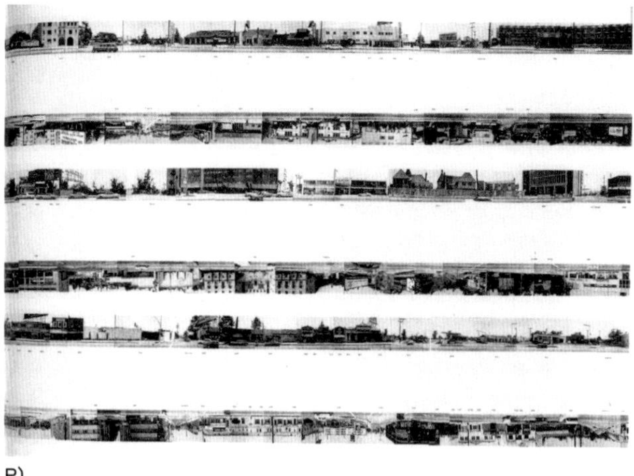

P)

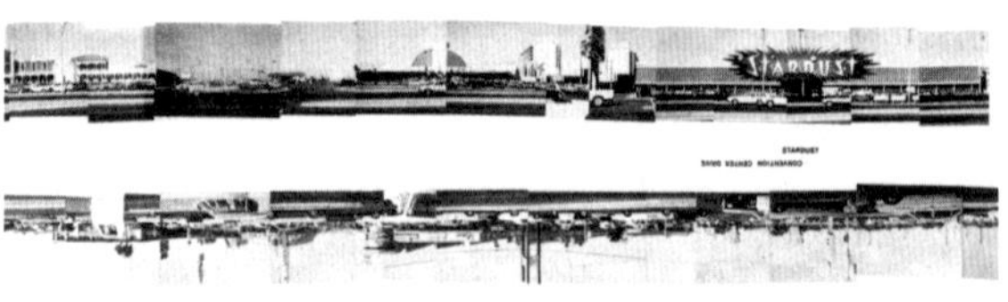

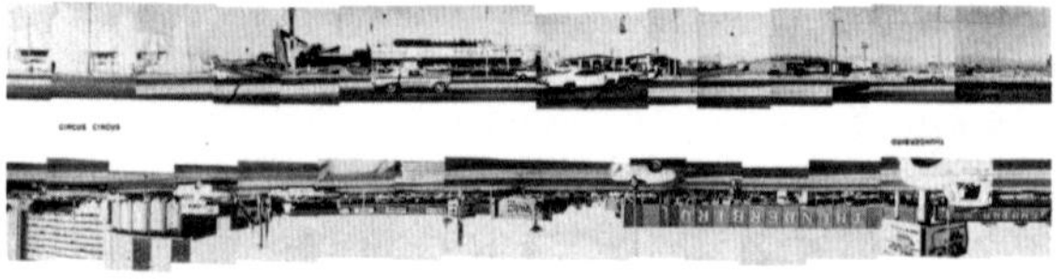

Q)

P) Edward Ruscha: *Every Building on the Sunset Strip,* concertina fold-out, 1965, detail

Q) "'Edward Ruscha' elevation of the Strip" from *Learning from Las Vegas,* detail

particularly on Fremont Street in the center of Las Vegas. In contrast to the urban sprawl along the Strip, the aspect of relative urban density on Fremont Street is articulated here, showing the leap in scale between a pedestrian-oriented and an automobile-oriented form of the city. The sequences, all shot at night, emphasize an interest in the aesthetics of the architecture of light. In comparison with the "deadpan" film, this film is marked by an extremely artistic and sometimes experimental approach. In one quasi-surreal sequence, the city's light spectacles, which stand out against the black background, are reflected on a horizontal axis. Another sequence shows a view from below of the brightly colored neon tubes above the Fremont Street pavement and transforms them into a psychedelic abstraction of color, shape, and light. The sequences appear at times to be almost "literal" quotations from the introductory sequence in George Sidney's 1964 production *Viva Las Vegas*.

In emphasizing the sequentiality of the perception of the contemporary city from an automobile, Venturi and Scott Brown related directly to a research project at the Massachusetts Institute of Technology (MIT) on the "Perceptual Form of the City," directed by György Kepes and Kevin Lynch. Lynch published his research findings in 1960 in the now-famous book *The Image of the City*, where he drew attention to the fact that the contemporary city was "experienced" in film-like image sequences. [68] Kepes and Lynch emphasized the central significance of this hypothesis for the whole research project in their concluding report, which described an "analysis of the perceptual impact of the urban highway on the driver and his passengers." [69] For this purpose, journeys on various highways in New England were documented using a combination of photography, film, and written records. The car thus became a machine for a new way of perceiving the city, for a "vision in motion." The link between automobility, perception, and the form of the city ultimately became the central topic of research in the study *The View from the Road*, which Lynch published along with Donald Appleyard and John Myer in 1964, following on directly from the MIT research program. [S] Venturi and Scott Brown referenced the book in *Learning from Las Vegas*. [70]

The aim of *The View from the Road* was to develop design guidelines for urban highways, which would enable drivers to perceive the city as an aesthetically pleasing whole. The architect becomes a director of the gaze. *Learning from Las Vegas* took this as its starting-point. For Venturi and Scott Brown, as well as the authors of *The View from the Road*, the perception of the city was a sequential experience related to cinema: "The sense of spatial sequence is like that of large-scale architecture; the continuity and insistent temporal flow are akin to music and the cinema." [71] Accordingly, in the authors' view, the medium of film was the one most appropriate for depicting the contemporary city. [72] The significance of *The View from the Road* in relation to *Learning from Las Vegas* is additionally underlined by the fact that Venturi and Scott Brown made use of notation techniques that Appleyard, Lynch, and Myer had developed in order to depict the sequentiality of the dynamic perception of the city. This applies, in particular, to the arrangement of image sequences into vertical rows. The authors of *The View from the Road* also provided their readers with a "reading guide" in the form of arrows arranged laterally. [T] Although this representational technique itself is not used in *Learning from Las Vegas*, it does appear in the little-known "Alameda Report" of 1977, which was based on the Las Vegas study in many ways. [73]

Learning from Las Vegas in context

In terms of both content and methodology, Venturi and Scott Brown in *Learning from Las Vegas* connected to problems in contemporary architectural discourse in many ways. Beyond that, the book succeeded in establishing a firm place for itself in 20th-century architectural and urbanistic theory. There were important reasons for this. Venturi and Scott Brown were among the first to introduce aspects of the everyday, the ugly and ordinary into Modernist debates on architecture and urbanism. Las Vegas served as a symbol for this undertaking. The aim of *Learning from Las Vegas* was to study and to present the aesthetics of the Strip as the product of an authentic American popular culture—a popular culture that had found a valid form for the idea of a city "from below"; a city that had evolved spontaneously and without the assistance of an architect or any other planning authority. In their manifesto, Venturi and Scott Brown argued not only that architects ought to accept the aesthetics of America's commercial popular culture, but also that this aesthetic could serve as the starting-point for a contemporary architectural design. Their decisive argument was that the city had to be acknowledged and accepted the way it actually was. Venturi and Scott Brown primarily saw themselves as readers and interpreters of an existing cultural and urban state. In taking this position, they distanced themselves from modern architects' preferred role-model—that of a godlike demiurge who was committed not to the reality of the city, but instead to a social and architectural utopia that had yet to be achieved. Venturi and Scott Brown's approach was revolutionary precisely in

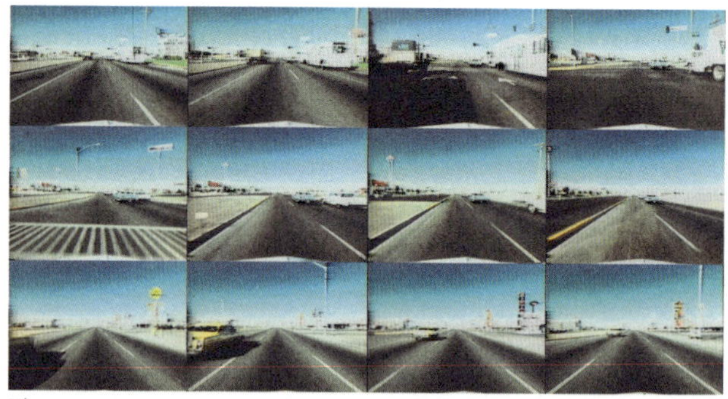

R)

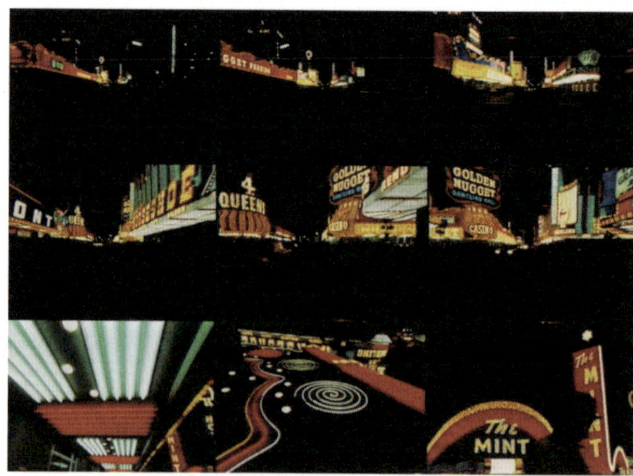

S)

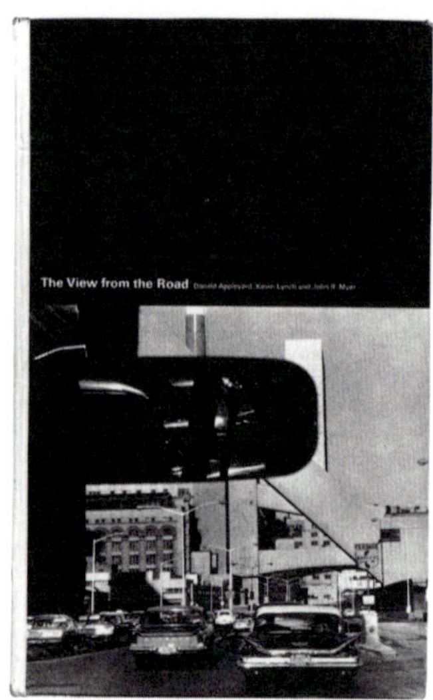

T)

R) Sequence from the film *Las Vegas Deadpan,* produced by students of the "Learning from Las Vegas Research Studio," 1968

S) Sequence from the film *Las Vegas Electric,* produced by students of the "Learning from Las Vegas Research Studio," 1968

T) Donald Appleyard, John Myer, Kevin Lynch: *The View from the Road,* 1964, cover

its renunciation of the rhetoric of revolution in favor of focusing architectural thought and action on the here and now. They captured this visually in their photographic and filmic research on the Strip. Working with the image of the city, and working *on* the image of the city, became one of their central concerns. It is this insistence on the city as it actually is that is the lasting legacy of *Learning from Las Vegas.*

Images from the Archives of Robert Venturi and Denise Scott Brown

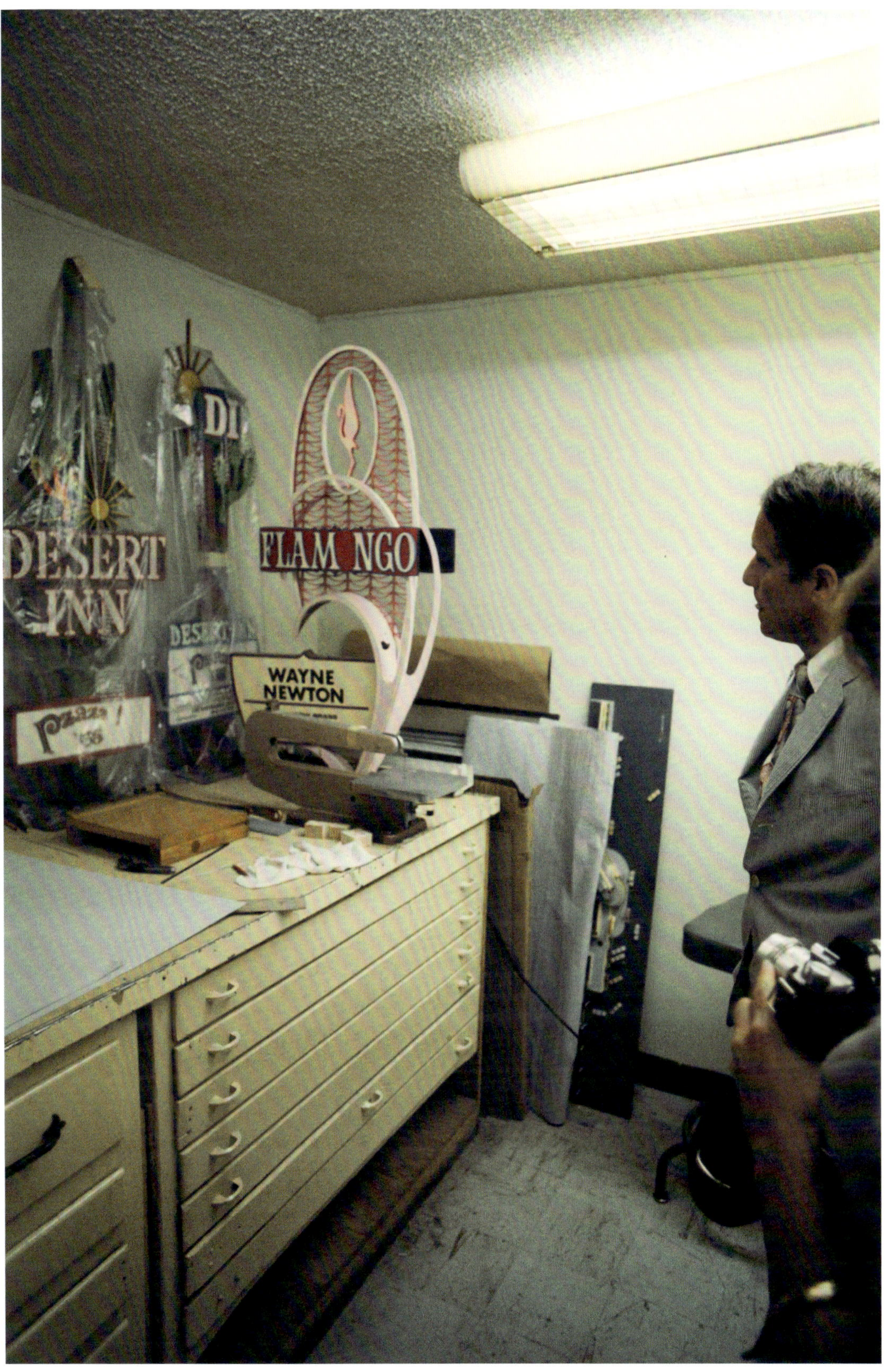
DESERT
INN
DI
FLAM NGO
WAYNE
NEWTON

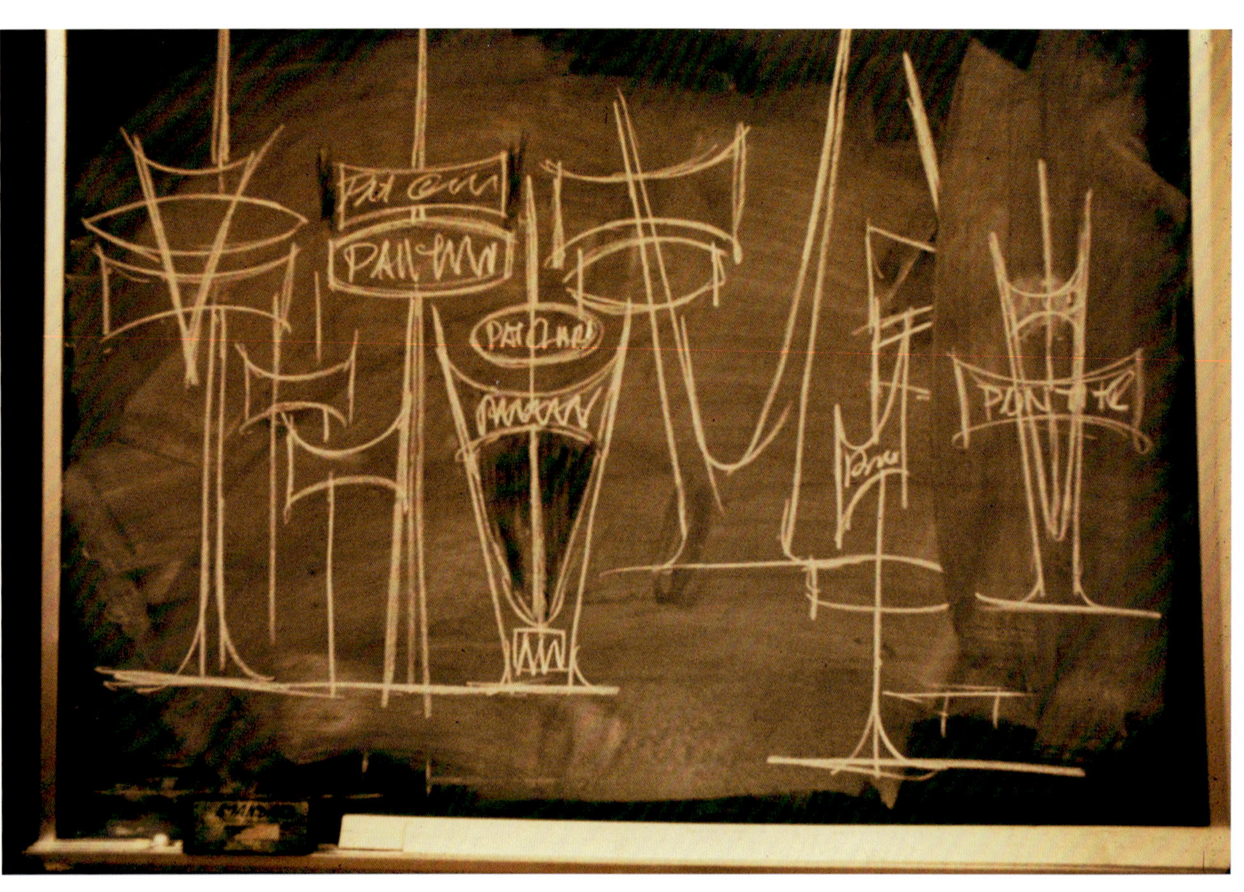

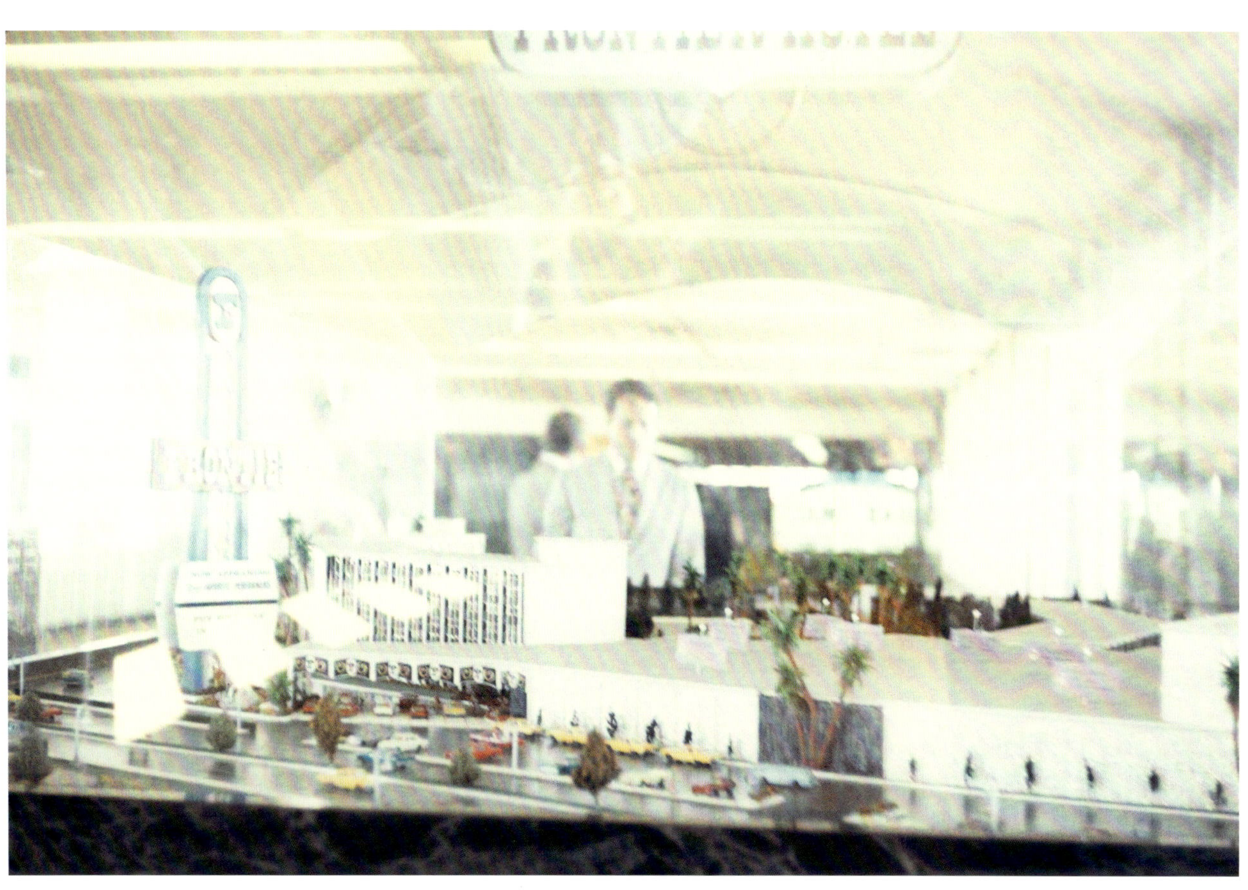

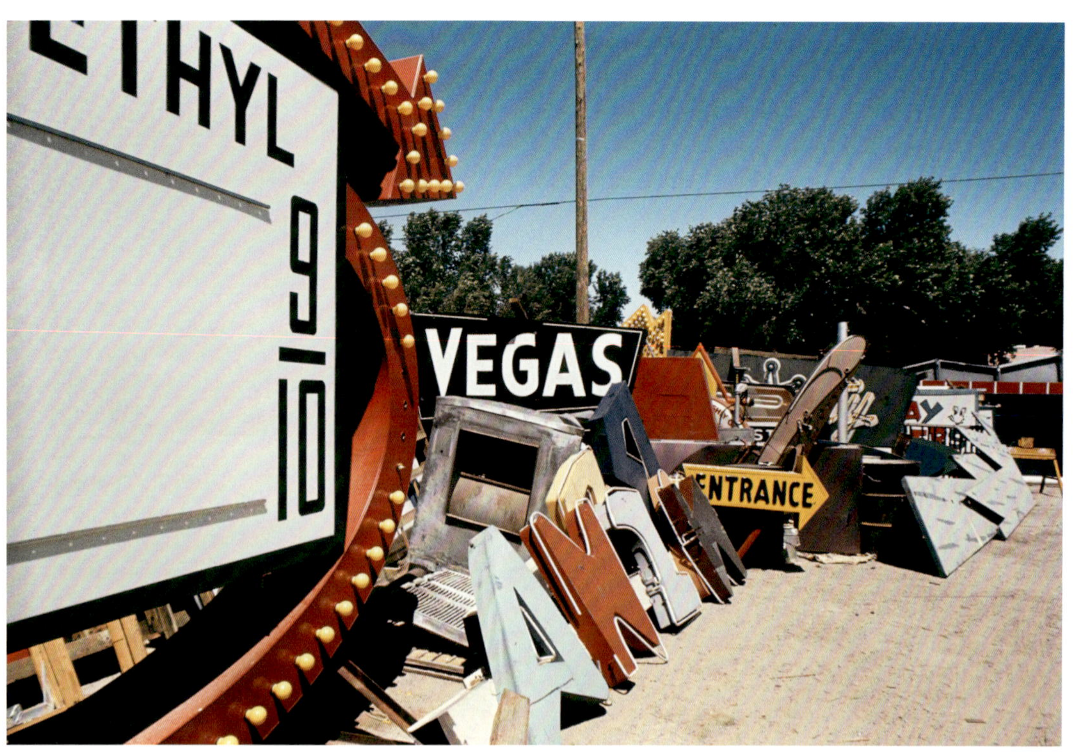
ETHYL
VEGAS
ENTRANCE

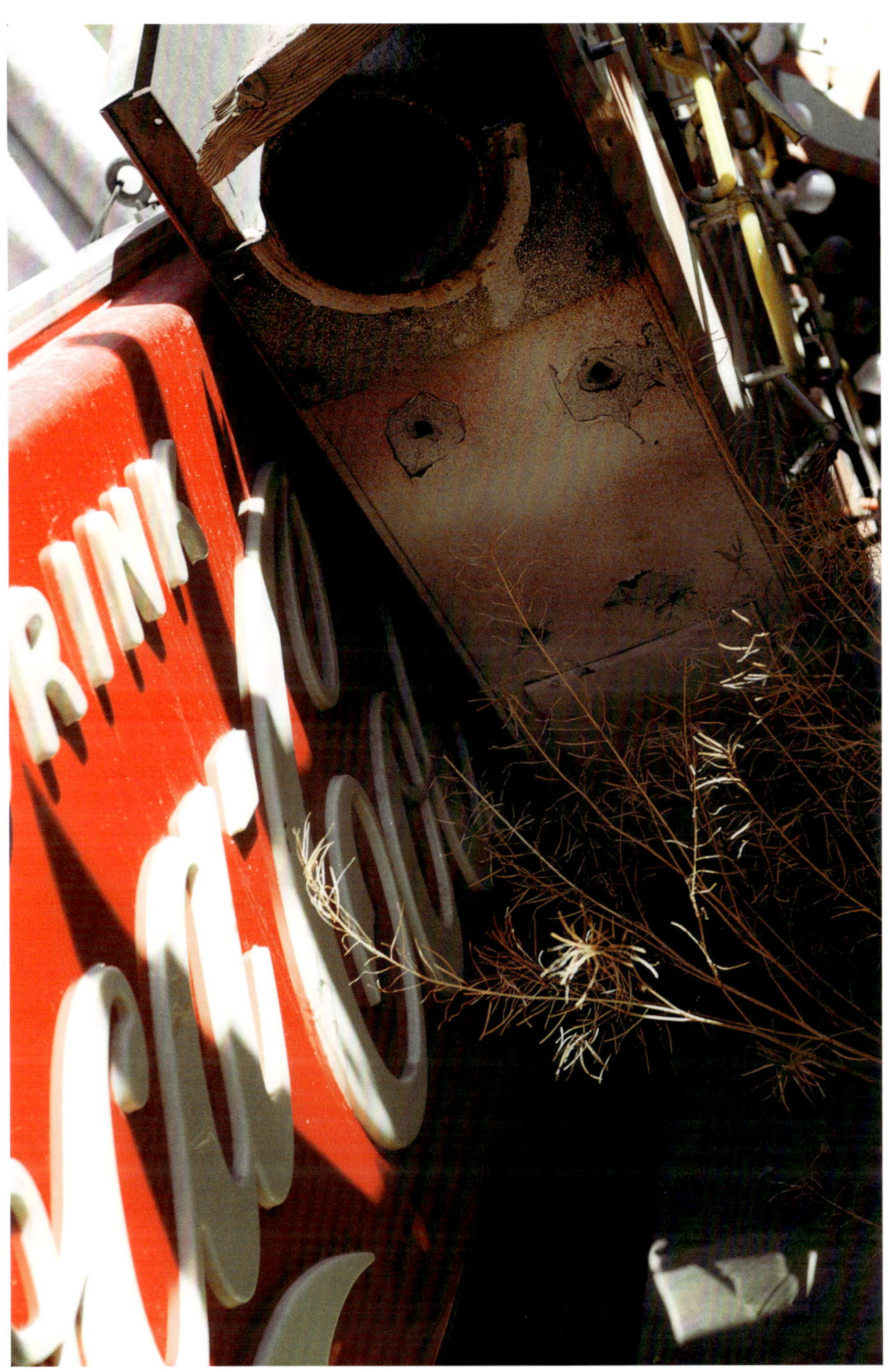
RINK

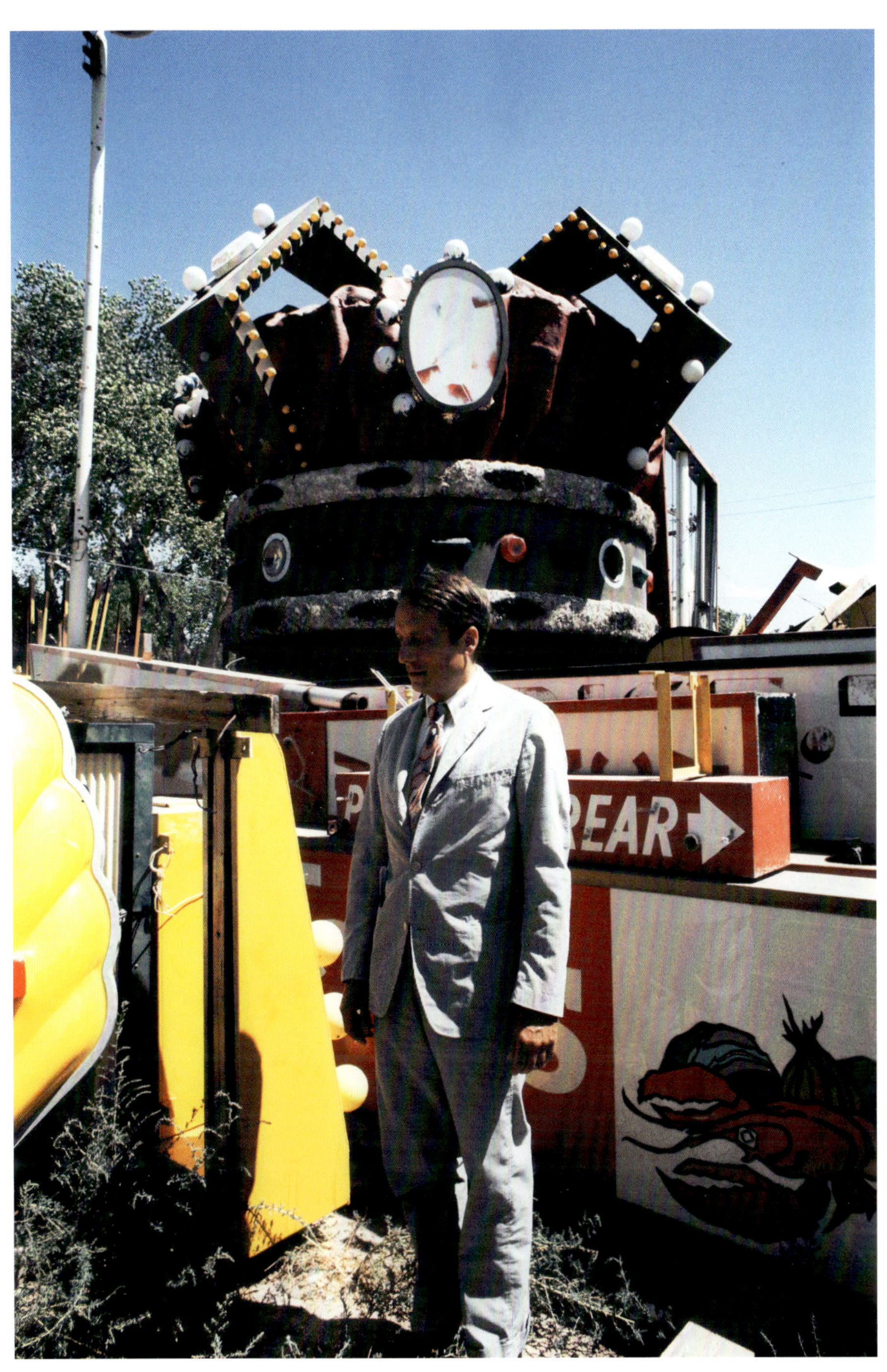
REAR

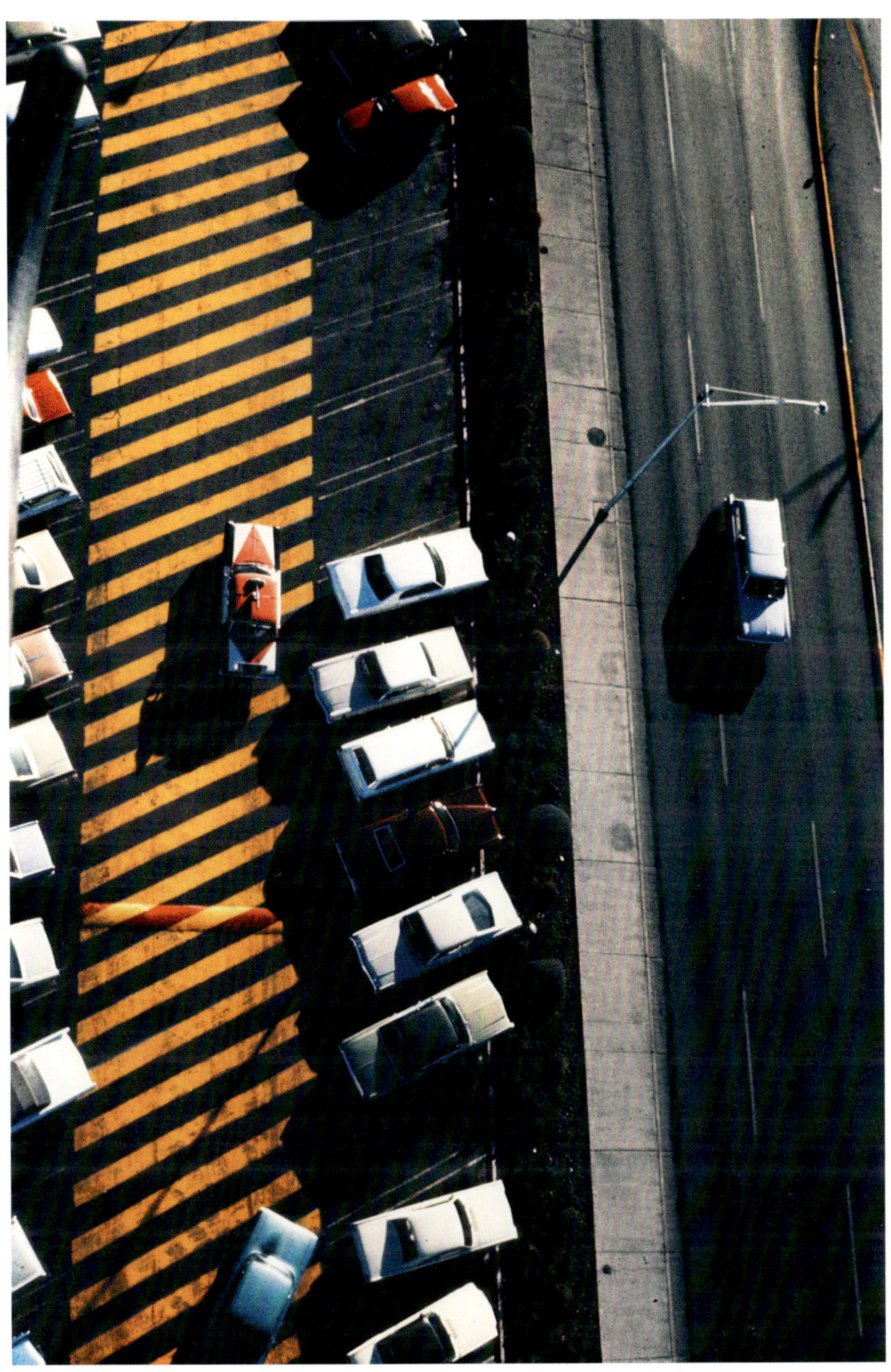

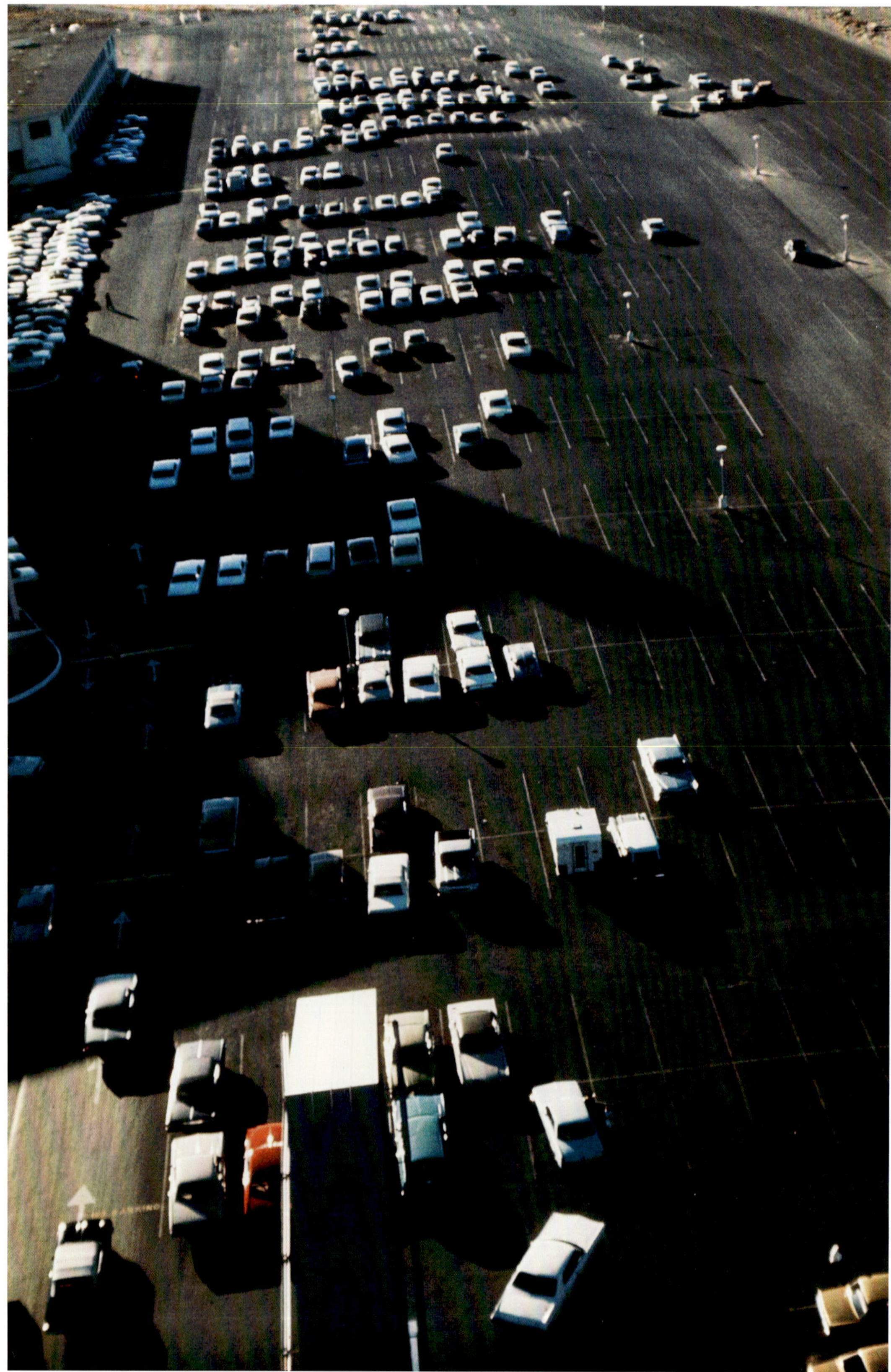

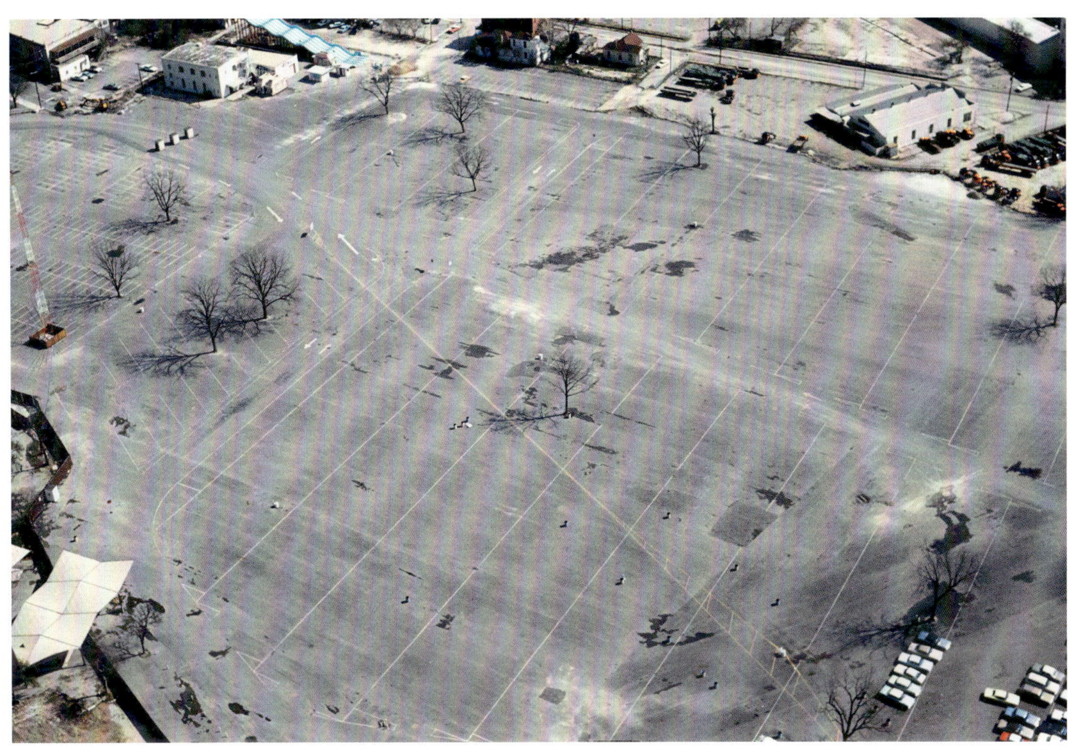

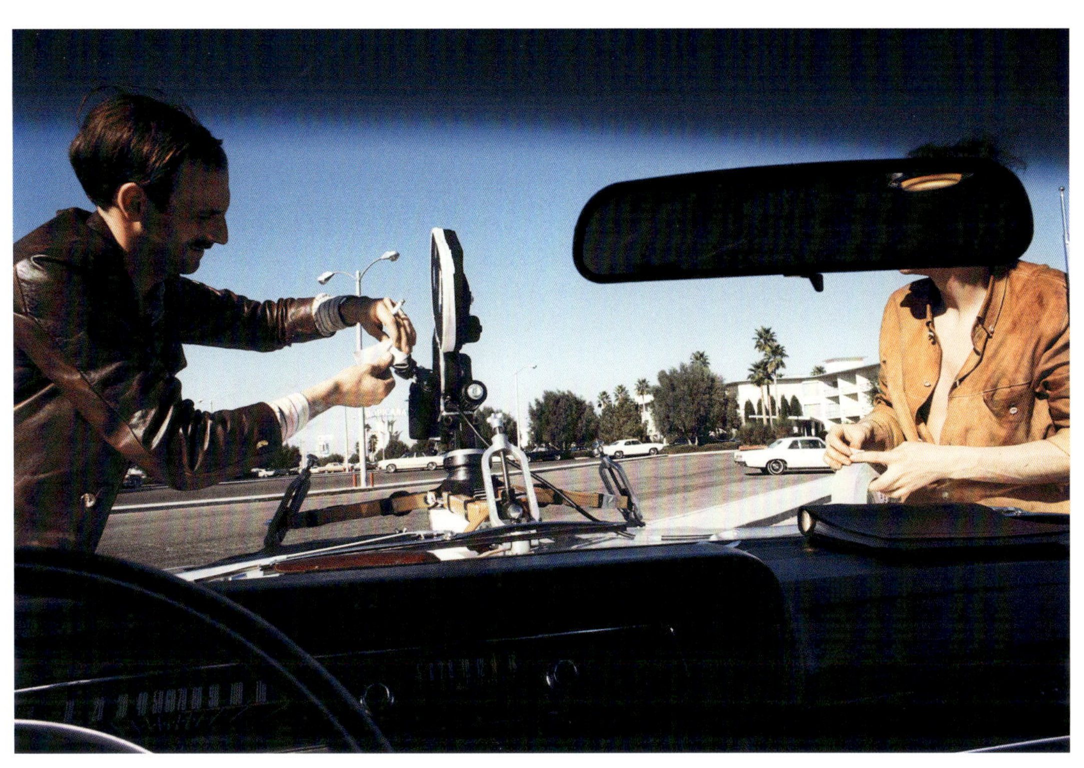

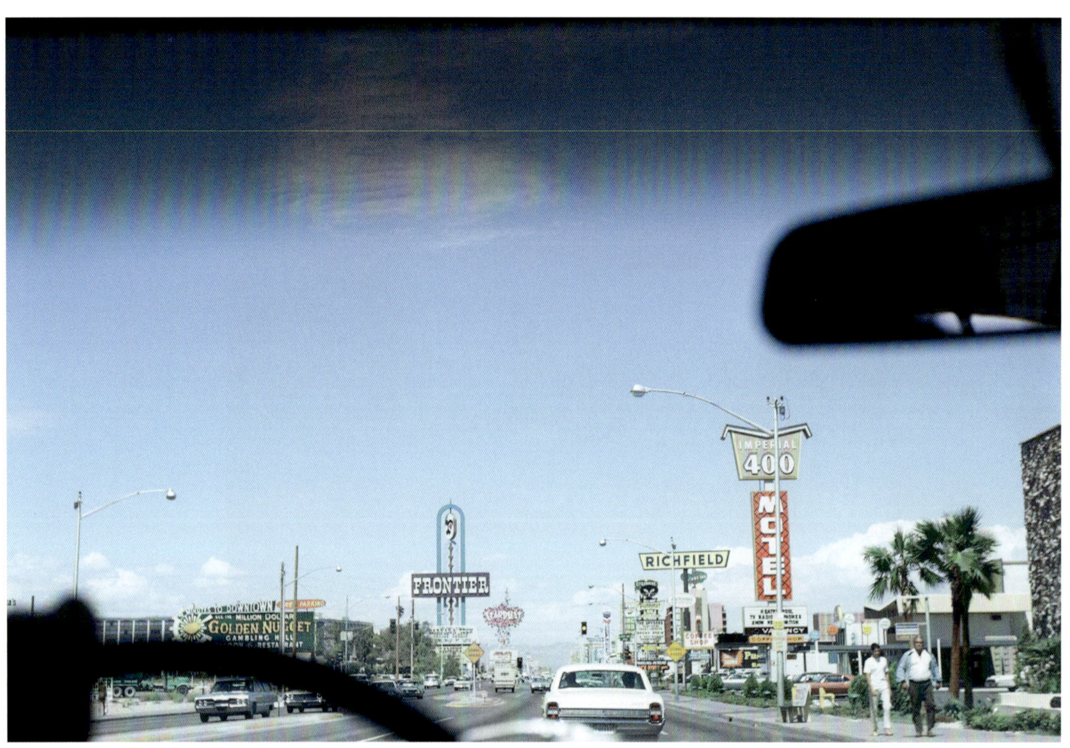
IMPERIAL
400
MOTEL
RICHFIELD
FRONTIER
GOLDEN NUGGET

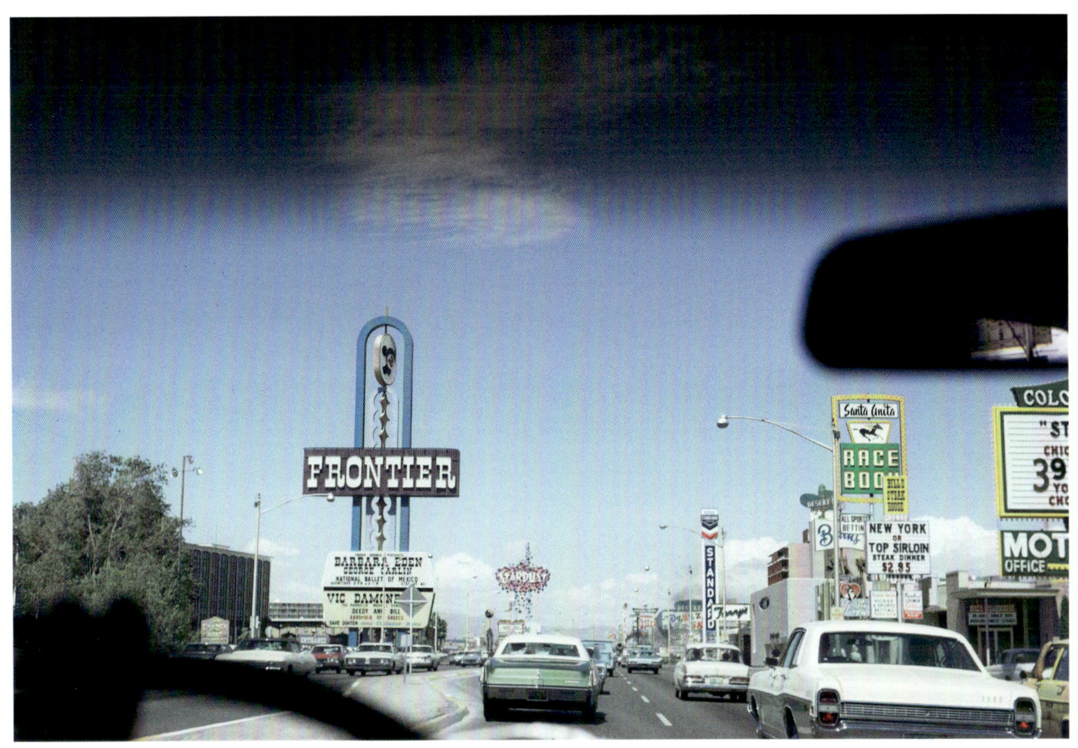
FRONTIER
BARBARA EDEN
GEORGE CARLIN
NATIONAL BALLET OF MEXICO
VIC DAMONE
DEEDY AND BILL
STARDUST
STANDARD
Santa Anita
RACE BOOK
NEW YORK
OR
TOP SIRLOIN
STEAK DINNER
$2.95
OFFICE

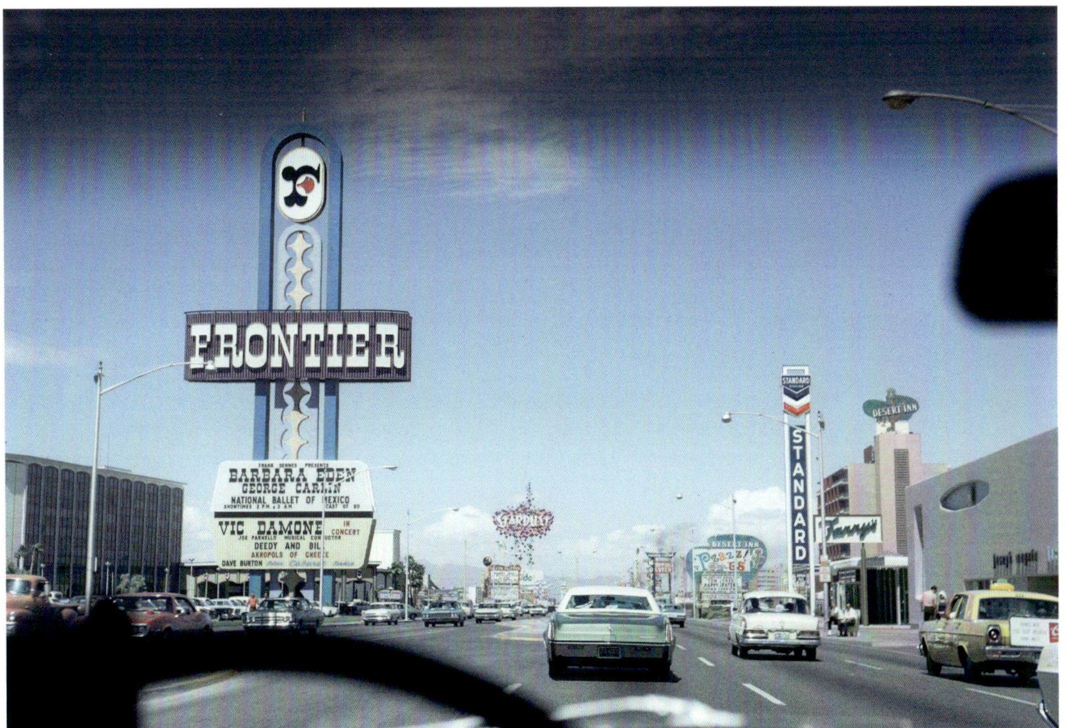
FRONTIER
FRANK SENNES PRESENTS
BARBARA EDEN
GEORGE CARLIN
NATIONAL BALLET OF MEXICO
VIC DAMONE
IN CONCERT
DEEDY AND BILL
STARDUST
STANDARD
DESERT INN

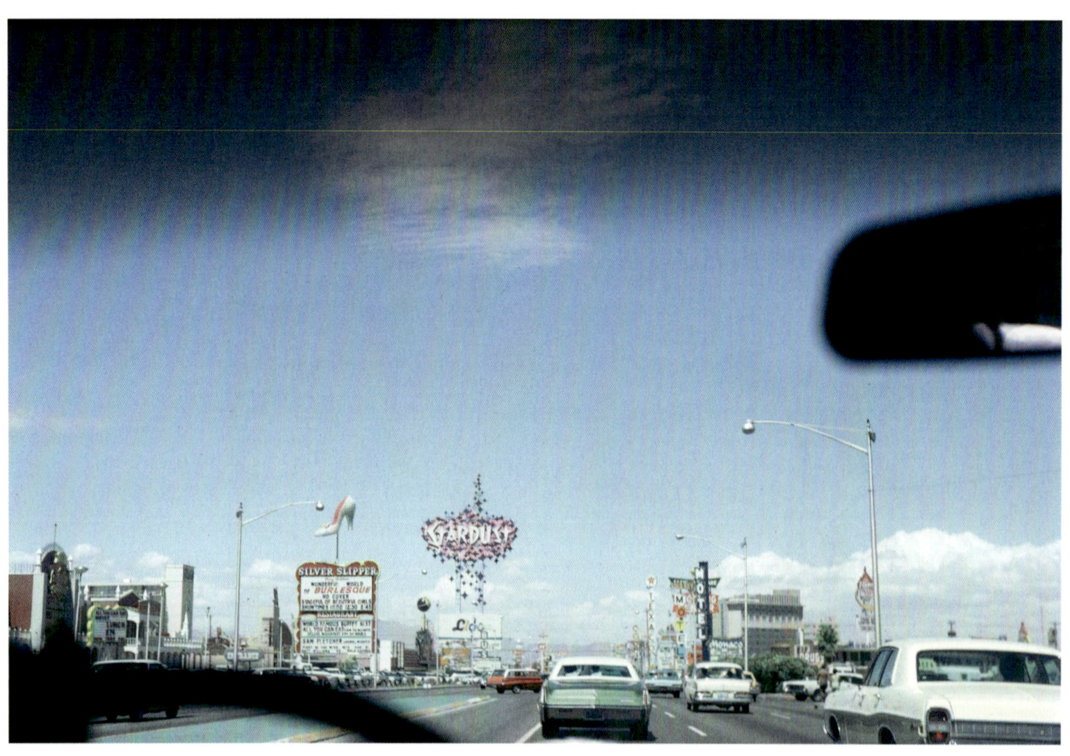
SILVER SLIPPER
WONDERFUL WORLD OF BURLESQUE
NO COVER
STARDUST
MOTEL

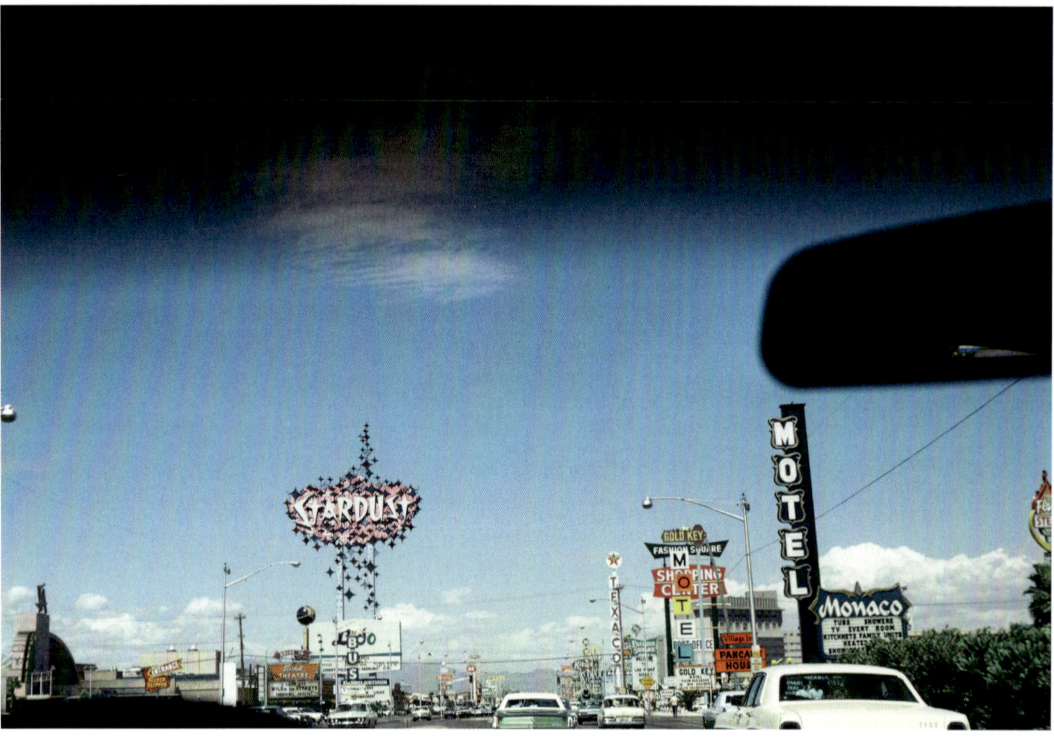
STARDUST
GOLD KEY
FASHION SQUARE
MOTEL
SHOPPING CENTER
TEXACO
MOTEL
Monaco
TUBS SHOWERS
TV EVERY ROOM
KITCHNETS FAMILY UNITS
GOLD KEY

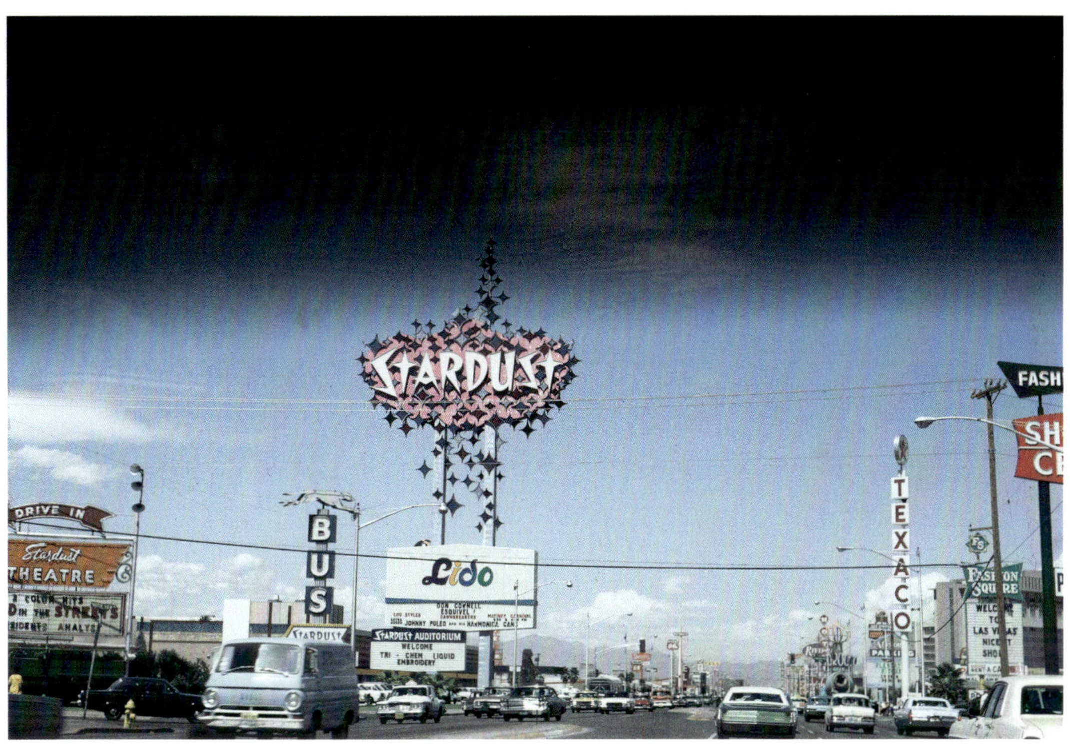
STARDUST
DRIVE IN
Stardust THEATRE
BUS
Lido
STARDUST AUDITORIUM
WELCOME
TRI - CHEM LIQUID
EMBROIDERY
TEXACO
FASHION SQUARE

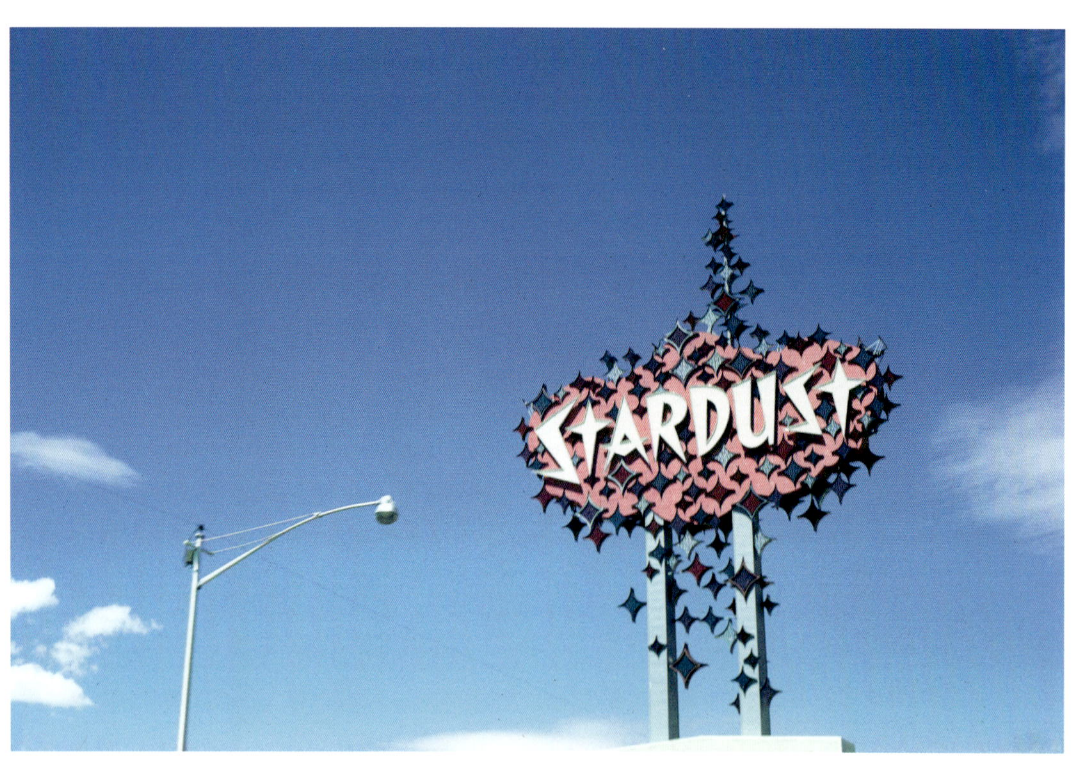
STARDUST

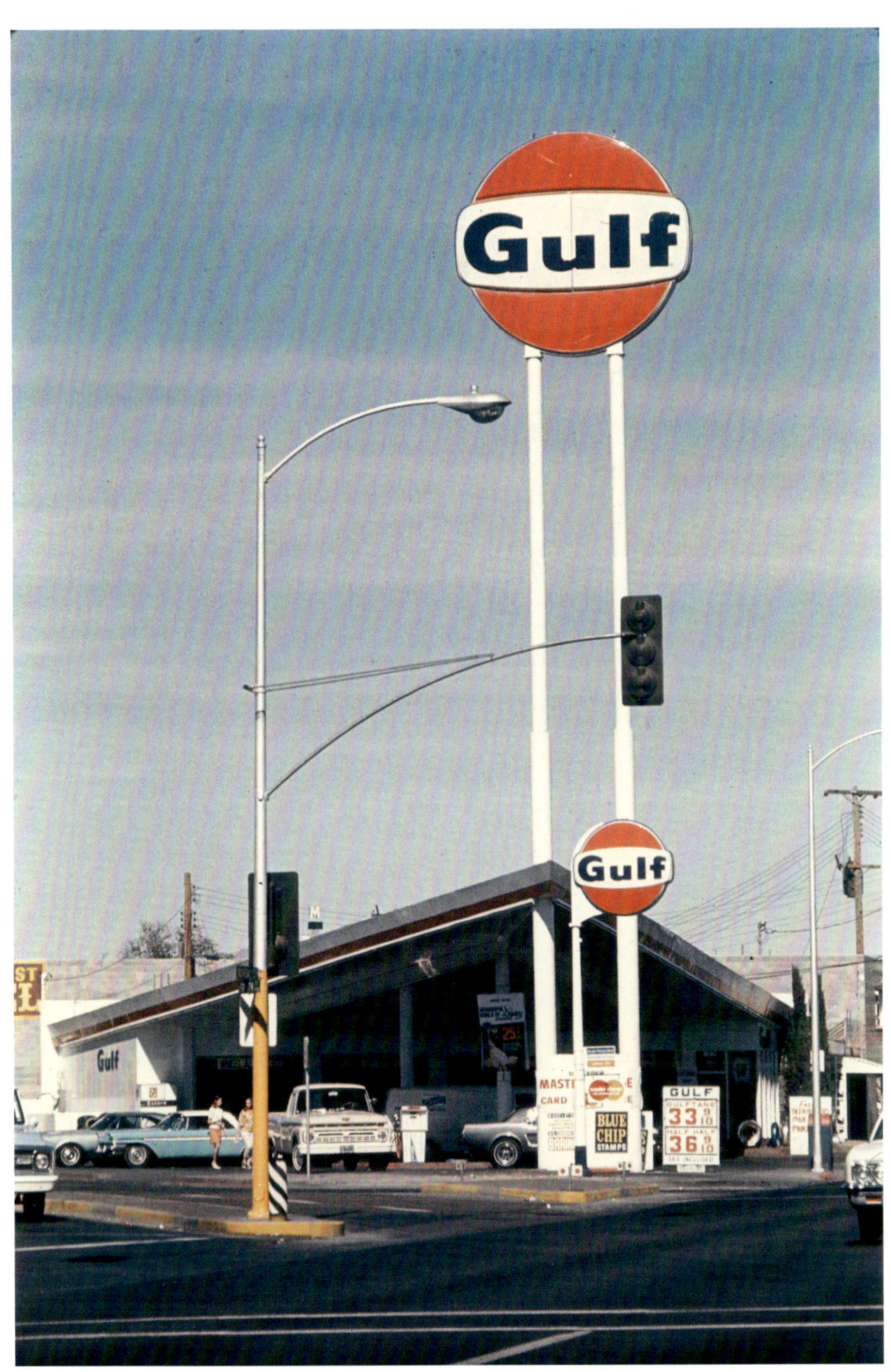
Gulf
Gulf
Gulf
BLUE CHIP STAMPS
GULF
GULFTANE
33 9/10
HALF HALF
36 9/10
TAX INCLUDED

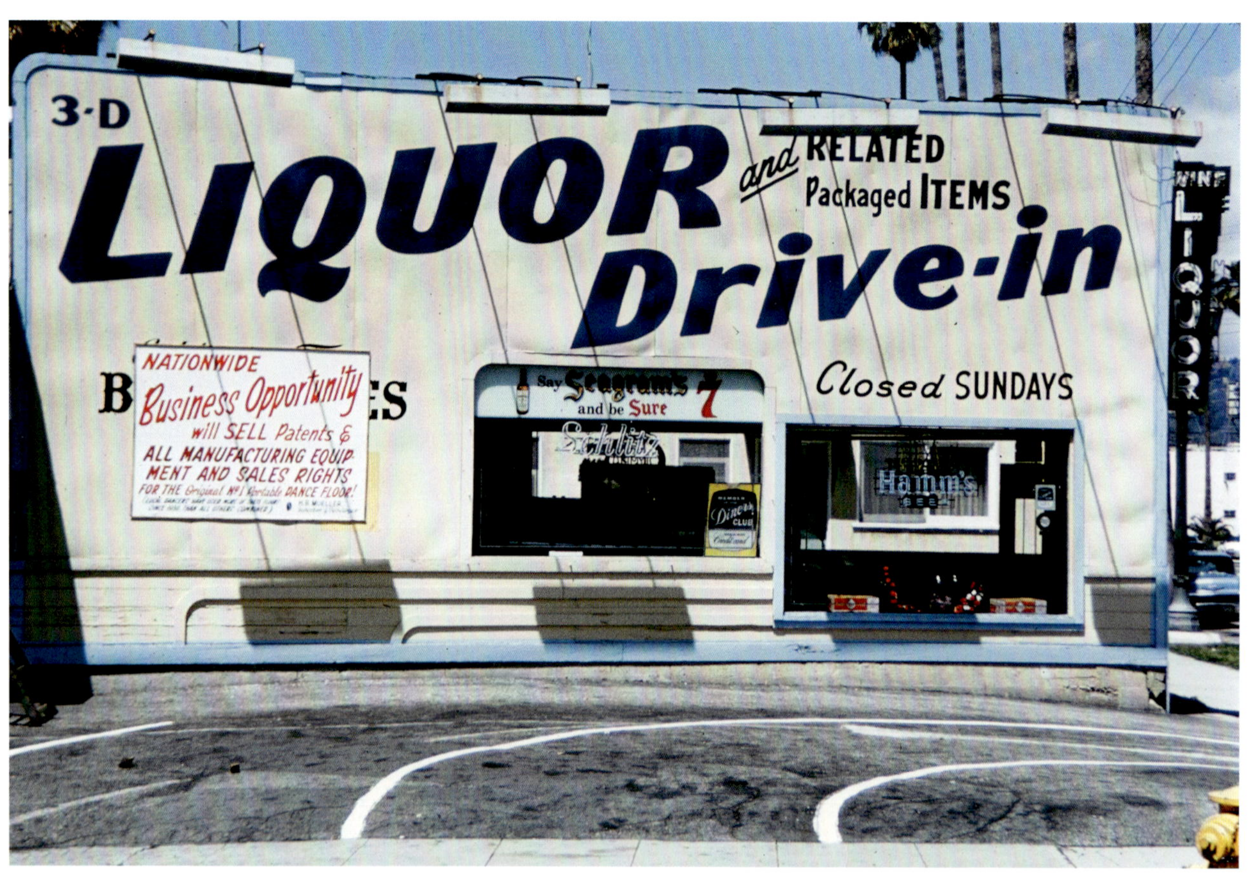
3-D
LIQUOR and RELATED
Packaged ITEMS
Drive-in
NATIONWIDE
Business Opportunity
will SELL Patents &
ALL MANUFACTURING EQUIP-
MENT AND SALES RIGHTS
FOR THE Original No1 Portable DANCE FLOOR!
Say Seagram's 7 and be Sure
Schlitz
Diners Club
Closed SUNDAYS
Hamm's
LIQUOR

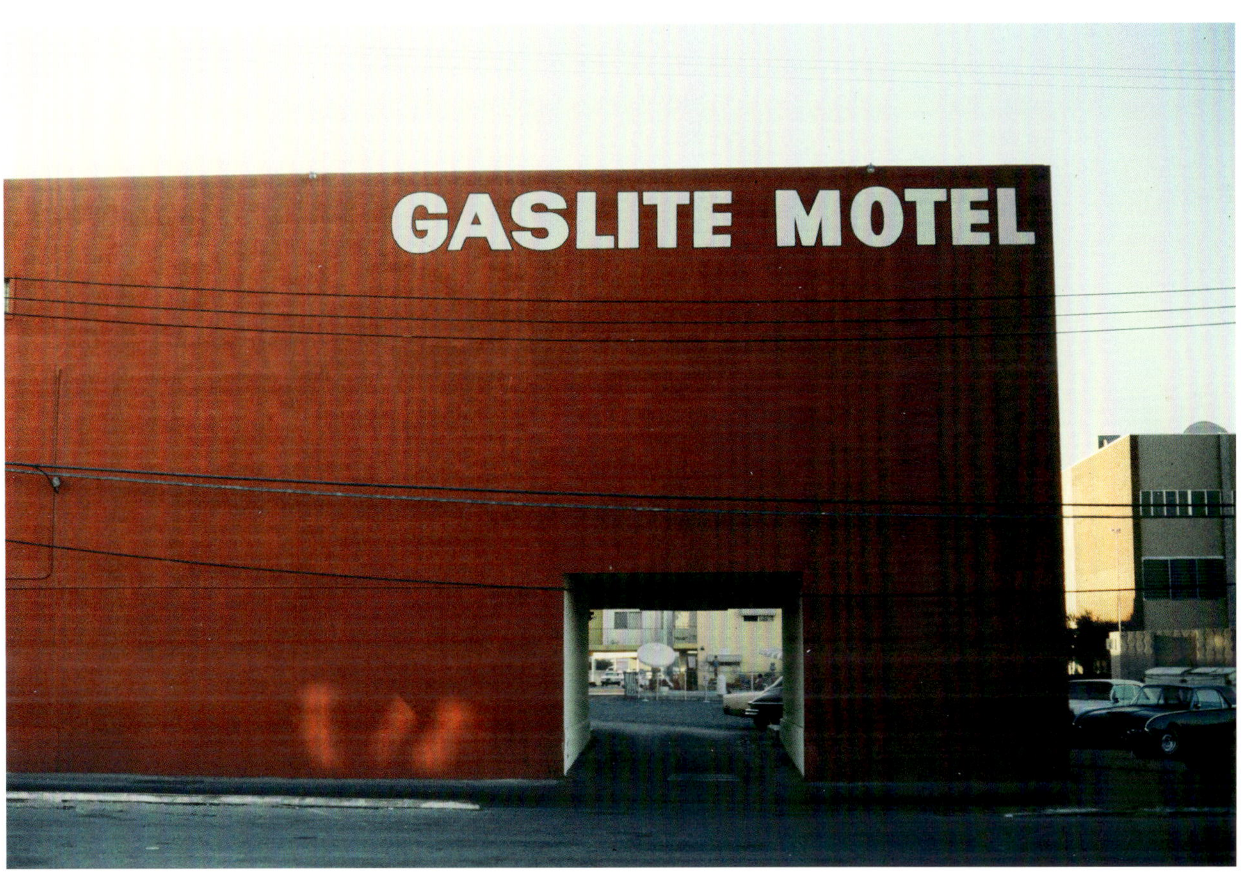
GASLITE MOTEL

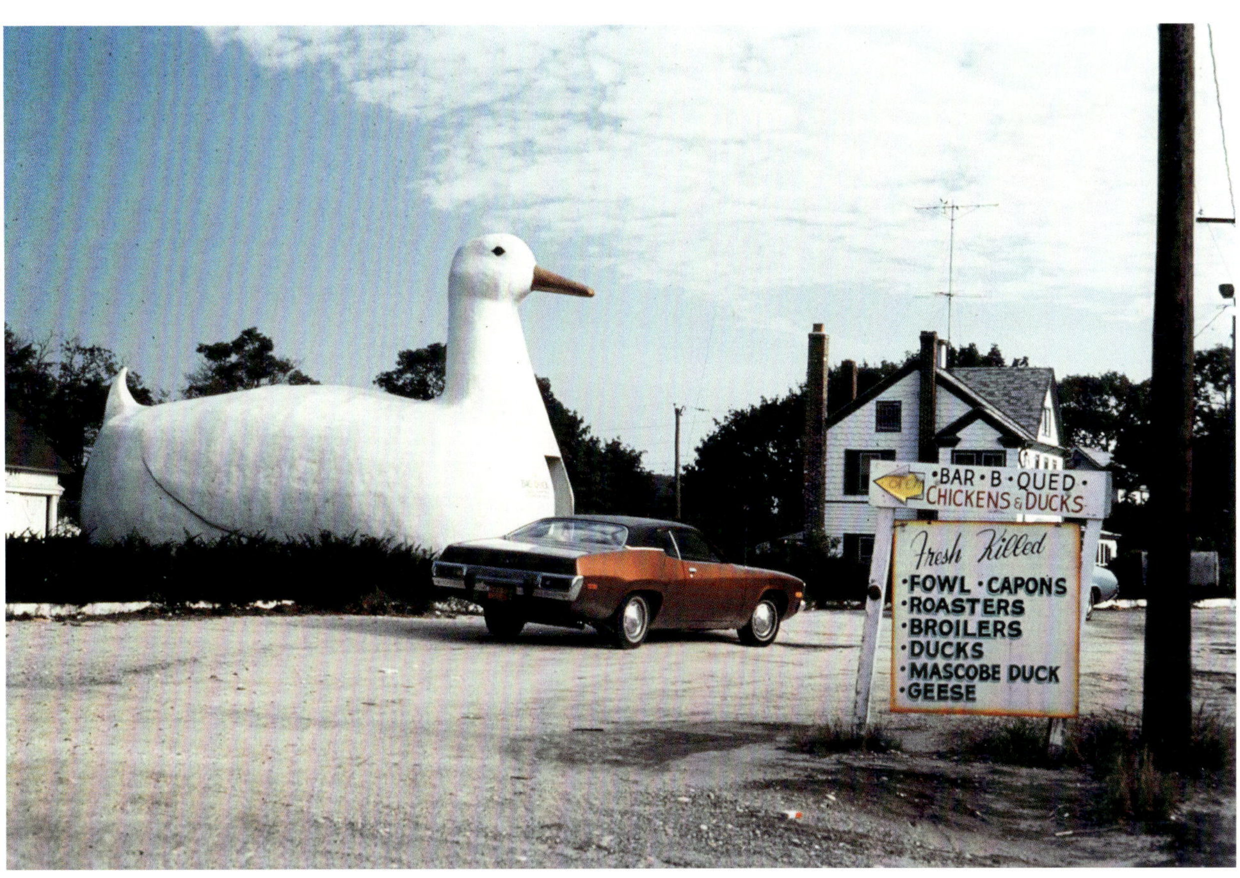
OPEN
BAR B QUED
CHICKENS & DUCKS
Fresh Killed
FOWL CAPONS
ROASTERS
BROILERS
DUCKS
MASCOBE DUCK
GEESE

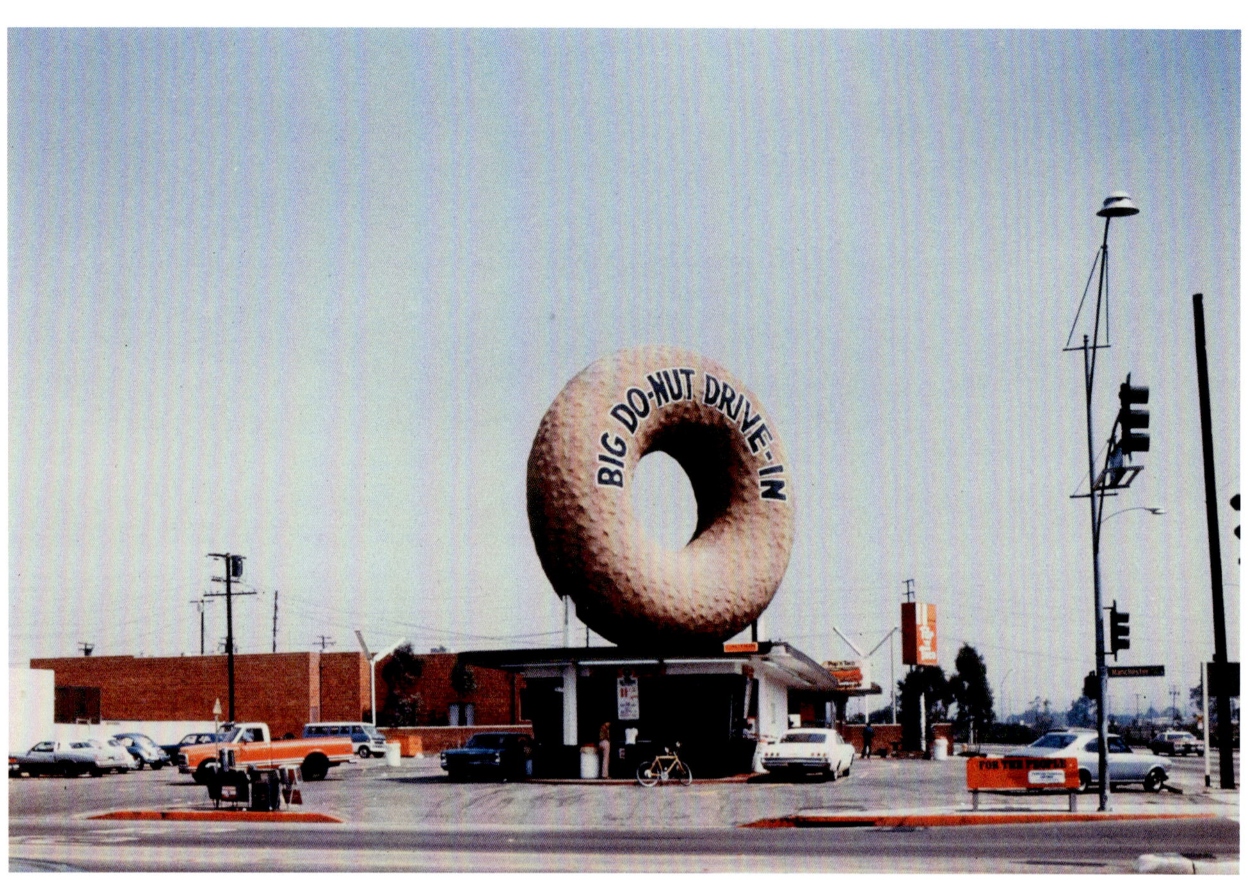
BIG DO-NUT DRIVE-IN

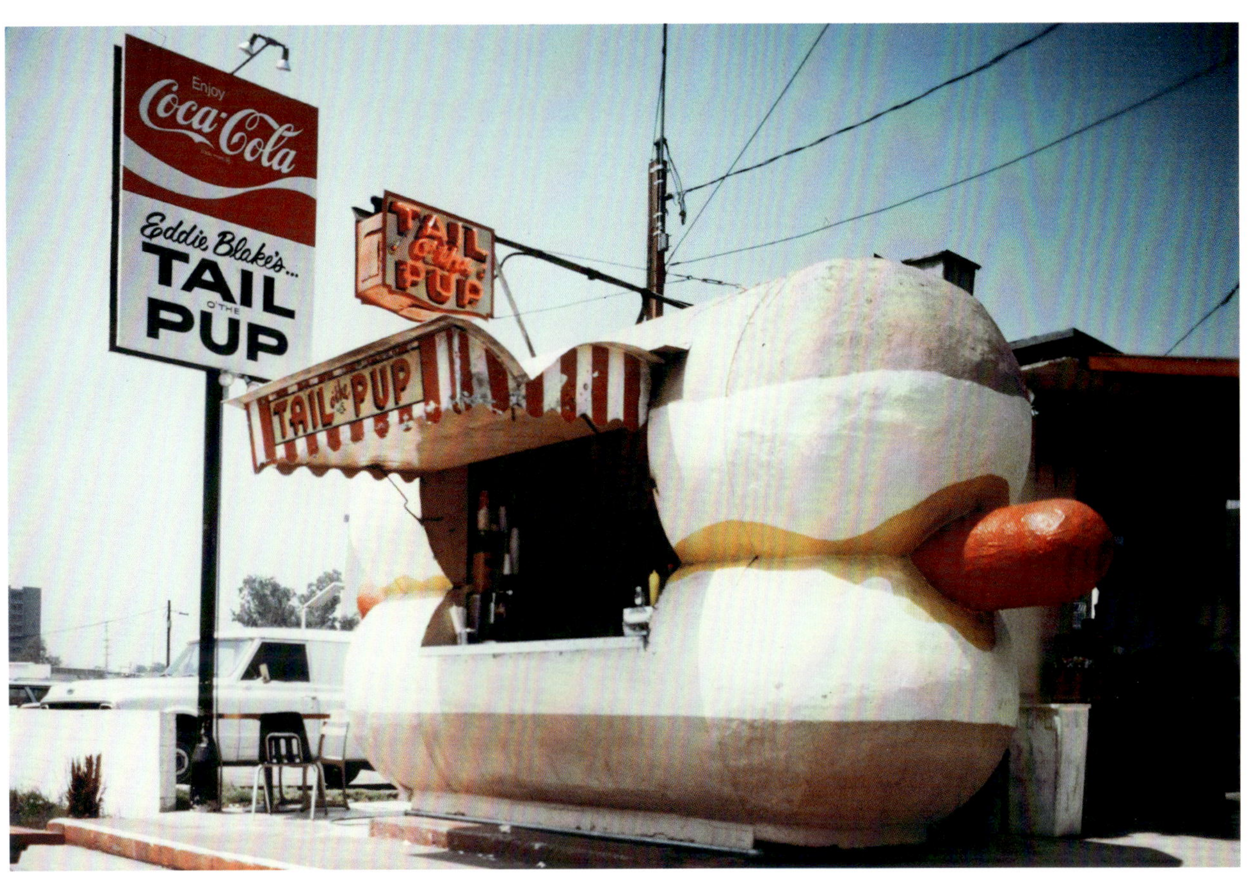
Enjoy
Coca-Cola
Eddie Blake's...
TAIL
O'THE
PUP
TAIL
PUP
TAIL
PUP

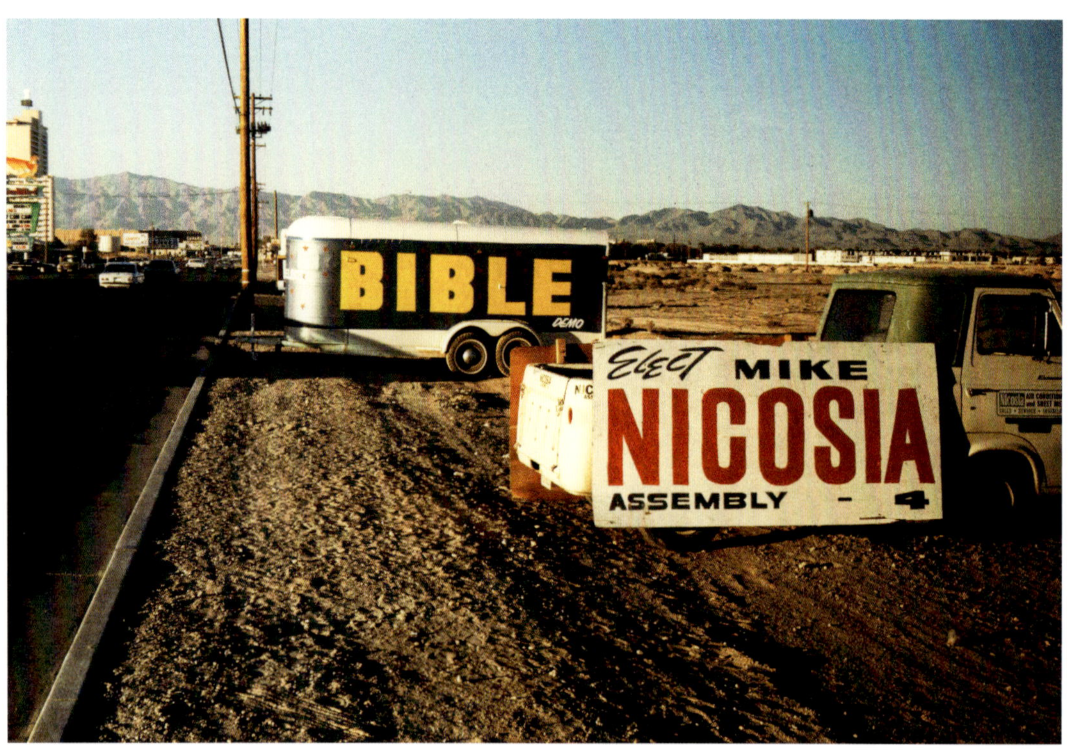
BIBLE
DEMO
ELECT MIKE
NICOSIA
ASSEMBLY - 4

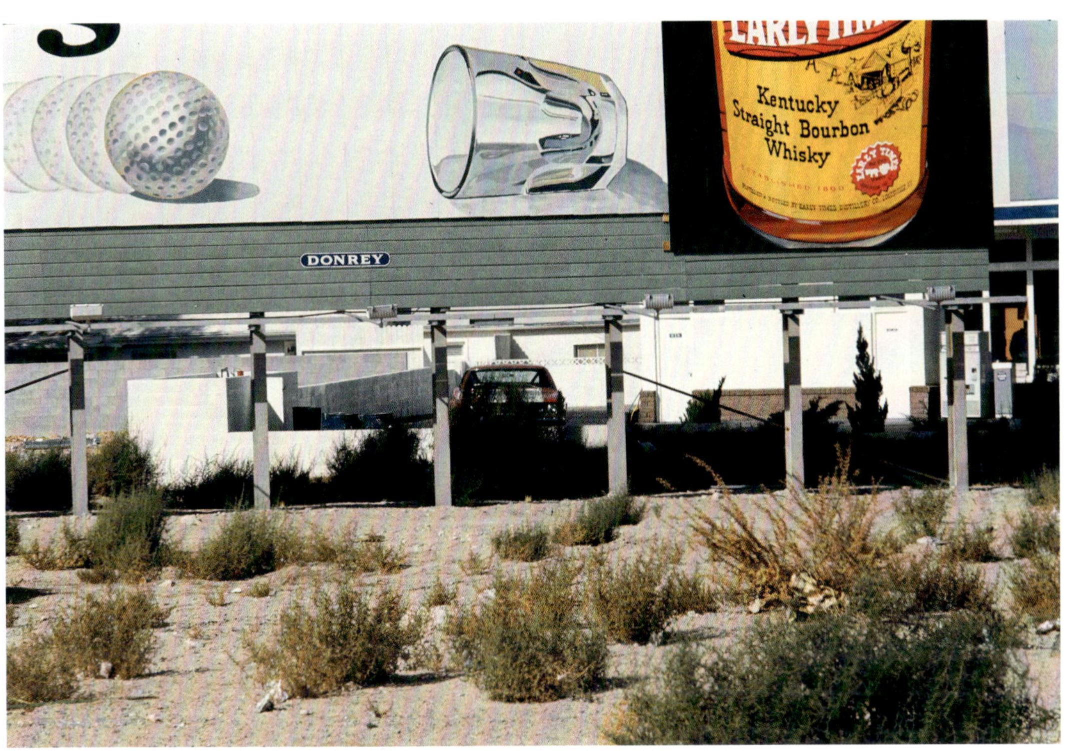
Kentucky
Straight Bourbon
Whisky
DONREY

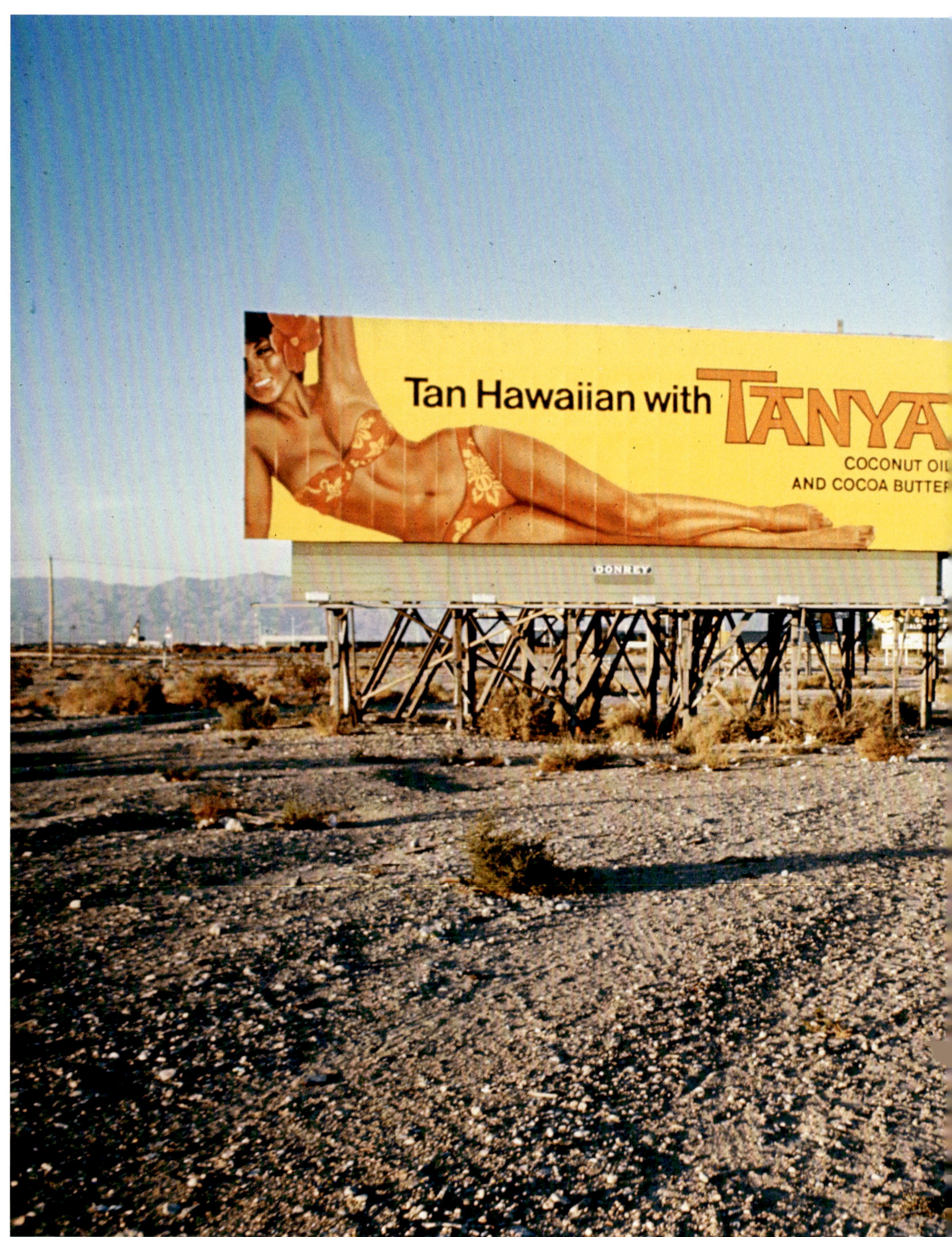
Tan Hawaiian with TANYA
COCONUT OIL
AND COCOA BUTTER
DONREY

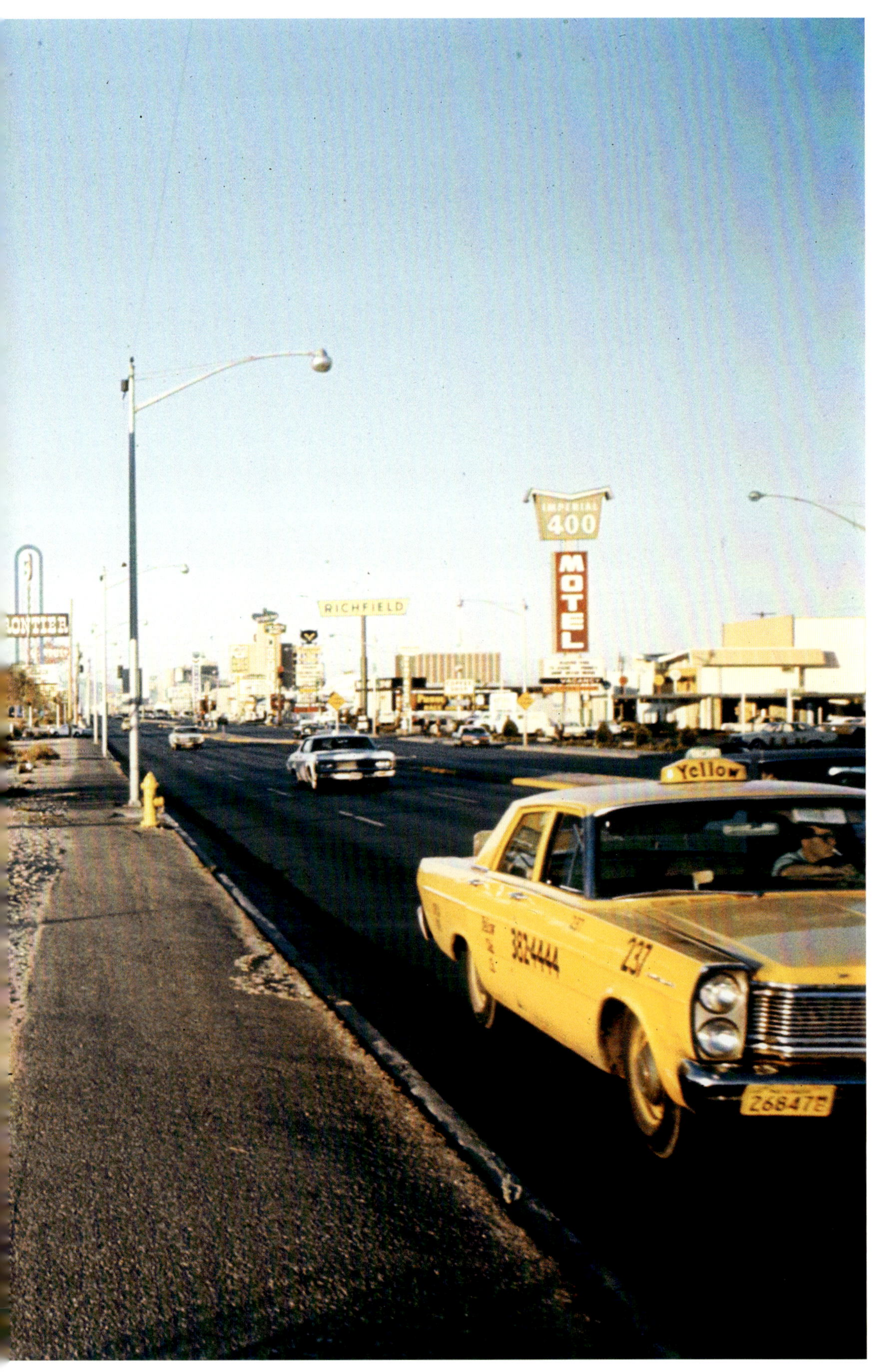
IMPERIAL
400
MOTEL
RICHFIELD
Yellow
382-4444
237

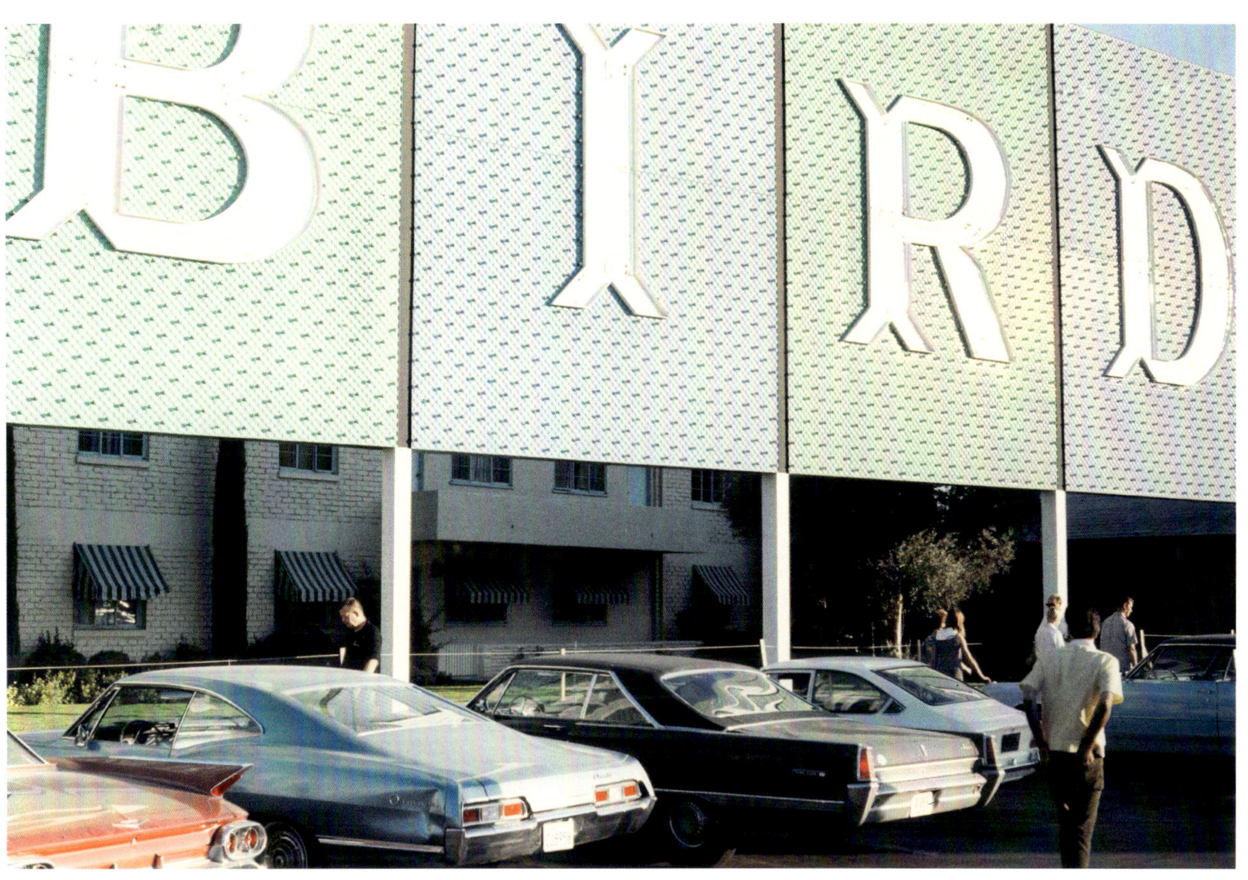
BIRD

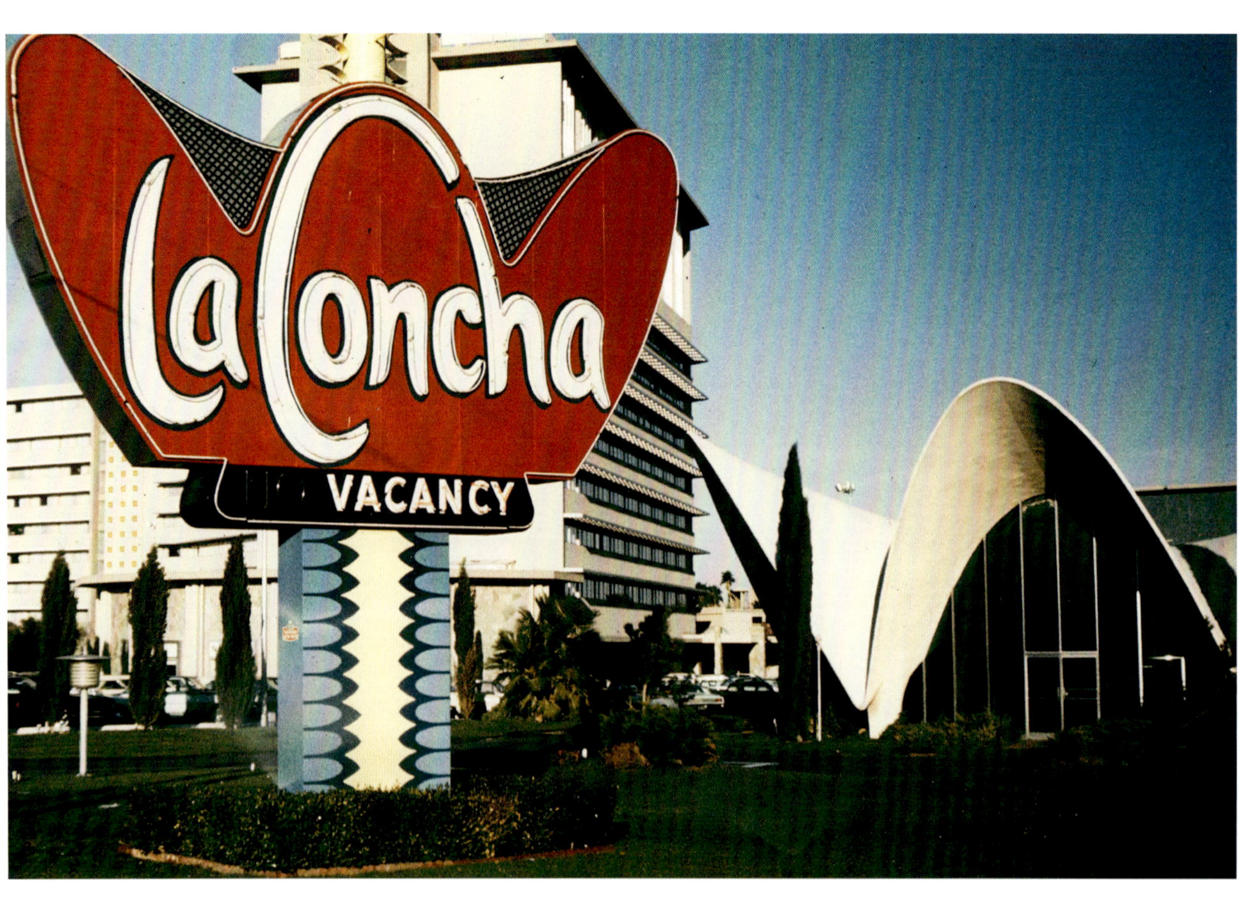
La Concha
VACANCY

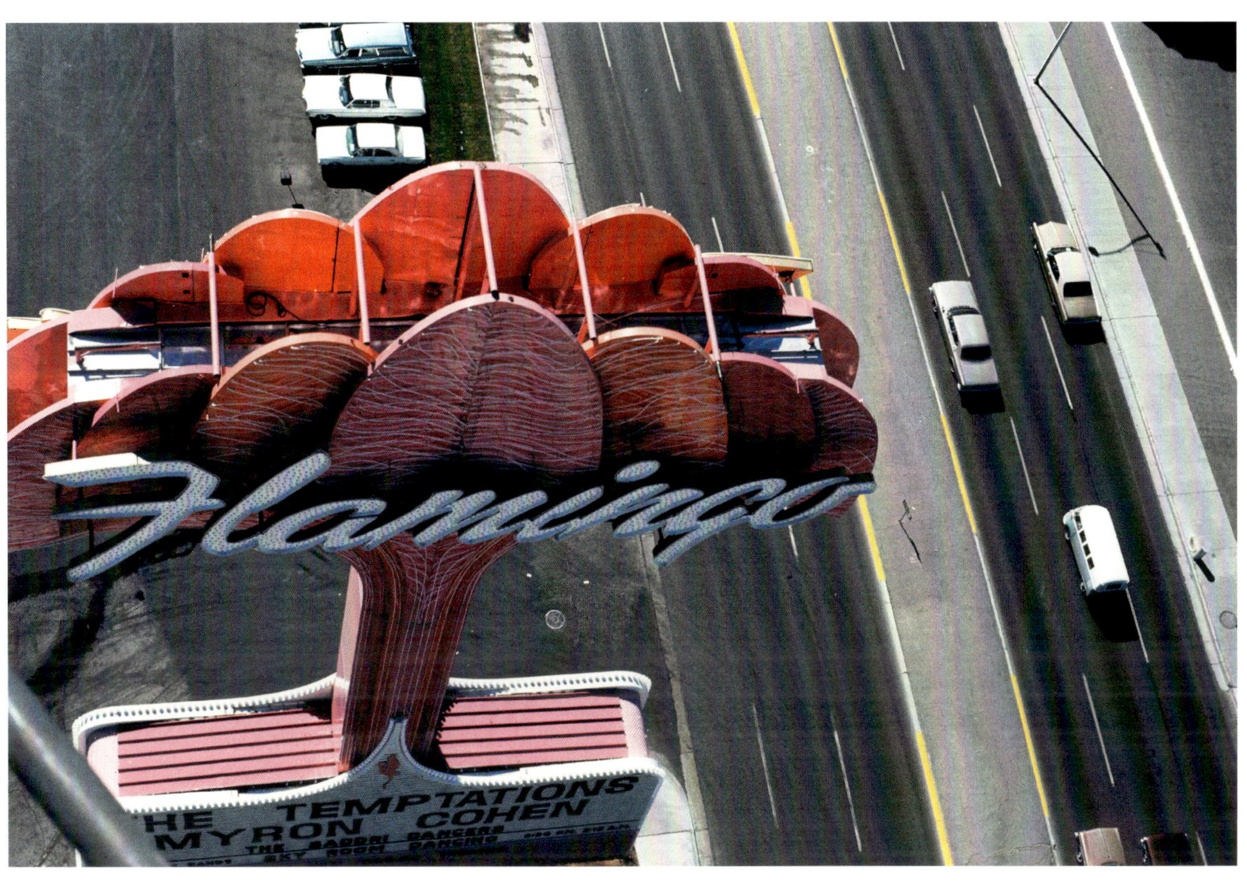
Flamingo
HE TEMPTATIONS
MYRON COHEN
DANCERS
THE
DANCING

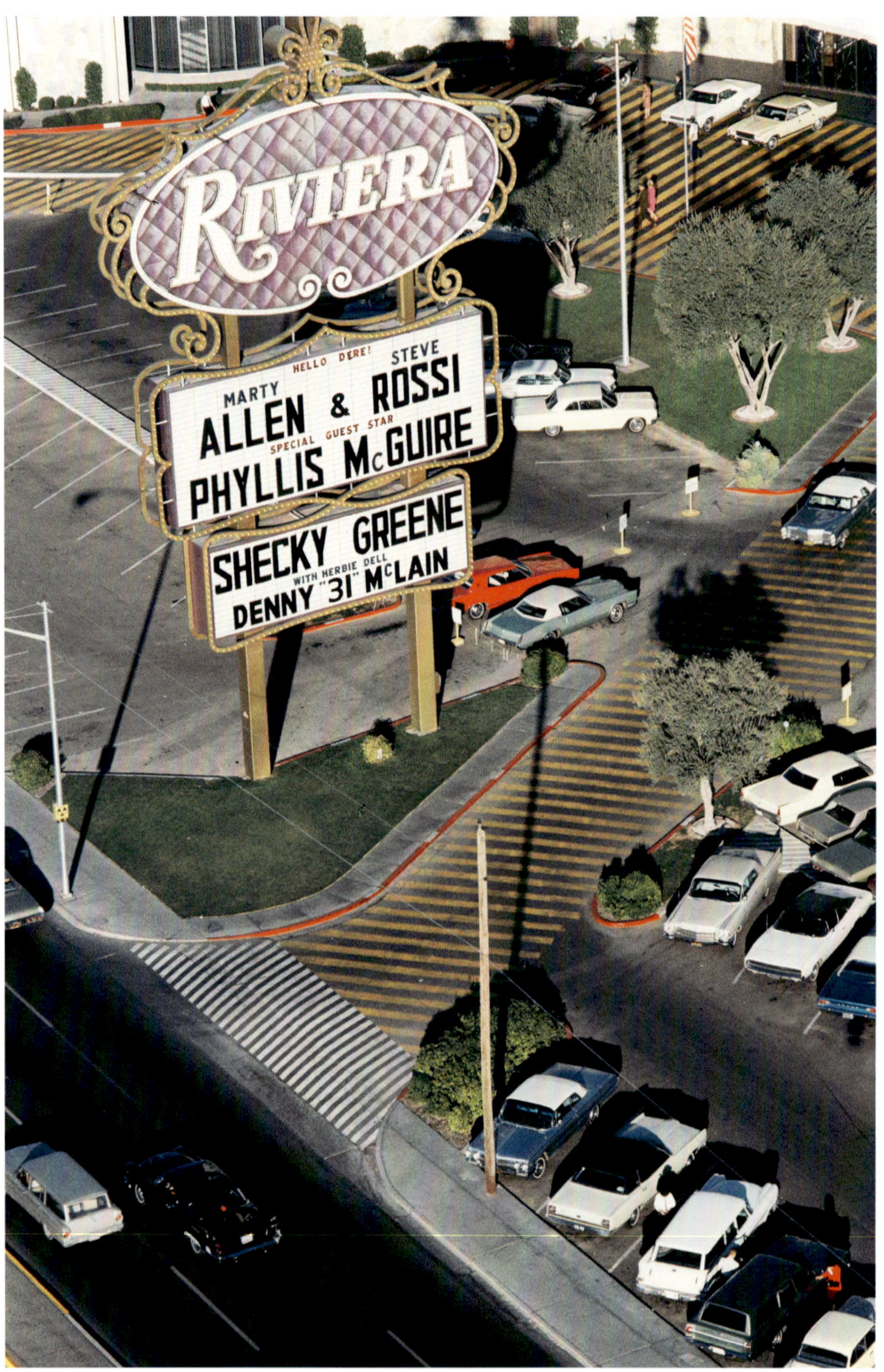
RIVIERA
HELLO DERE!
MARTY STEVE
ALLEN & ROSSI
SPECIAL GUEST STAR
PHYLLIS McGUIRE
SHECKY GREENE
WITH HERBIE DELL
DENNY "31" McLAIN

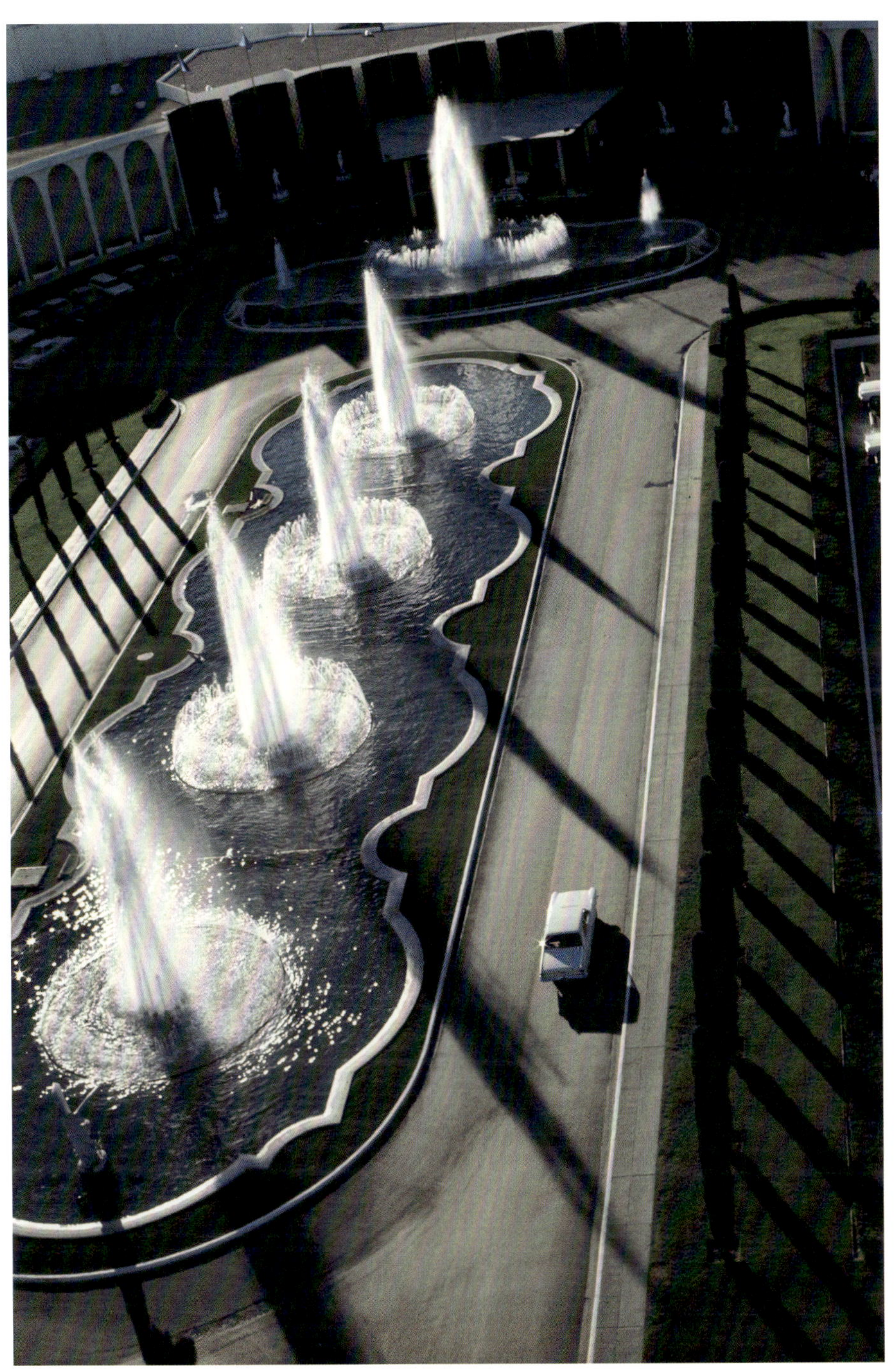

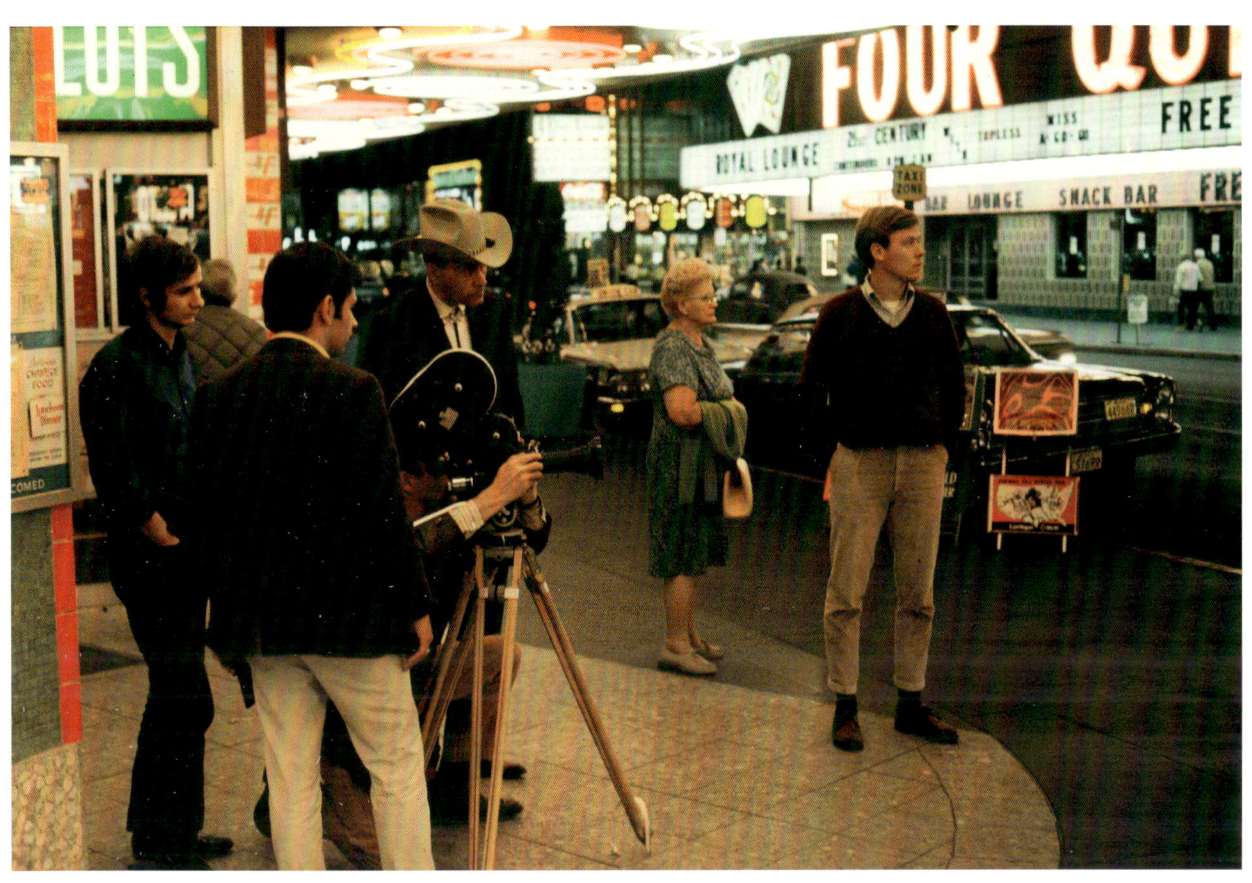
FOUR
FREE
ROYAL LOUNGE
CENTURY
TOPLESS
TAXI ZONE
BAR LOUNGE SNACK BAR

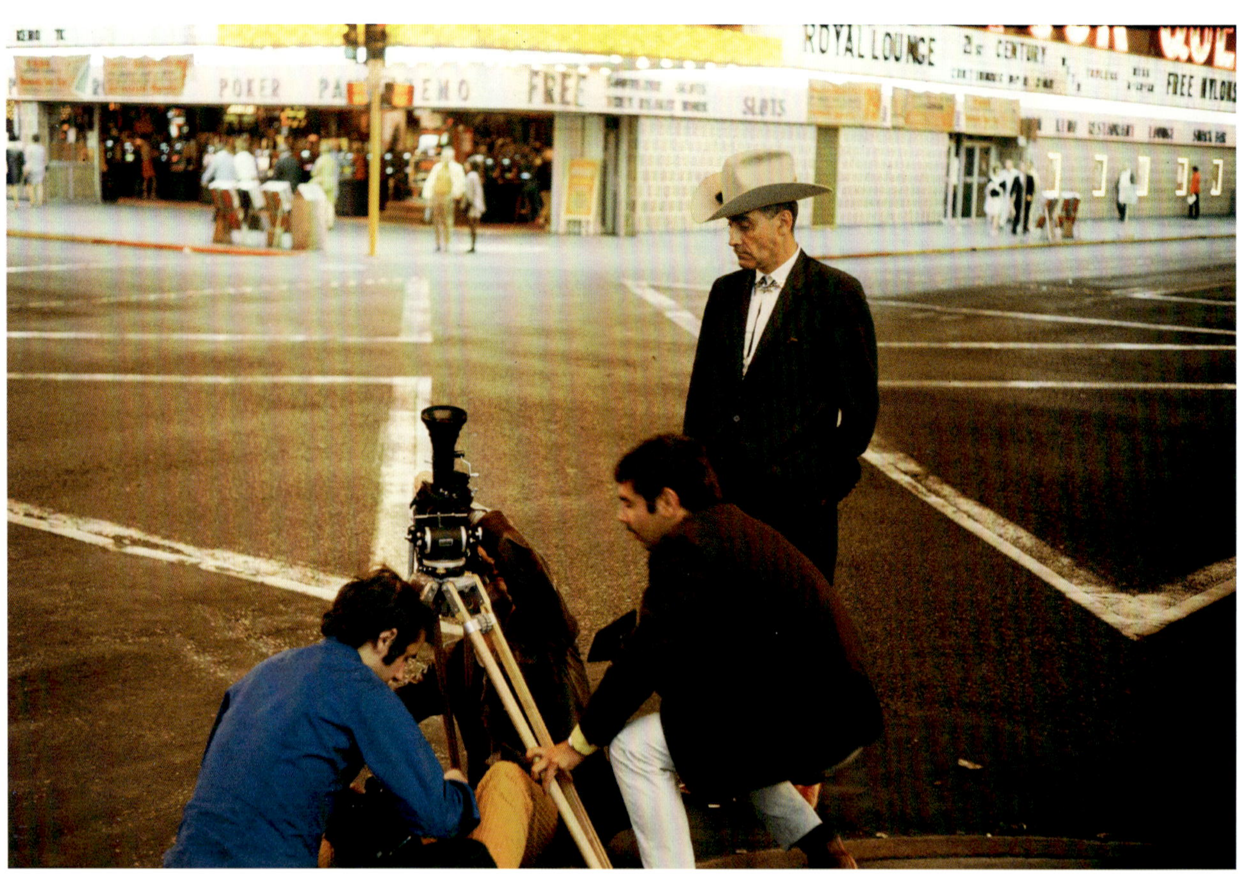
ROYAL LOUNGE
POKER
FREE
SLOTS
21st CENTURY

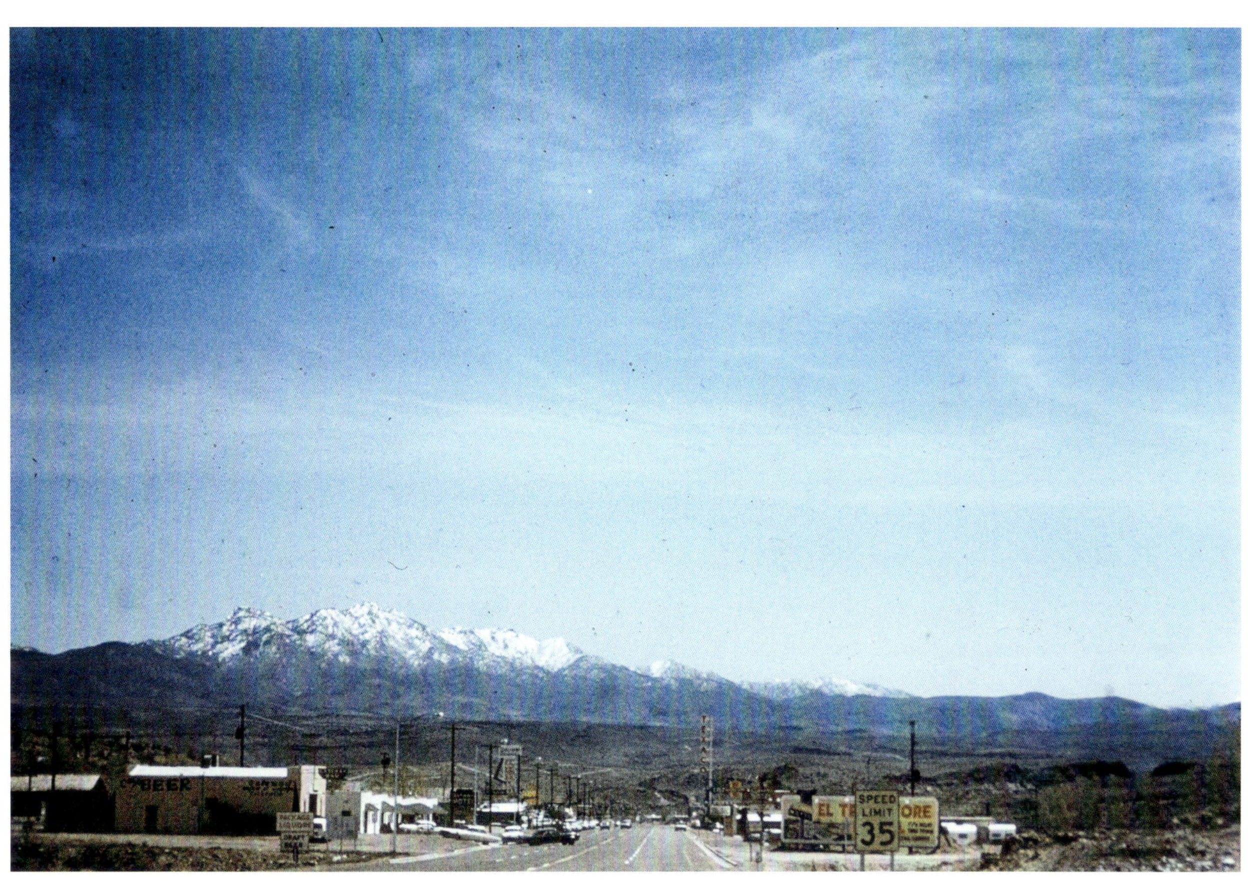
BEER
SPEED
LIMIT
35

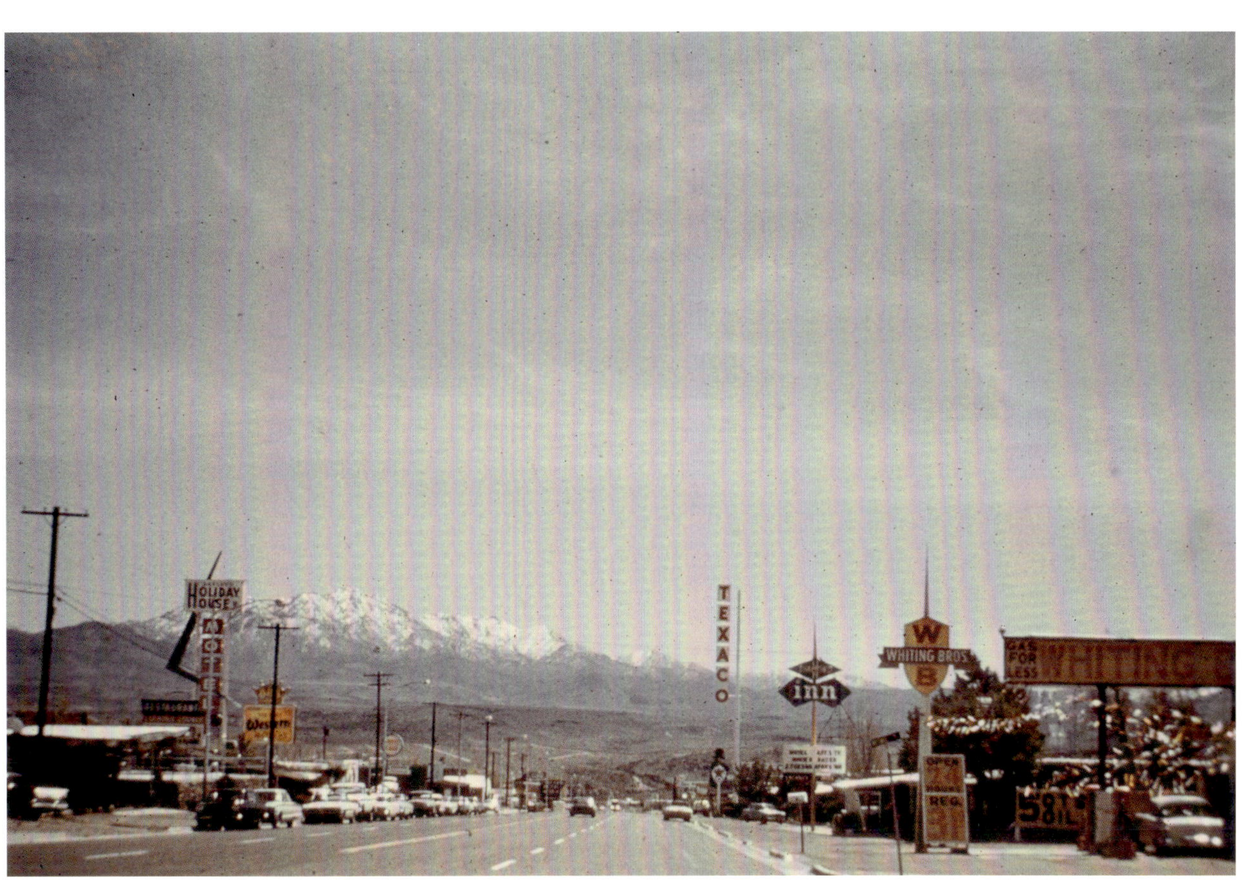
HOLIDAY HOUSE
TEXACO
inn
W
WHITING BROS
B
GAS FOR LESS
WHITING
OPEN
REG.

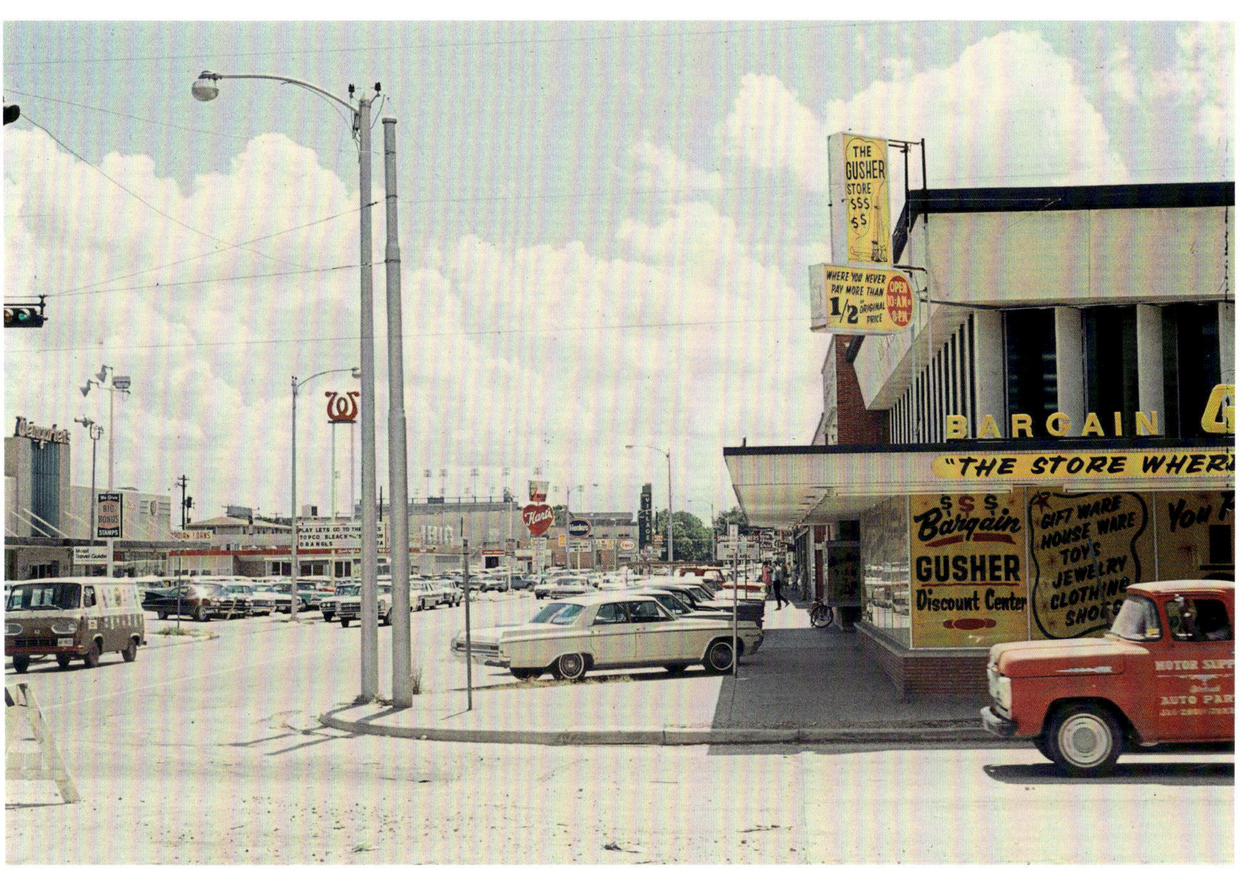
THE GUSHER STORE $$$ $$
WHERE YOU NEVER PAY MORE THAN 1/2 THE ORIGINAL PRICE
OPEN 10-AM 6-PM
BARGAIN
$$$ Bargain GUSHER Discount Center
GIFT WARE HOUSE WARE TOYS JEWELRY CLOTHING SHOES
BIG BONUS STAMPS

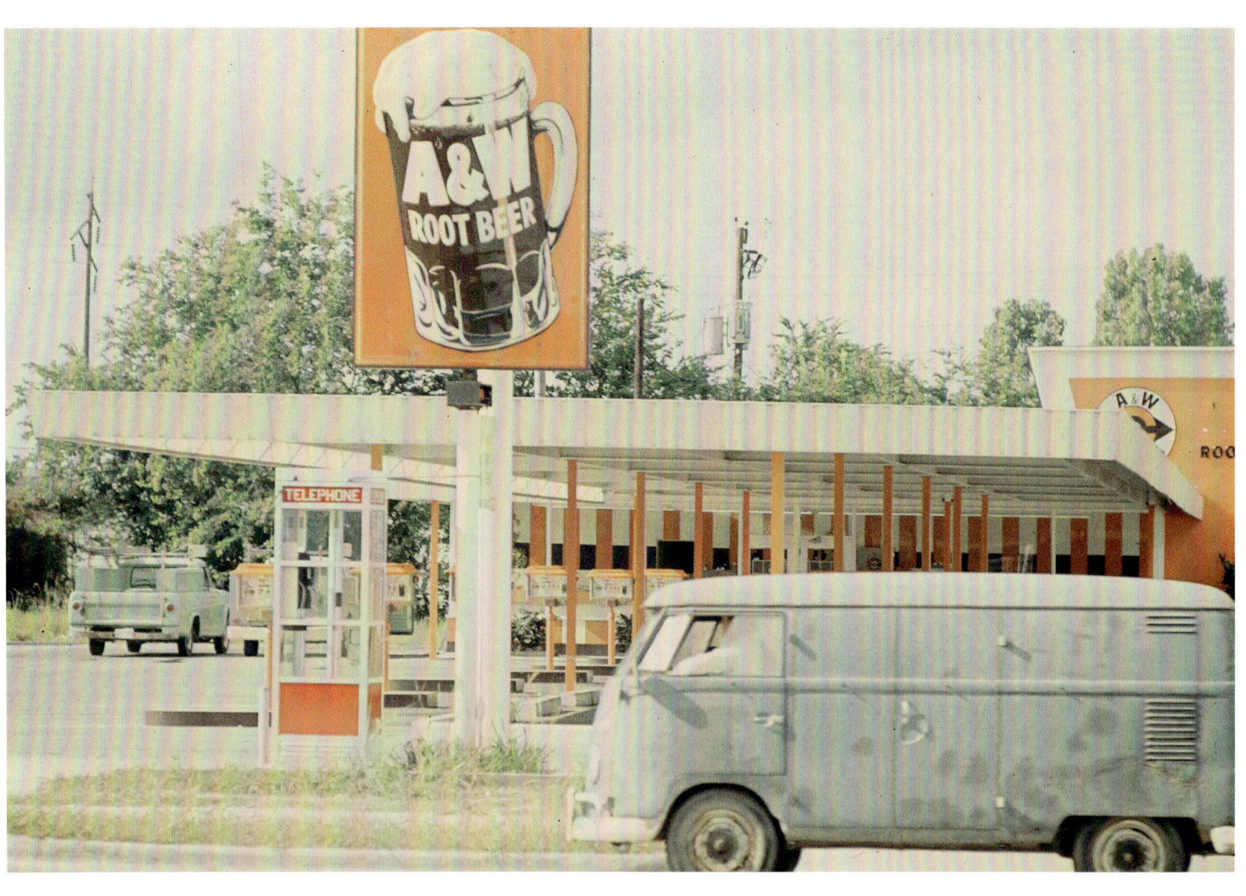
A&W
ROOT BEER
TELEPHONE
A&W

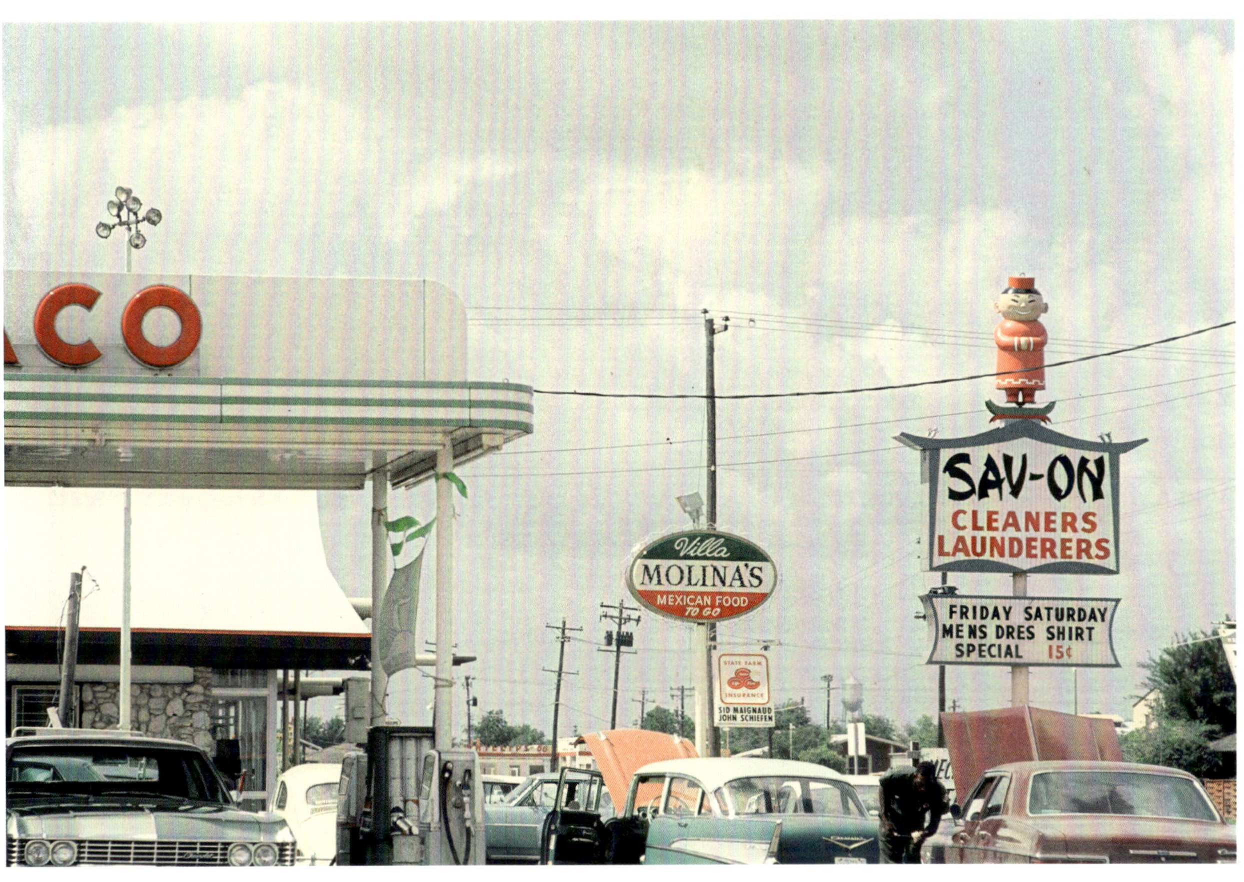
ACO
Villa
MOLINA'S
MEXICAN FOOD
TO GO
SAV-ON
CLEANERS
LAUNDERERS
FRIDAY SATURDAY
MENS DRES SHIRT
SPECIAL 15¢
SID MAIGNAUD
JOHN SCHIEFEN

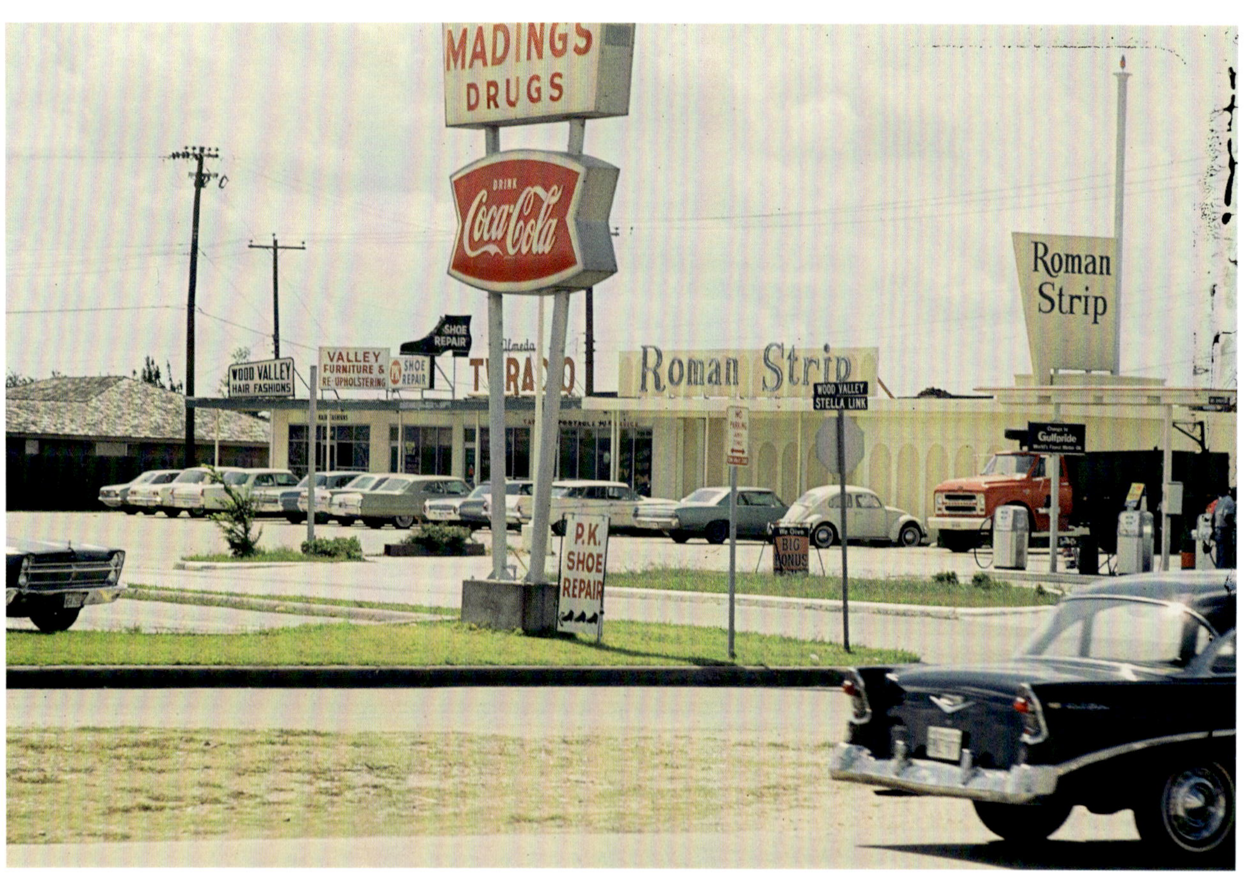
MADINGS
DRUGS
DRINK
Coca-Cola
Roman
Strip
WOOD VALLEY
HAIR FASHIONS
VALLEY
FURNITURE &
RE-UPHOLSTERING
SHOE
REPAIR
SHOE
REPAIR
Roman Strip
WOOD VALLEY
STELLA LINK
Gulfpride
P.K.
SHOE
REPAIR
BIG
BONUS

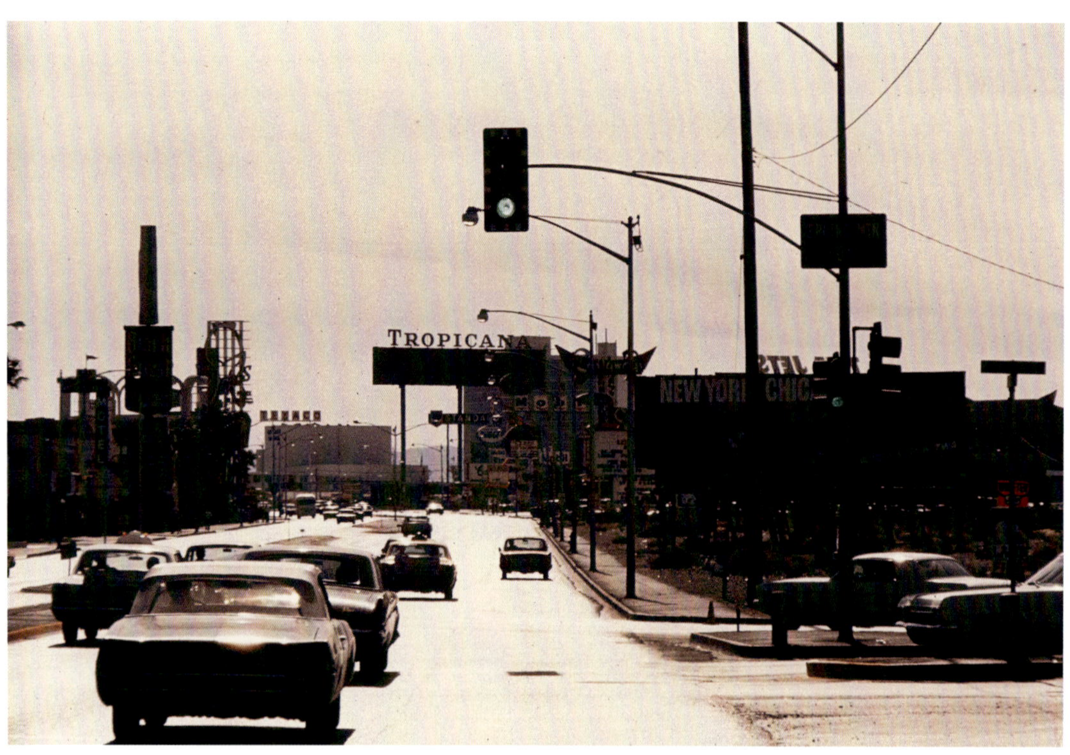
TROPICANA

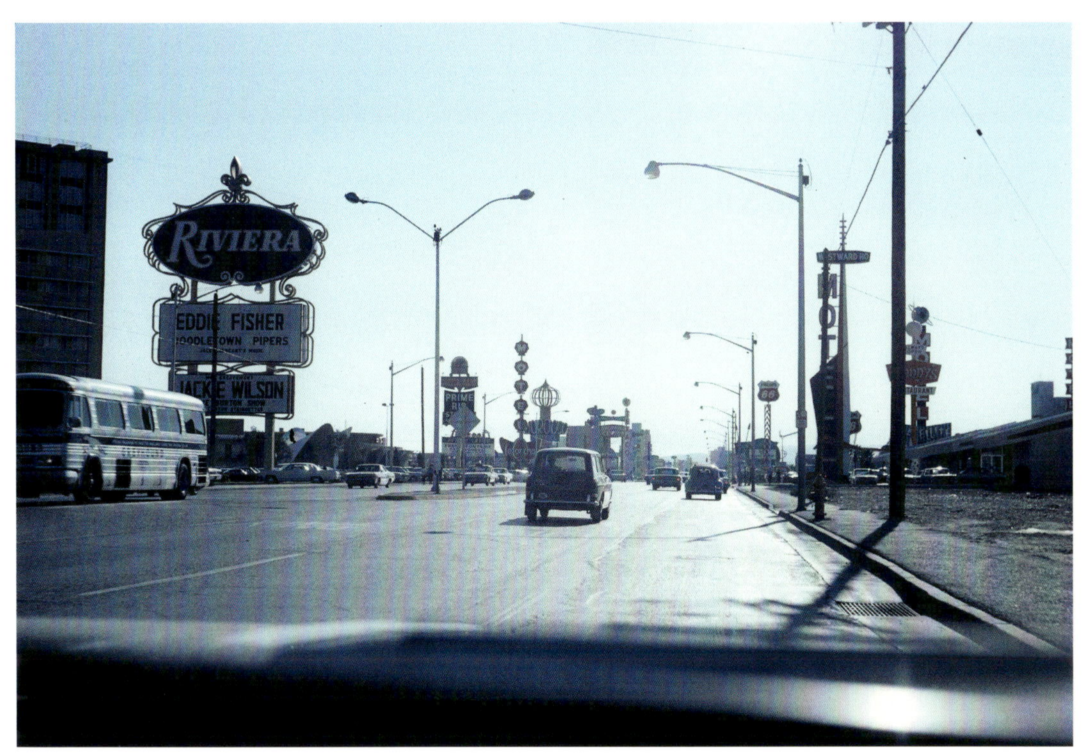
RIVIERA
EDDIE FISHER
DOODLETOWN PIPERS
JACKIE WILSON
MOTEL

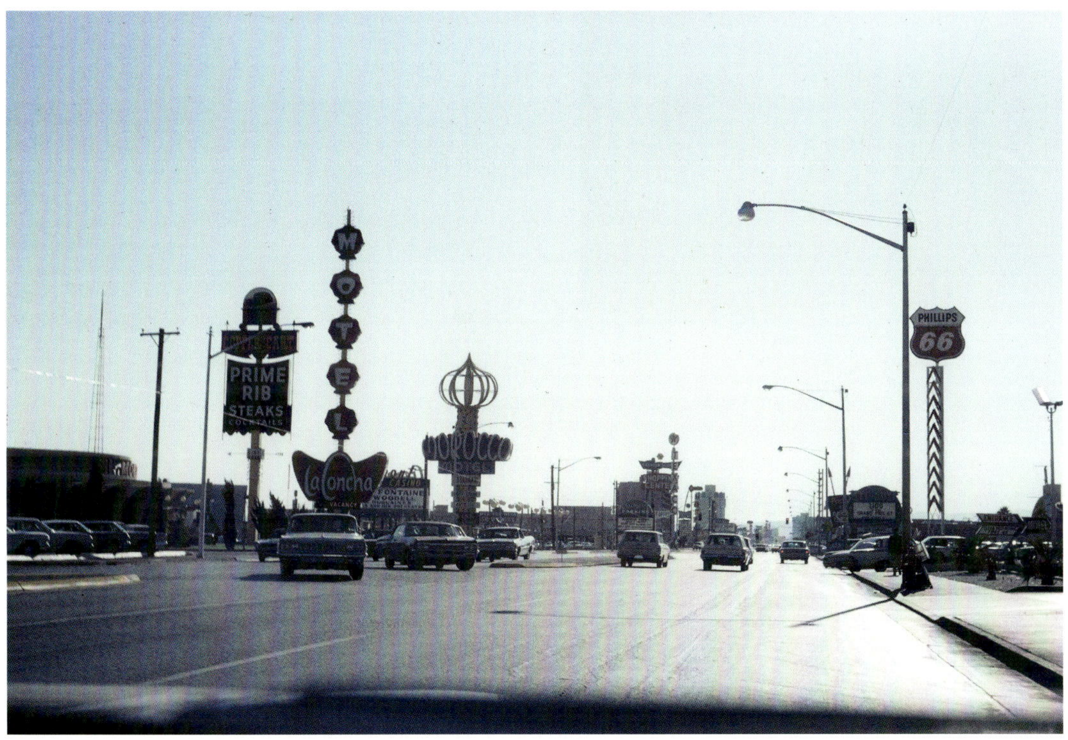
PRIME
RIB
STEAKS
MOTEL
La Concha
PHILLIPS
66

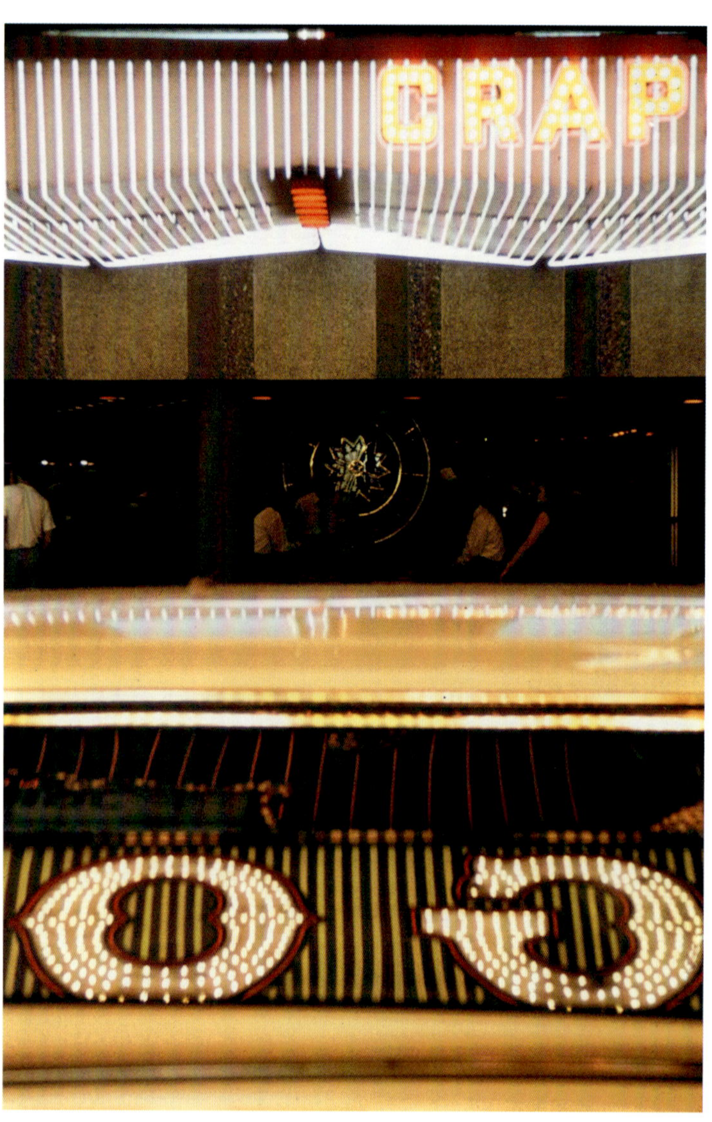
CRAP

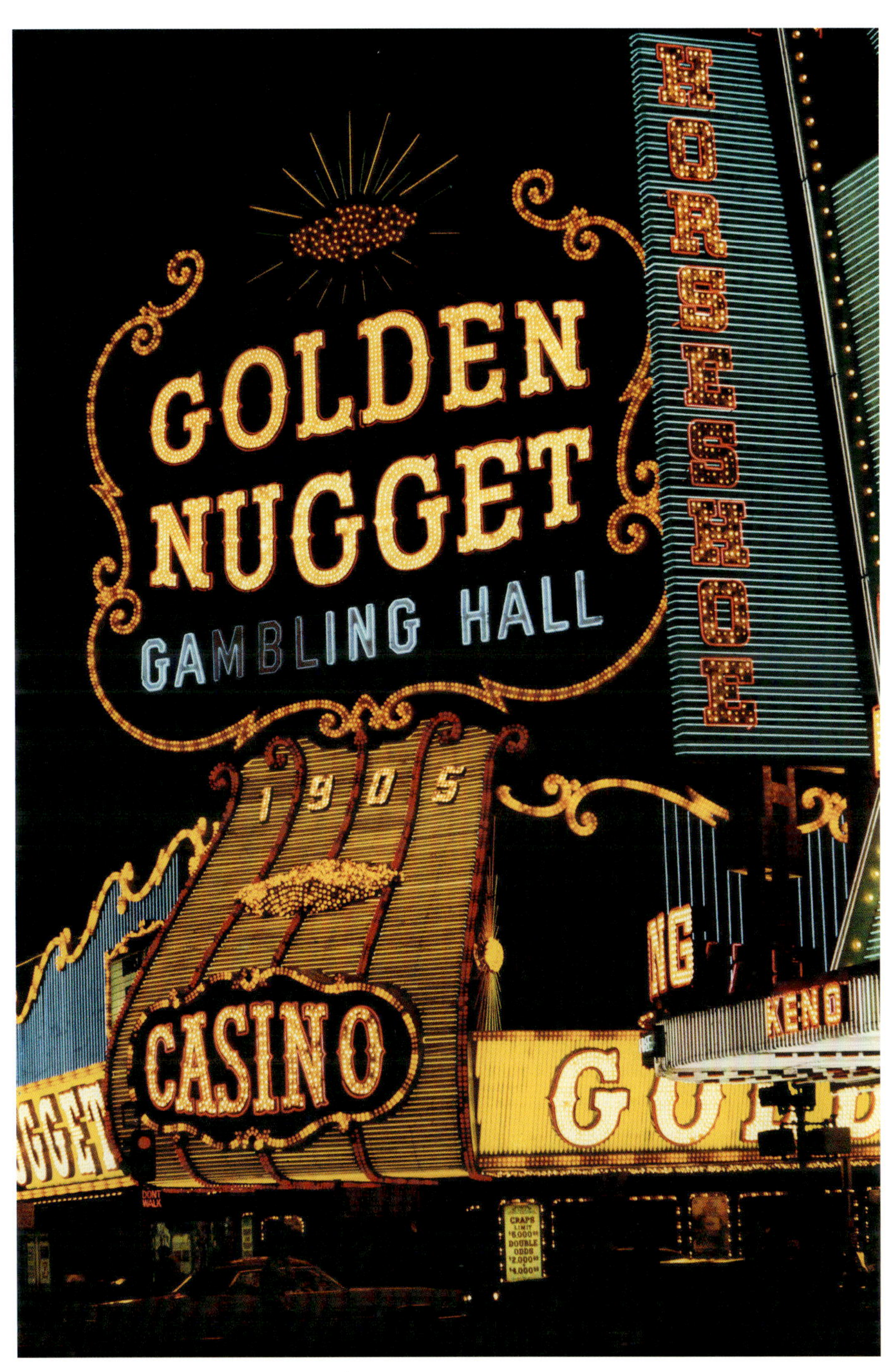
GOLDEN
NUGGET
GAMBLING HALL
HORSESHOE
1905
CASINO
KENO

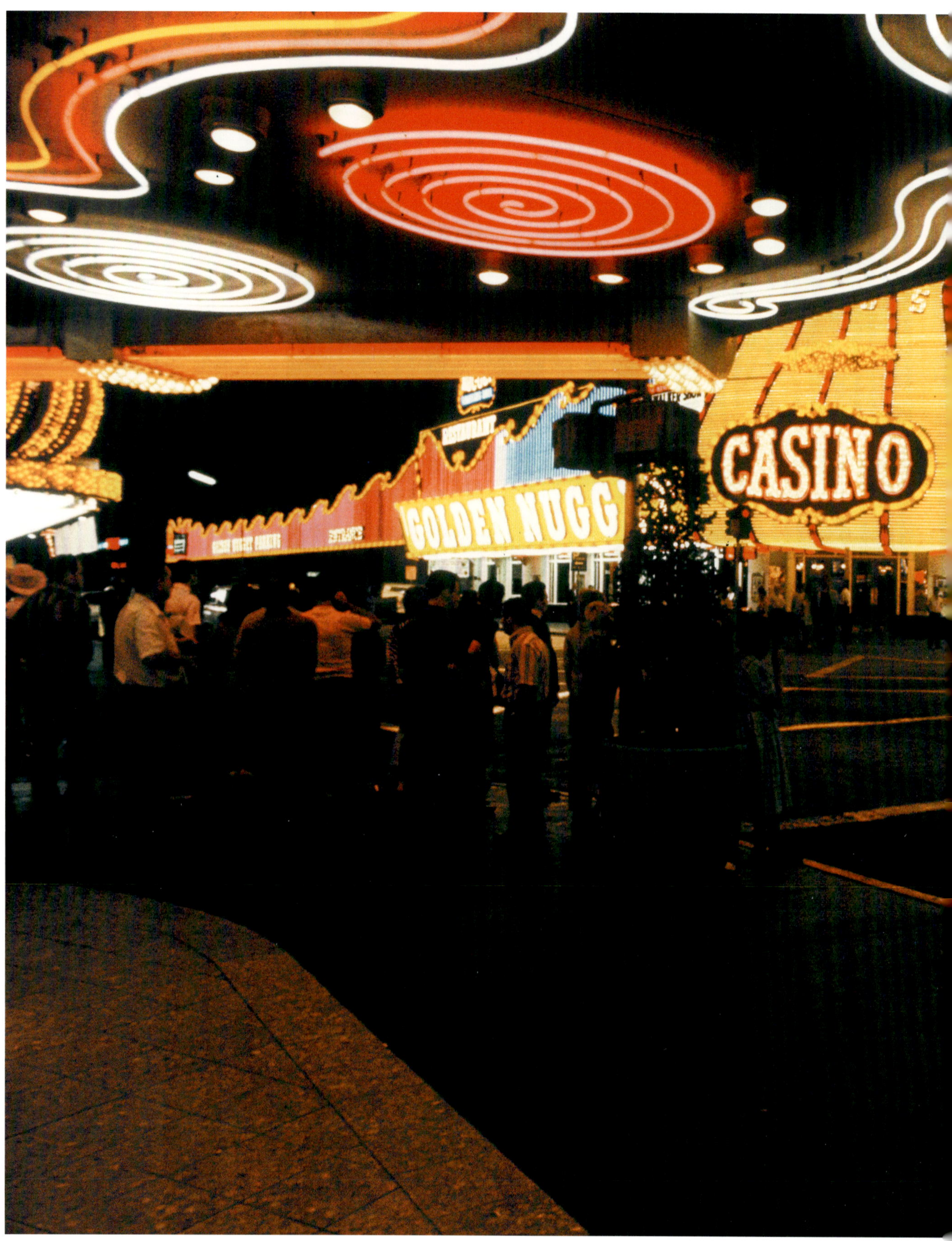
RESTAURANT
GOLDEN NUGG
CASINO

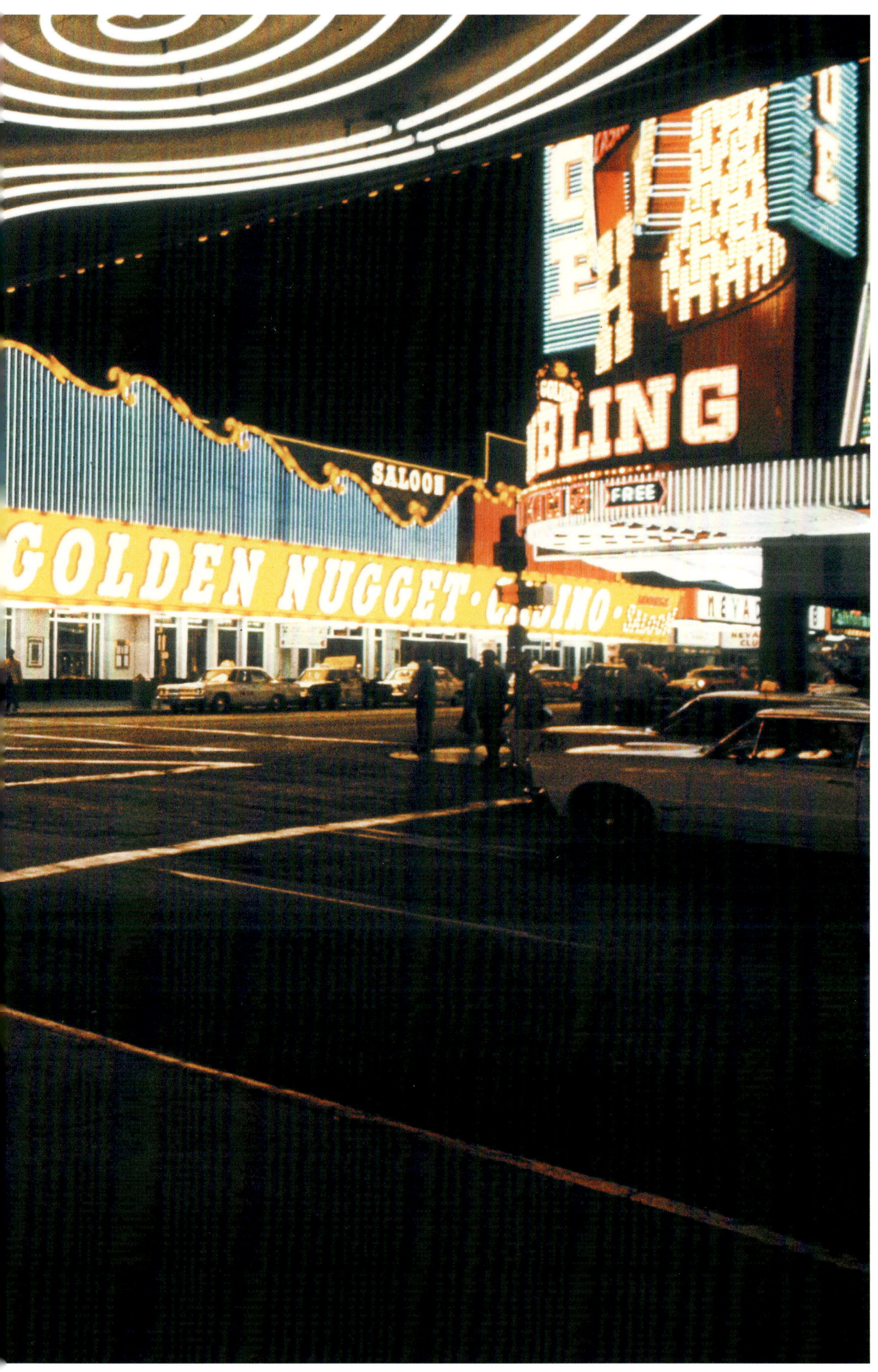
SALOON
GOLDEN NUGGET
BLING
FREE

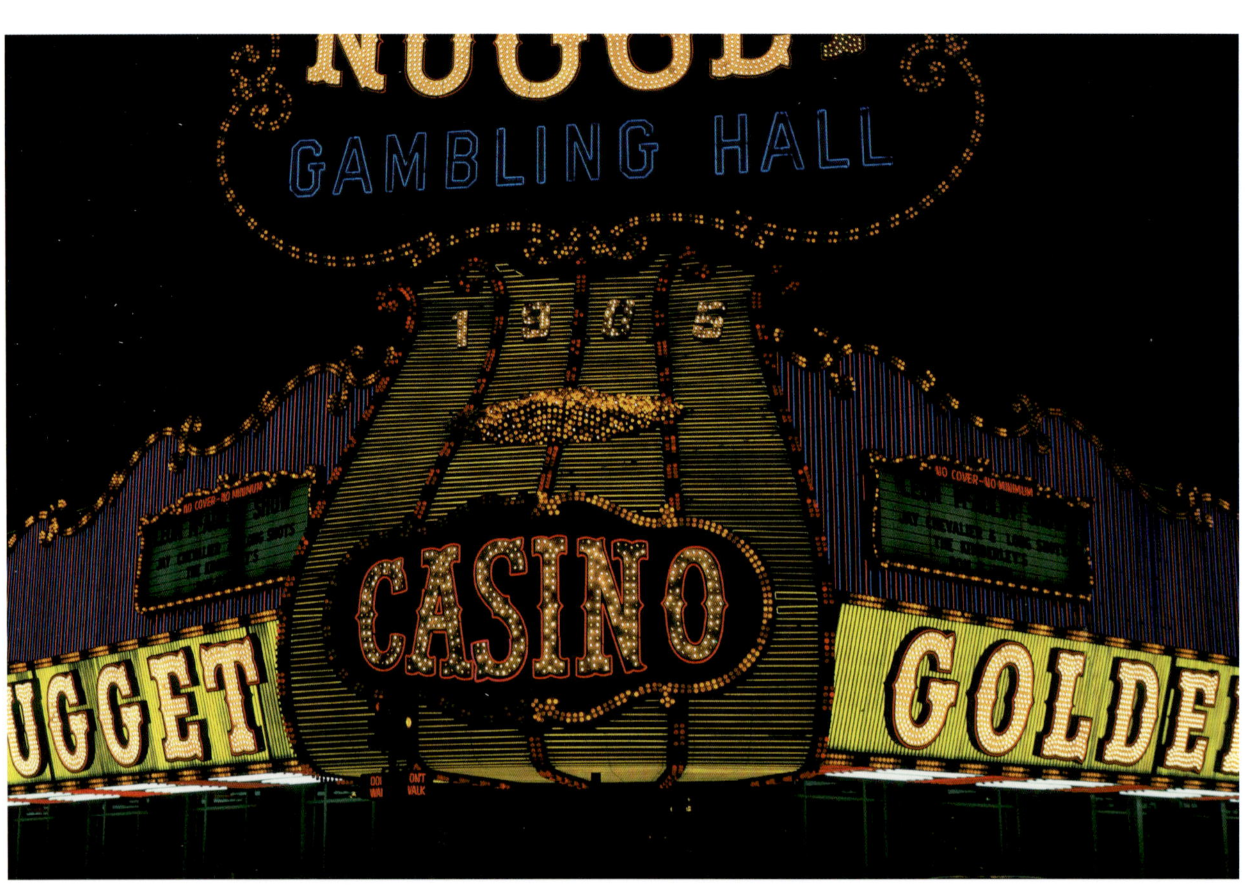
GAMBLING HALL
CASINO
NO COVER–NO MINIMUM

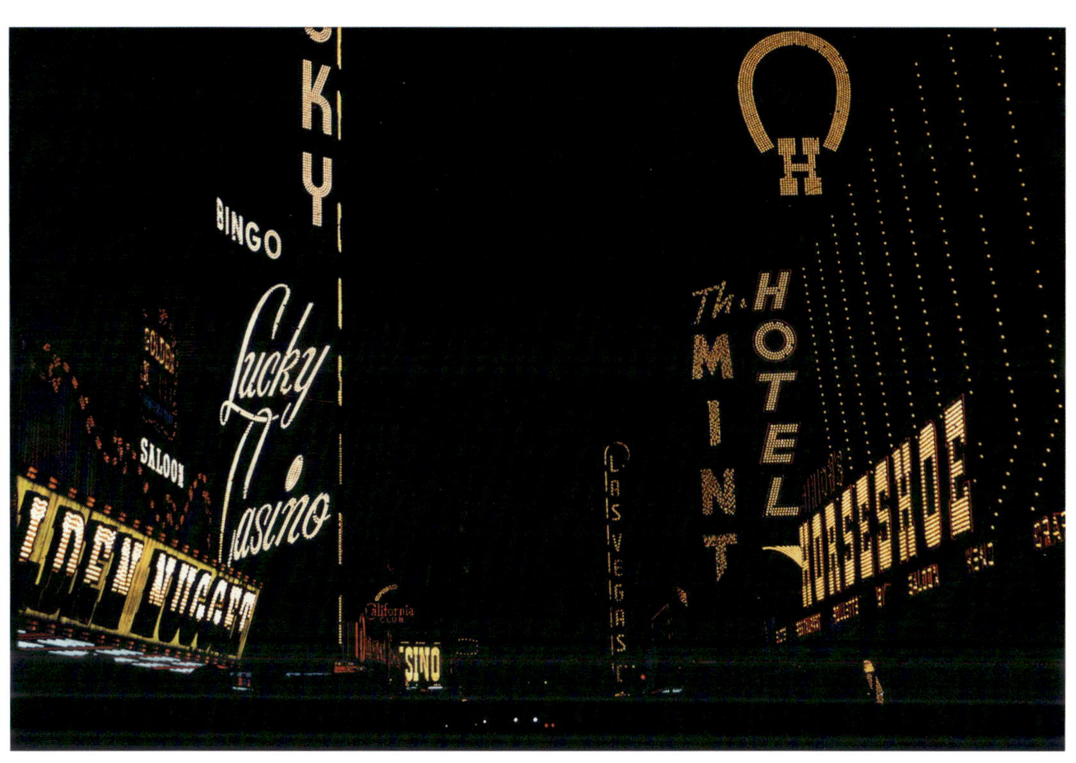
BINGO
Lucky Casino
SALOON
The MINT
HOTEL
HORSESHOE
LAS VEGAS
California CLUB

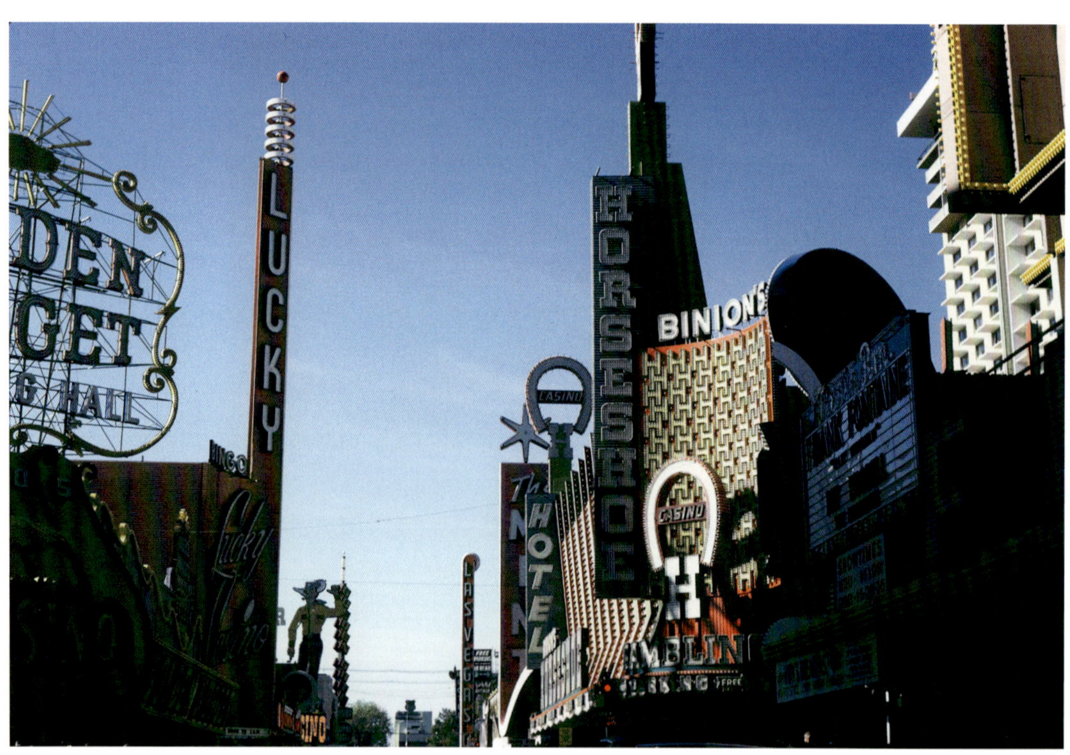
LUCKY
BINGO
HORSESHOE
BINION'S
CASINO
HOTEL
LAS VEGAS

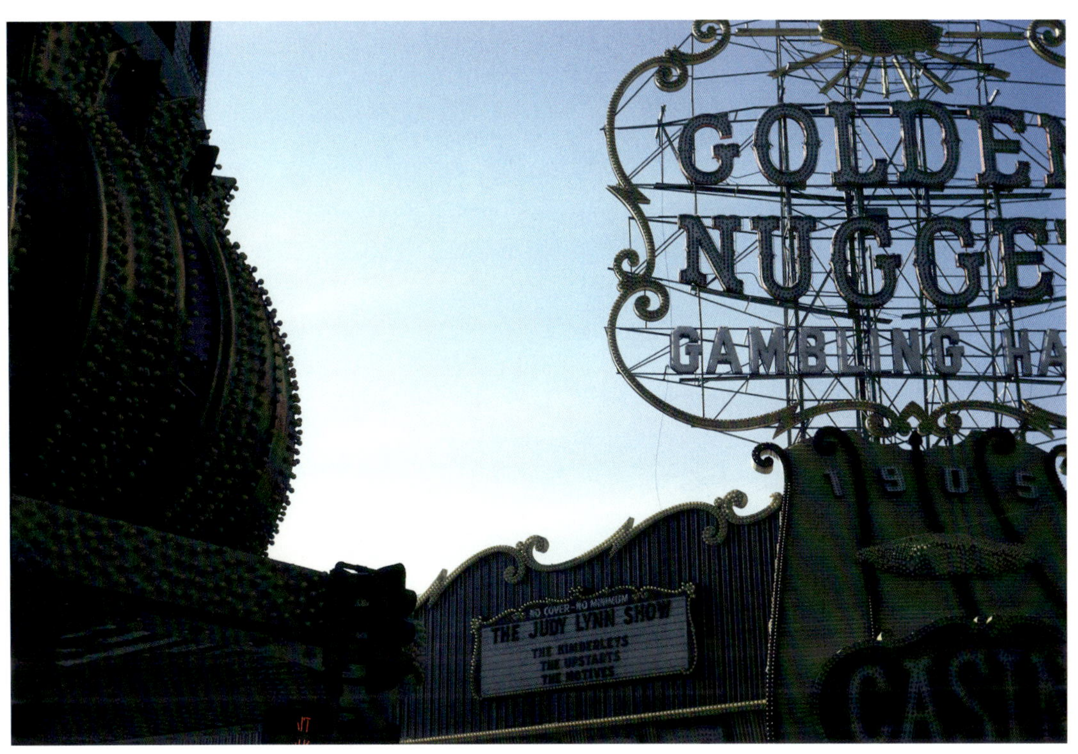
GOLDE
NUGGE
GAMBLING HA
1905
NO COVER–NO MINIMUM
THE JUDY LYNN SHOW
THE UPSTARTS

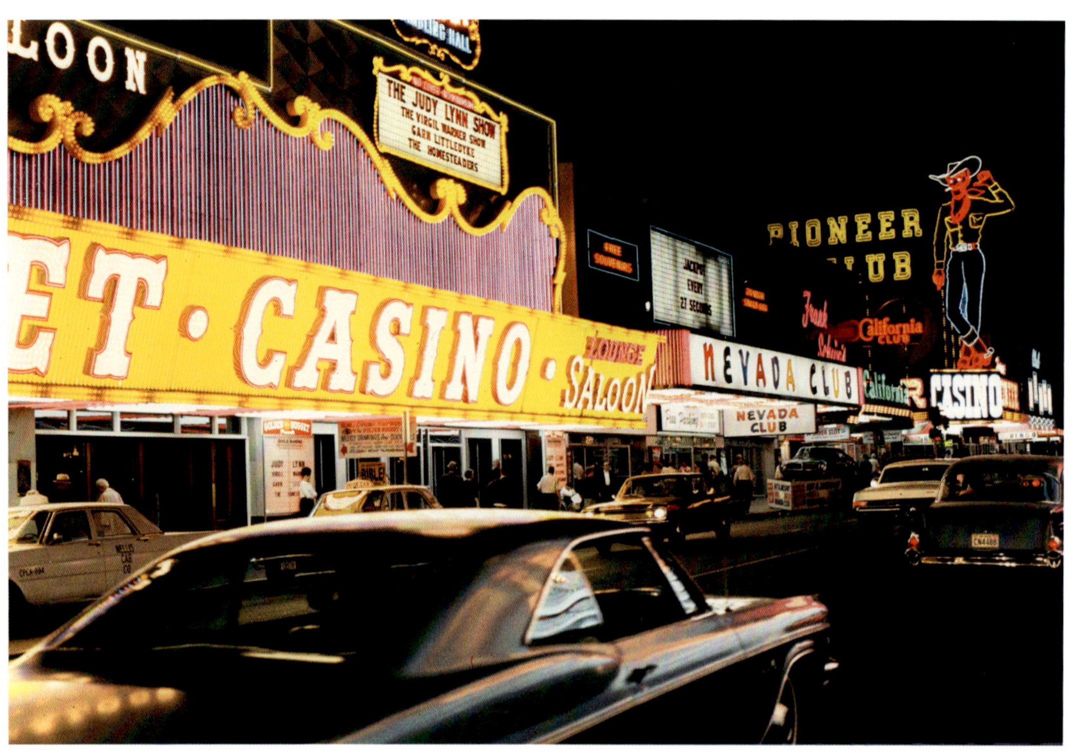
LOON
THE JUDY LYNN SHOW
THE VIRGIL WARNER SHOW
THE HOMESTEADERS
ET · CASINO · SALOON
LOUNGE
PIONEER
NEVADA CLUB
NEVADA CLUB
California
CASINO

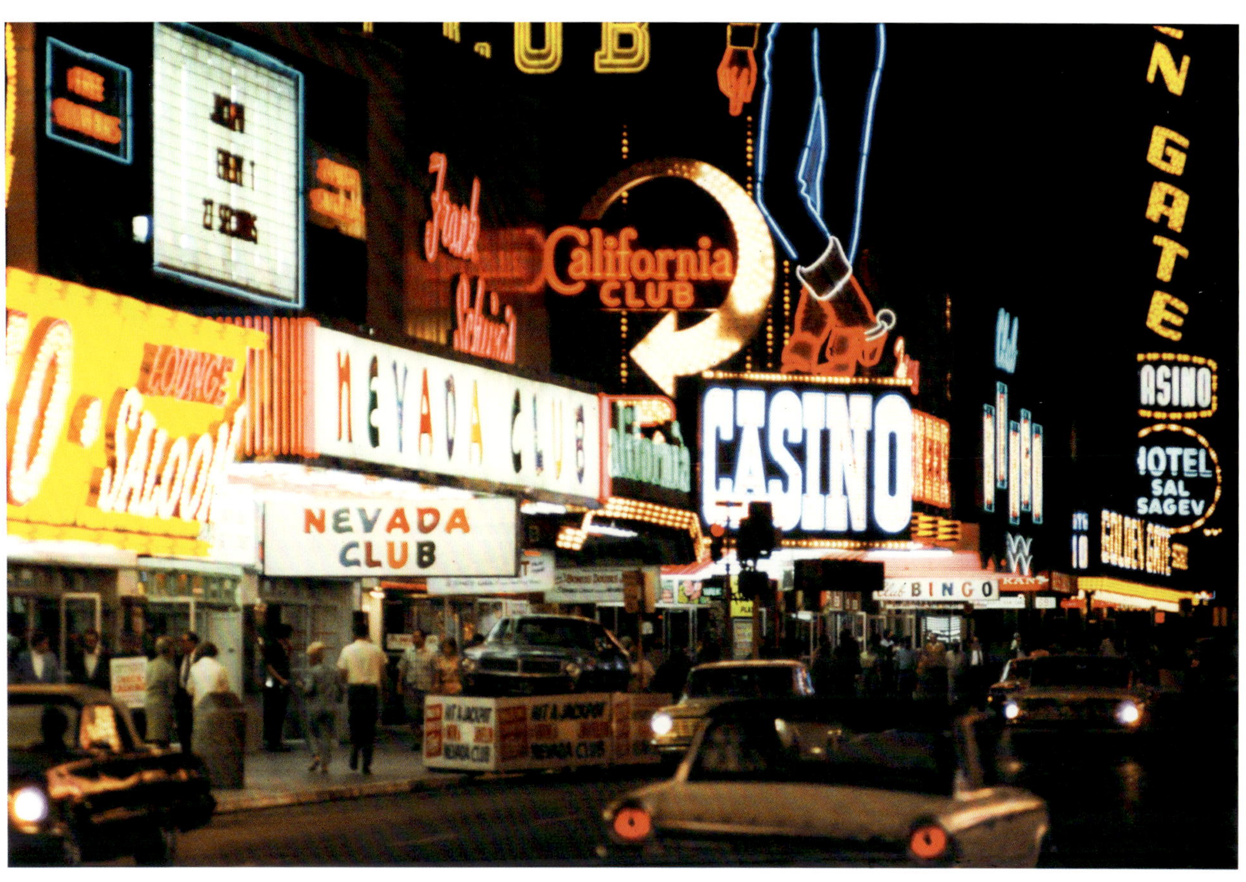
California
CLUB
NEVADA CLUB
NEVADA
CLUB
CASINO
LOUNGE
BINGO
N
GATE
ASINO
SAL
SAGEV

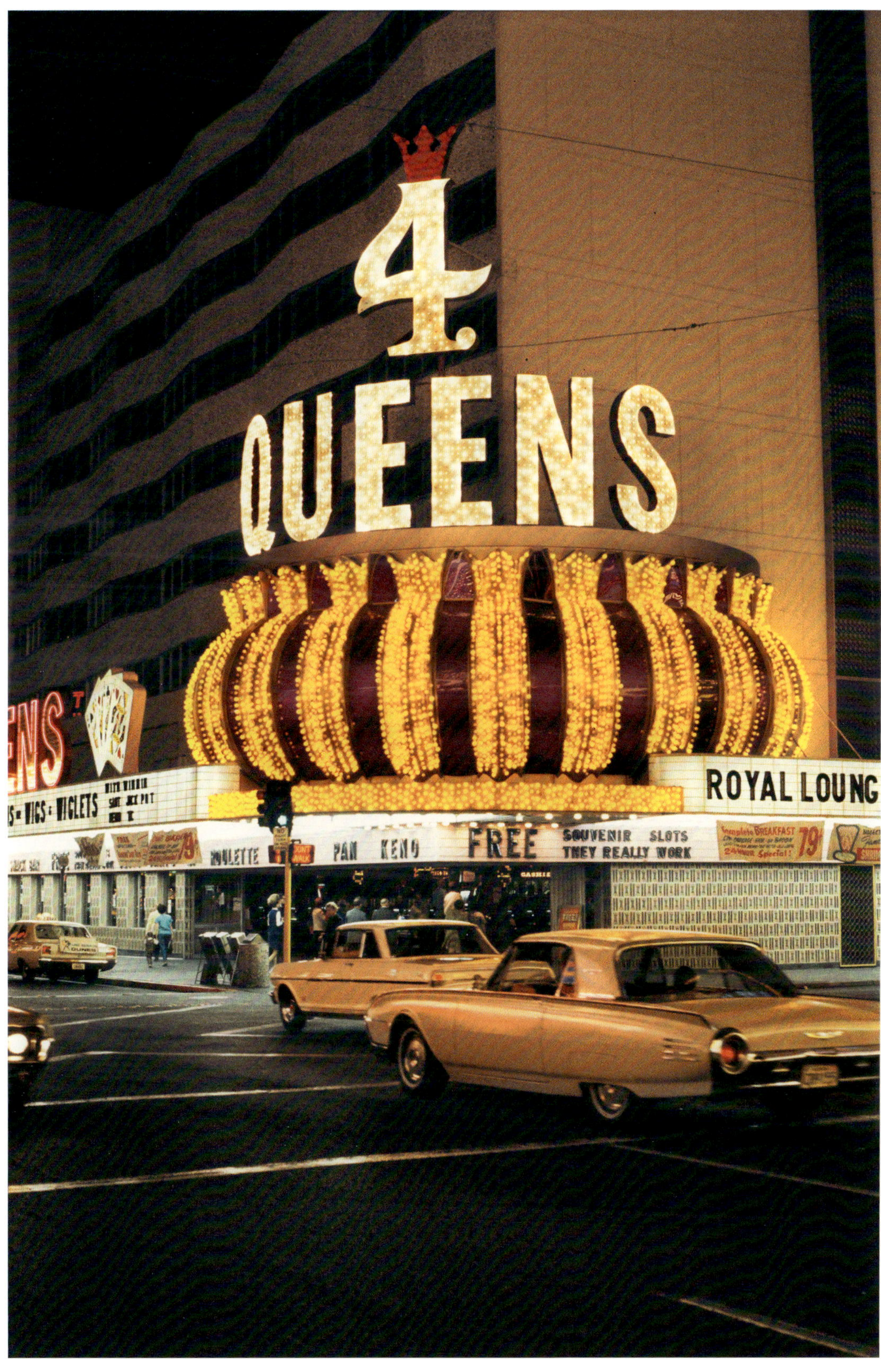
4
QUEENS
ROYAL LOUNG
ROULETTE
PAN
KENO
FREE
SOUVENIR SLOTS
THEY REALLY WORK

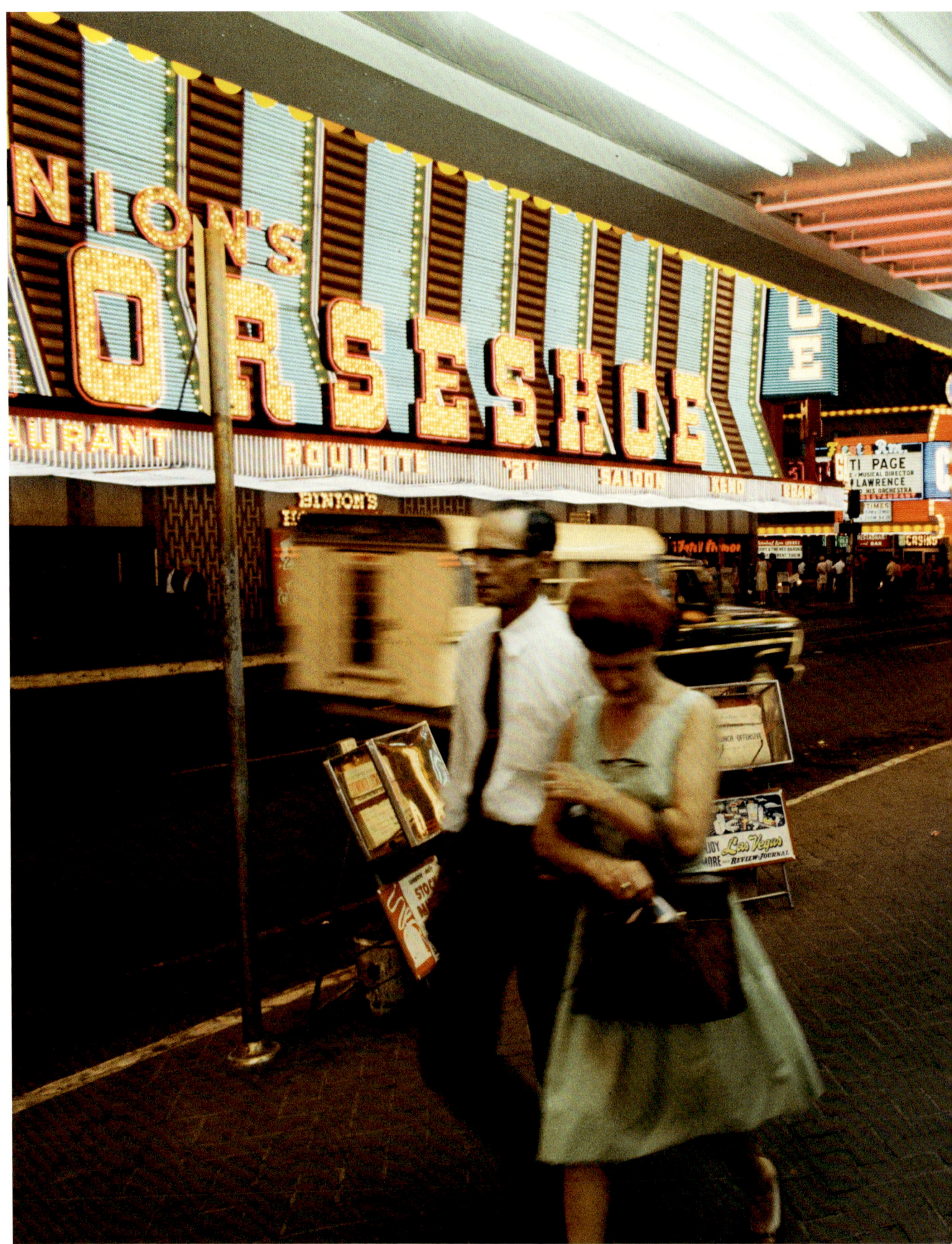
NION'S
ORSESHOE
AURANT
ROULETTE
SALOON
KENO
BINION'S
TI PAGE
LAWRENCE
CASINO
Las Vegas
REVIEW-JOURNAL

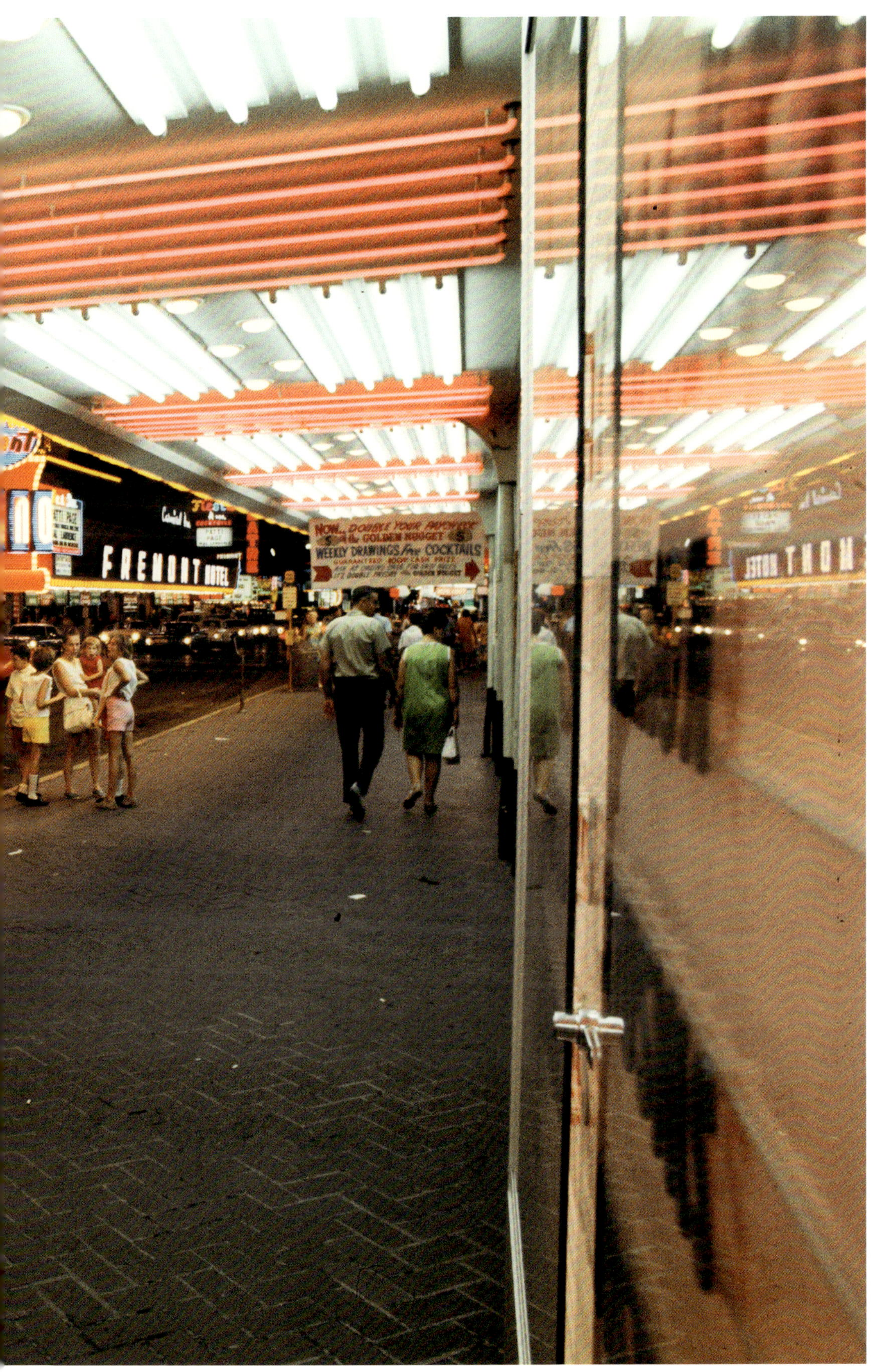
FREMONT HOTEL
WEEKLY DRAWINGS Free COCKTAILS

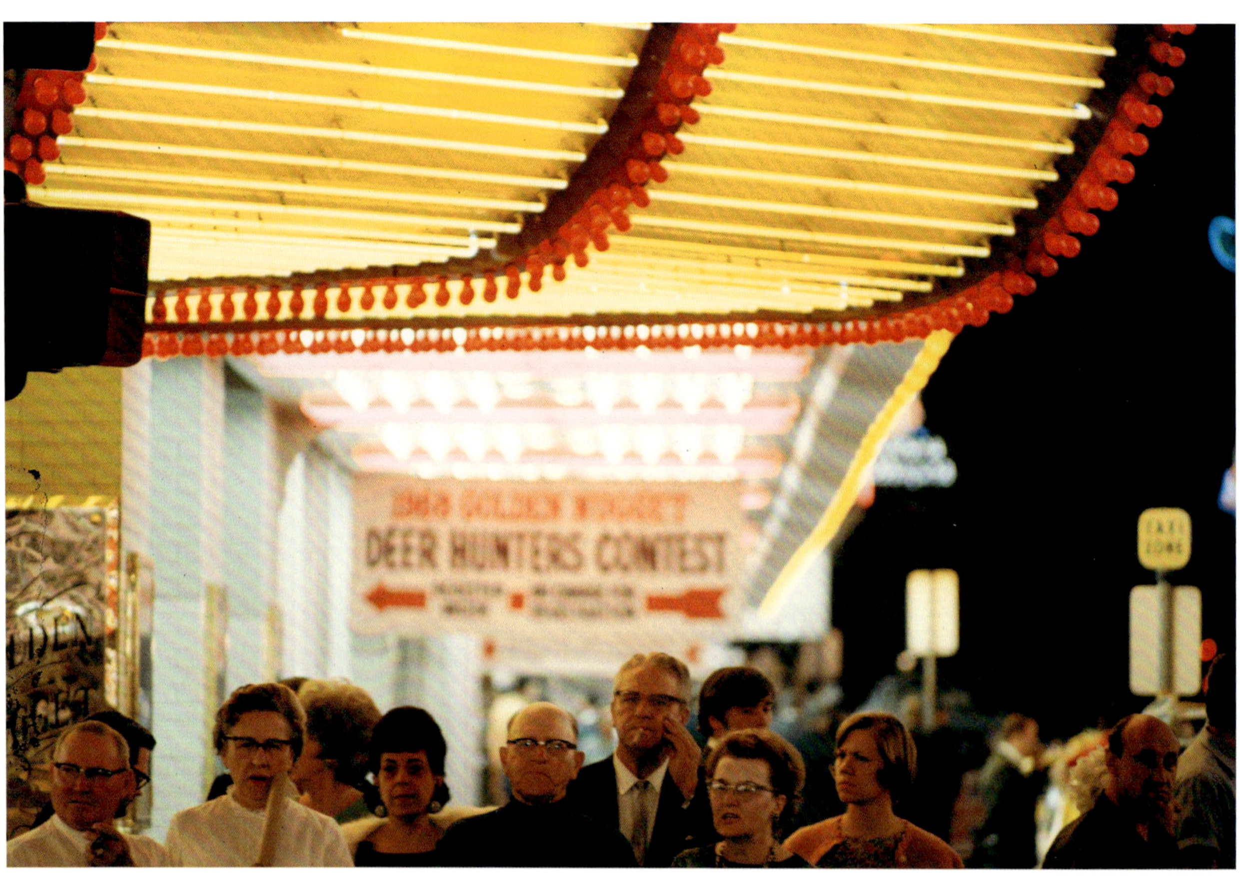
DEER HUNTERS CONTEST

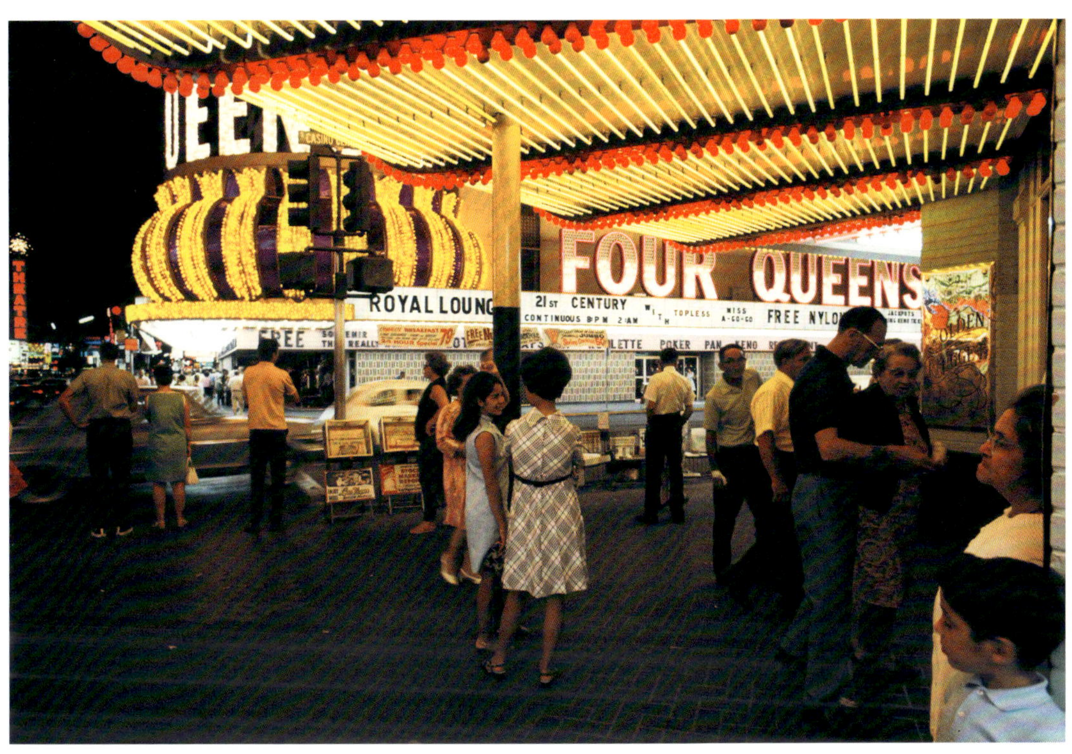
FOUR QUEENS
ROYAL LOUNG
21 ST CENTURY
CONTINUOUS 9 P M 2 AM
WITH TOPLESS
MISS A-GO-GO
FREE NYLON
POKER
KENO
THEATRE

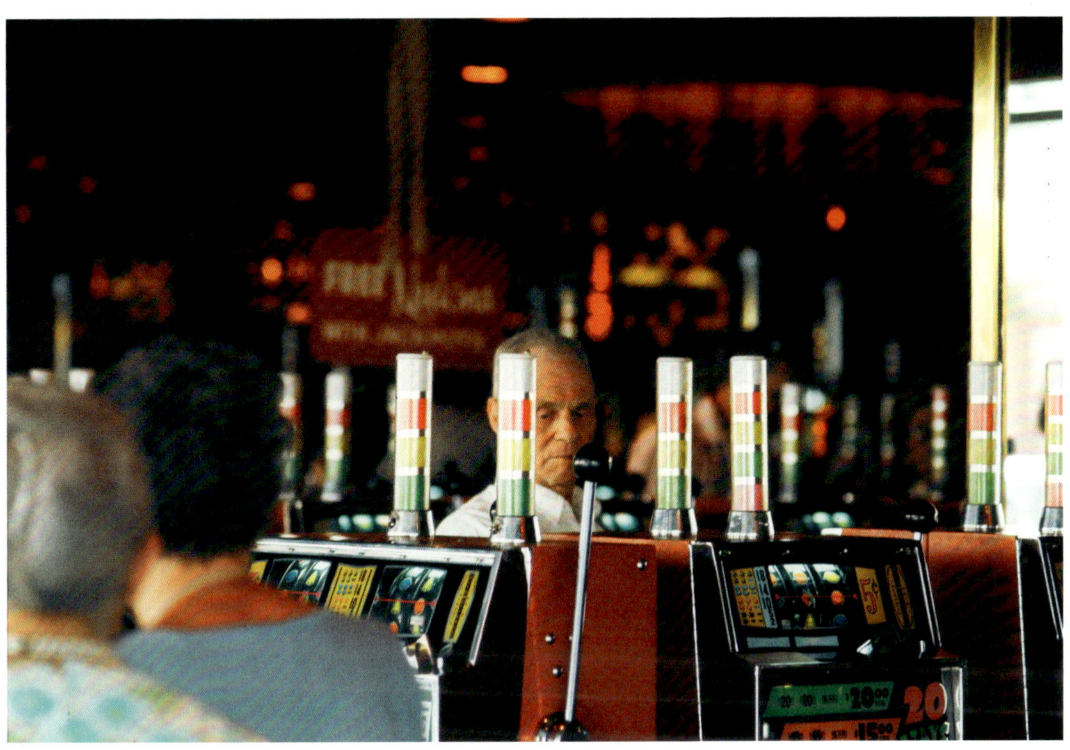

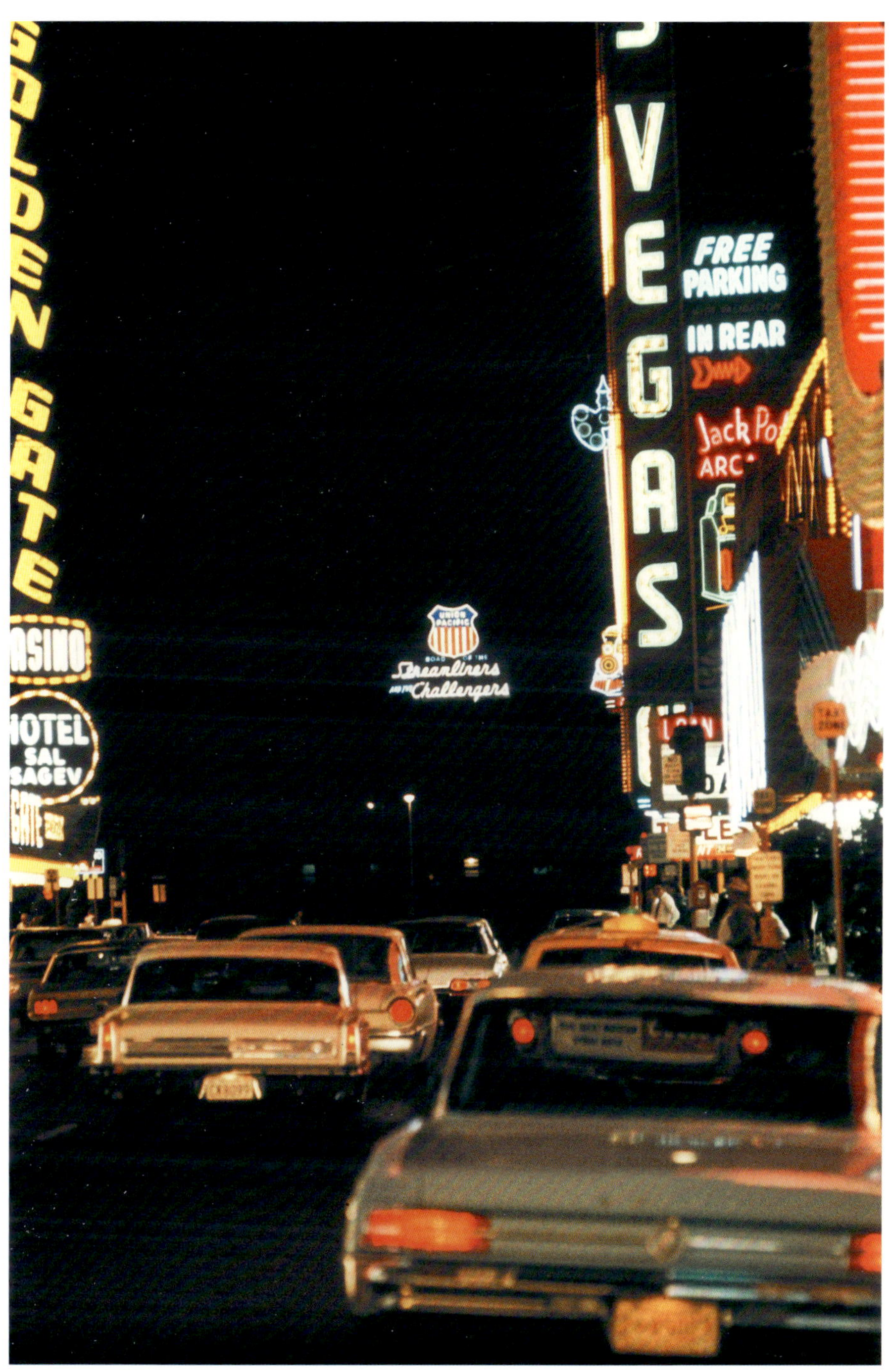
GOLDEN GATE
SAL
SAGEV
VEGAS
FREE
PARKING
IN REAR
UNION PACIFIC
Streamliners
Challengers

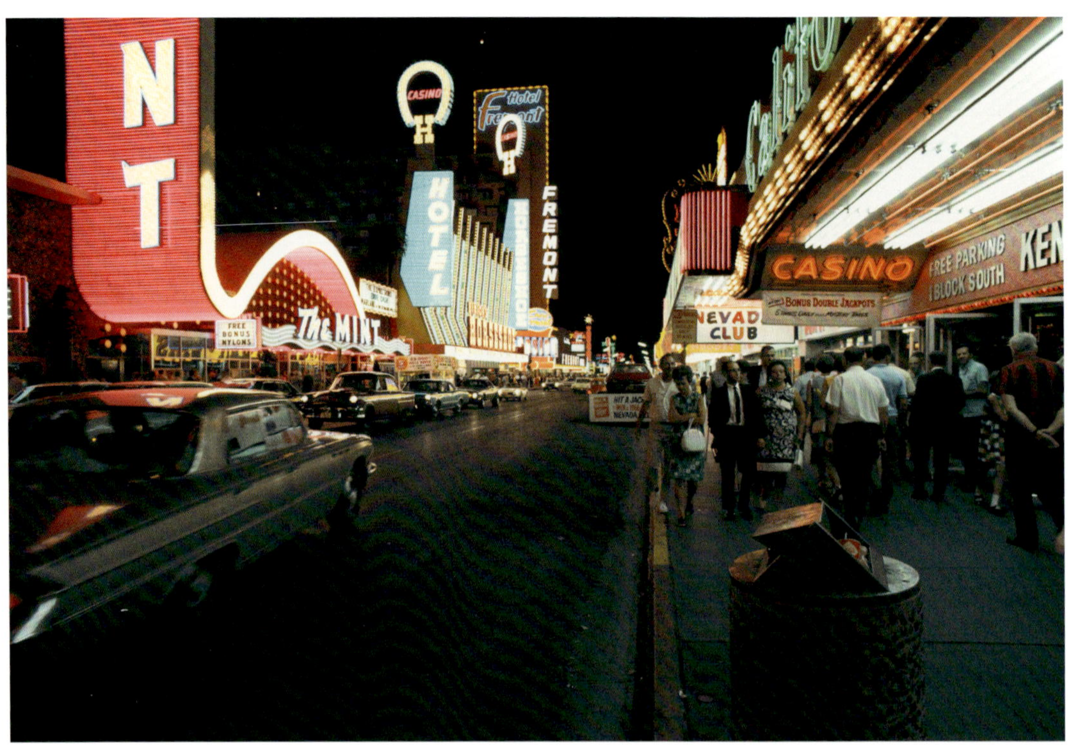
CASINO
Hotel Fremont
HOTEL
FREMONT
The MINT
FREE BONUS NYLONS
CASINO
FREE PARKING
1 BLOCK SOUTH
NEVAD
CLUB
BONUS DOUBLE JACKPOTS

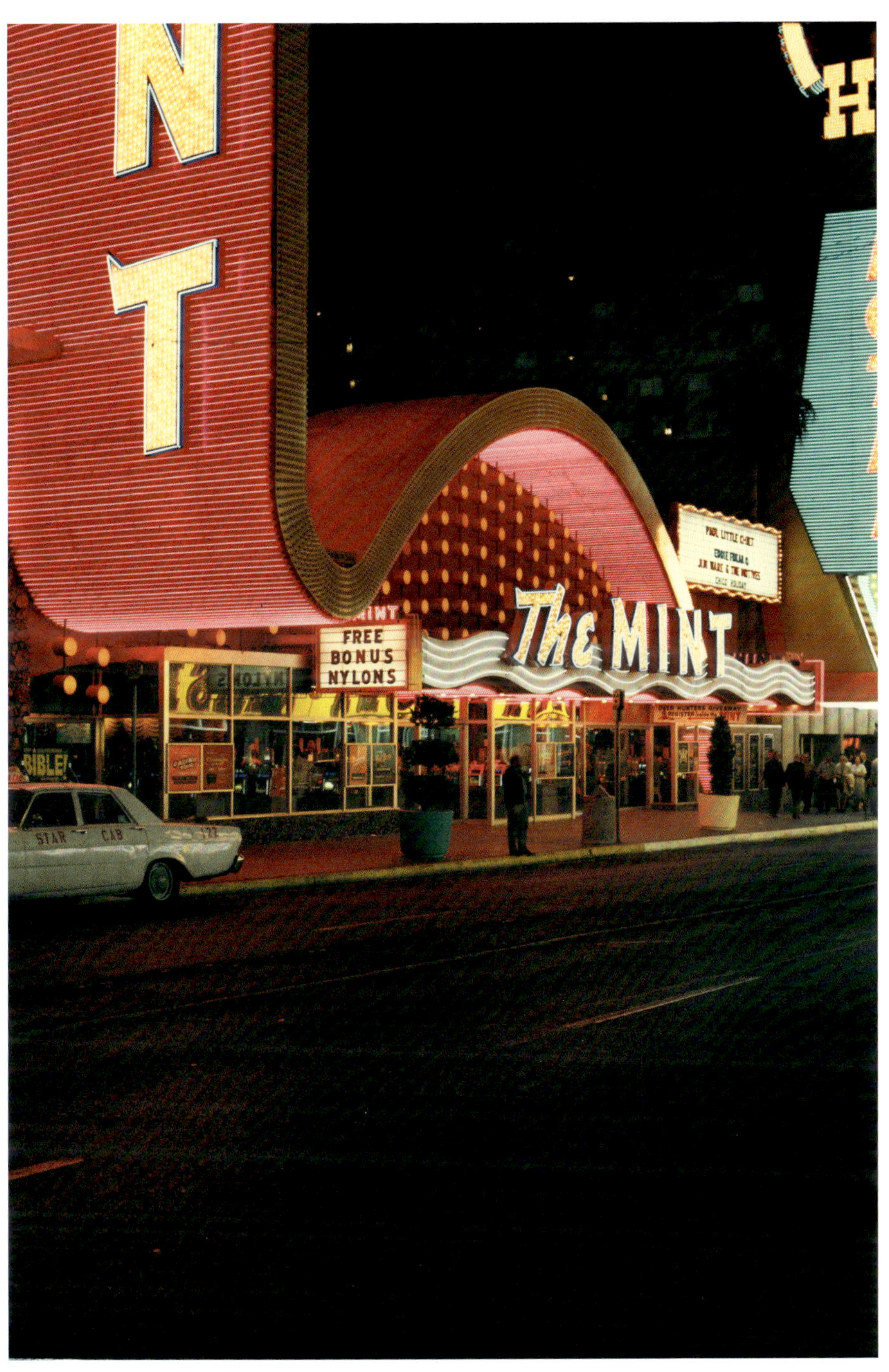
FREE
BONUS
NYLONS
The MINT
STAR CAB

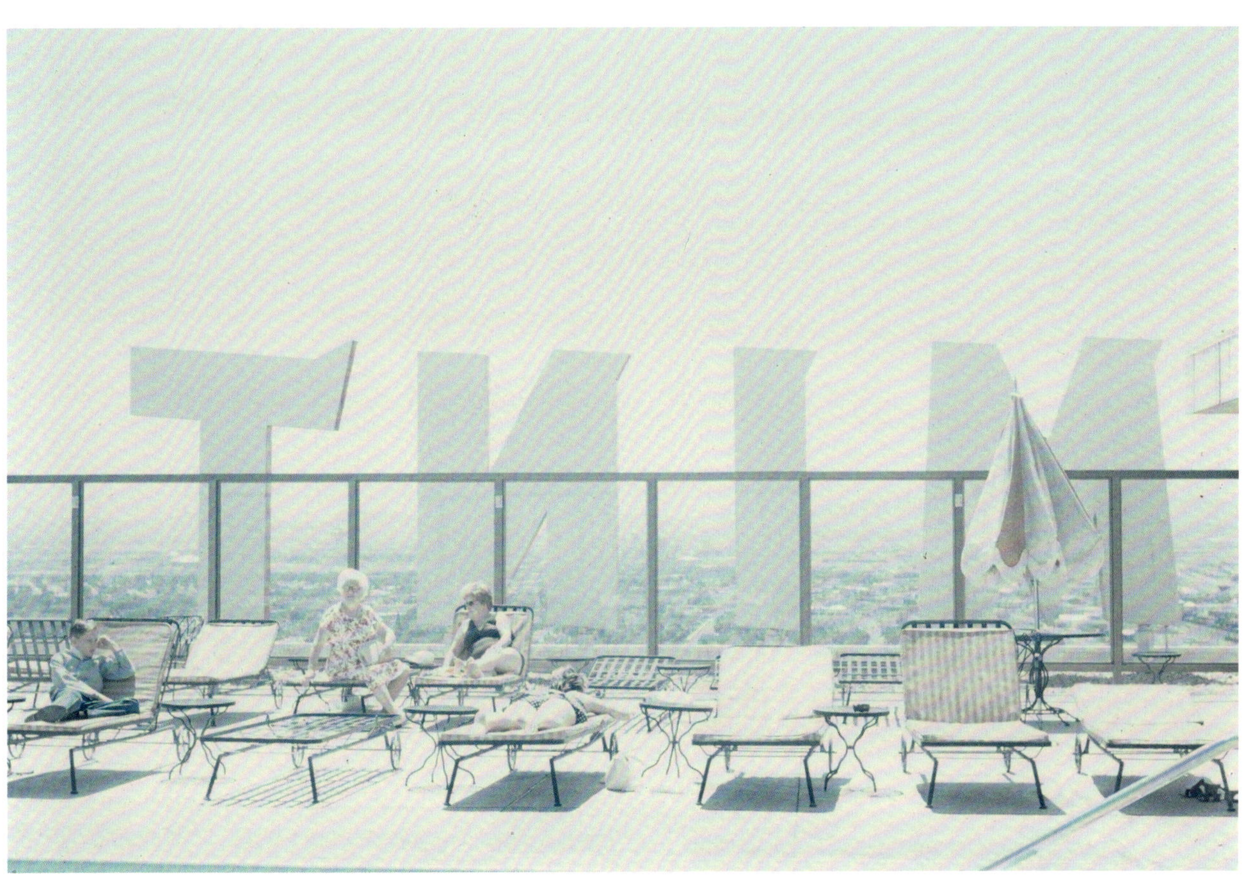

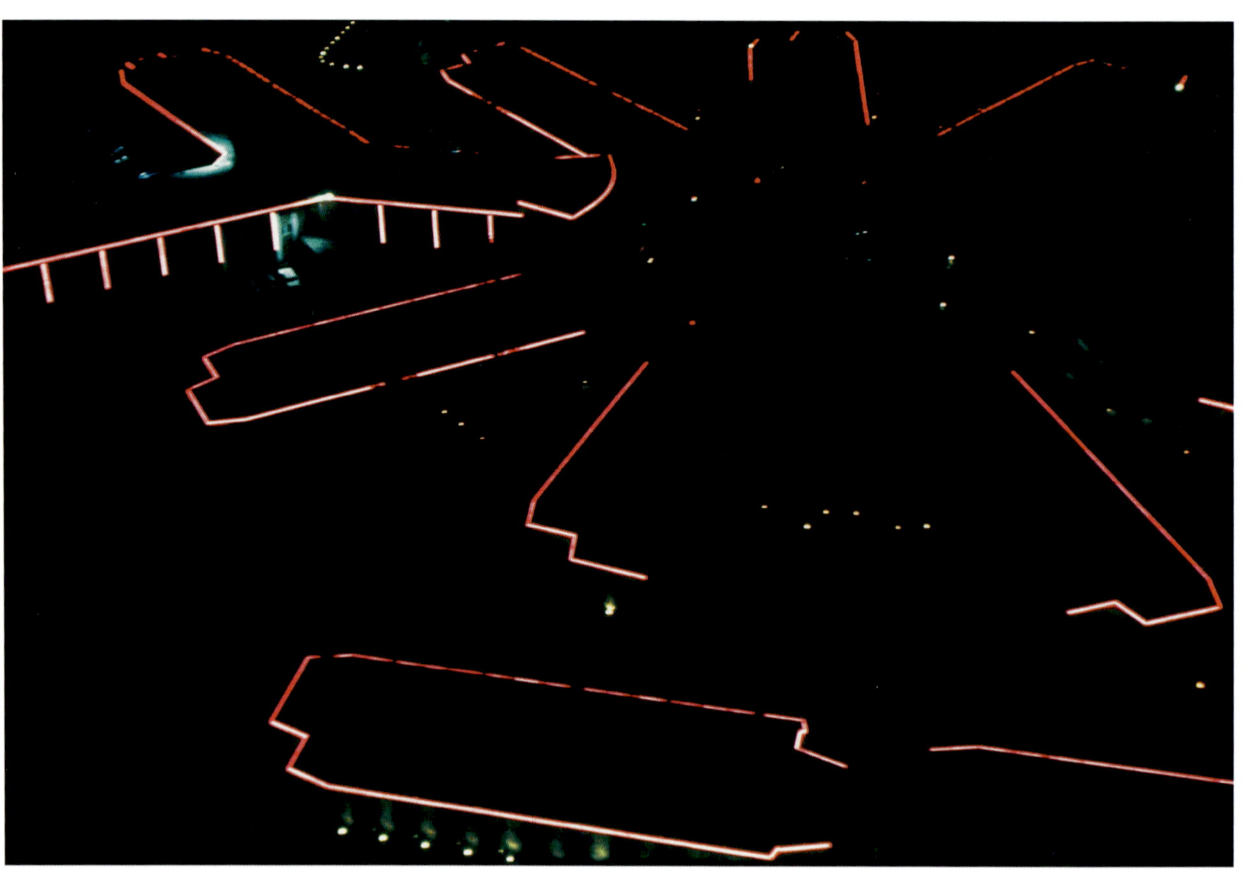

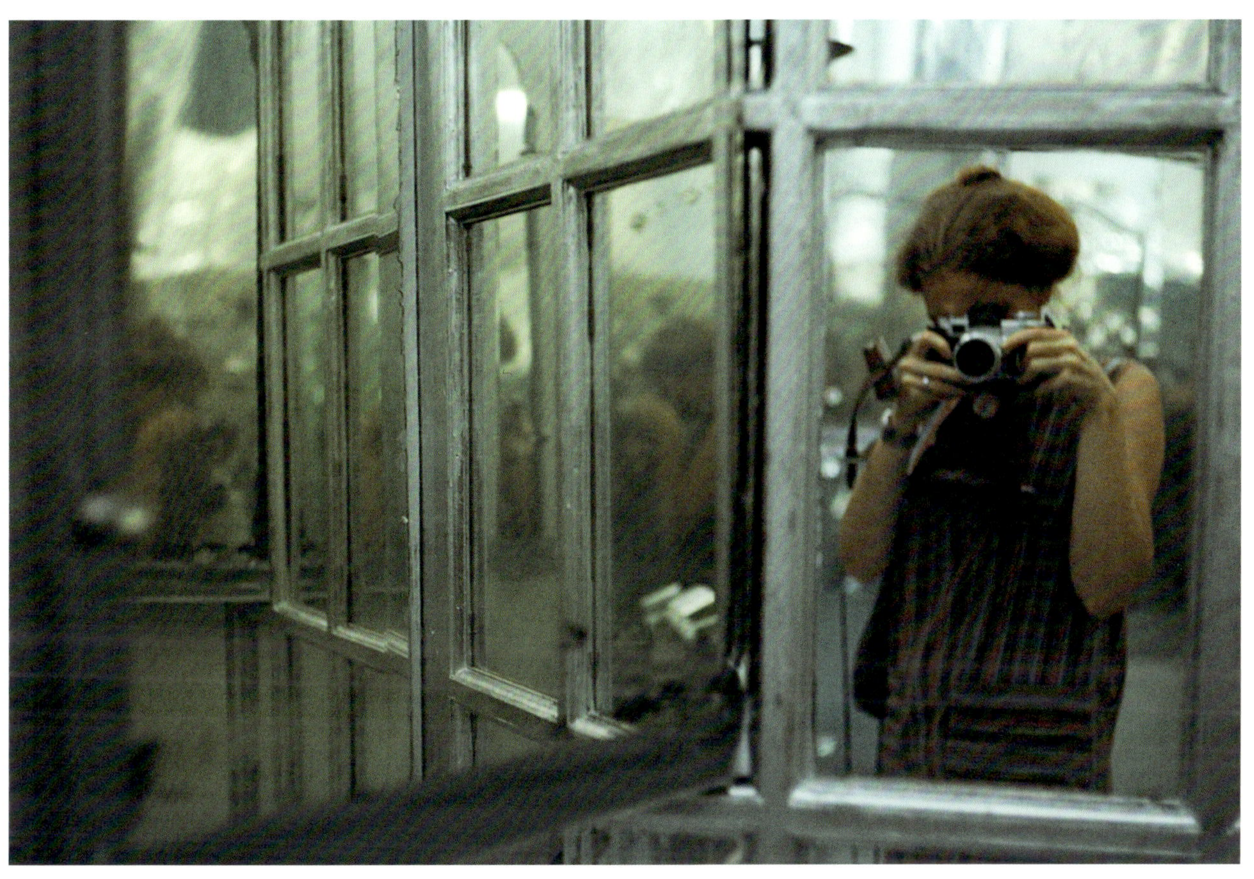

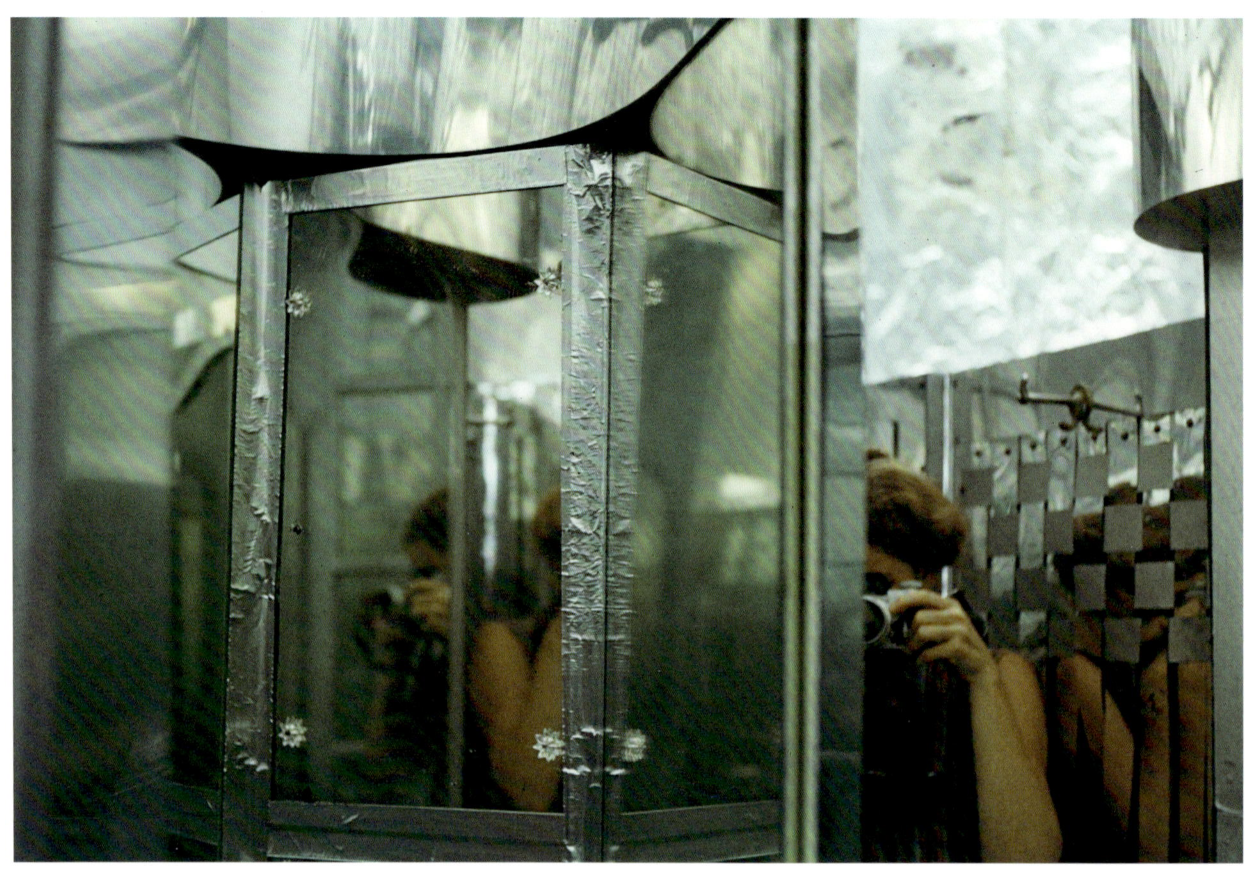

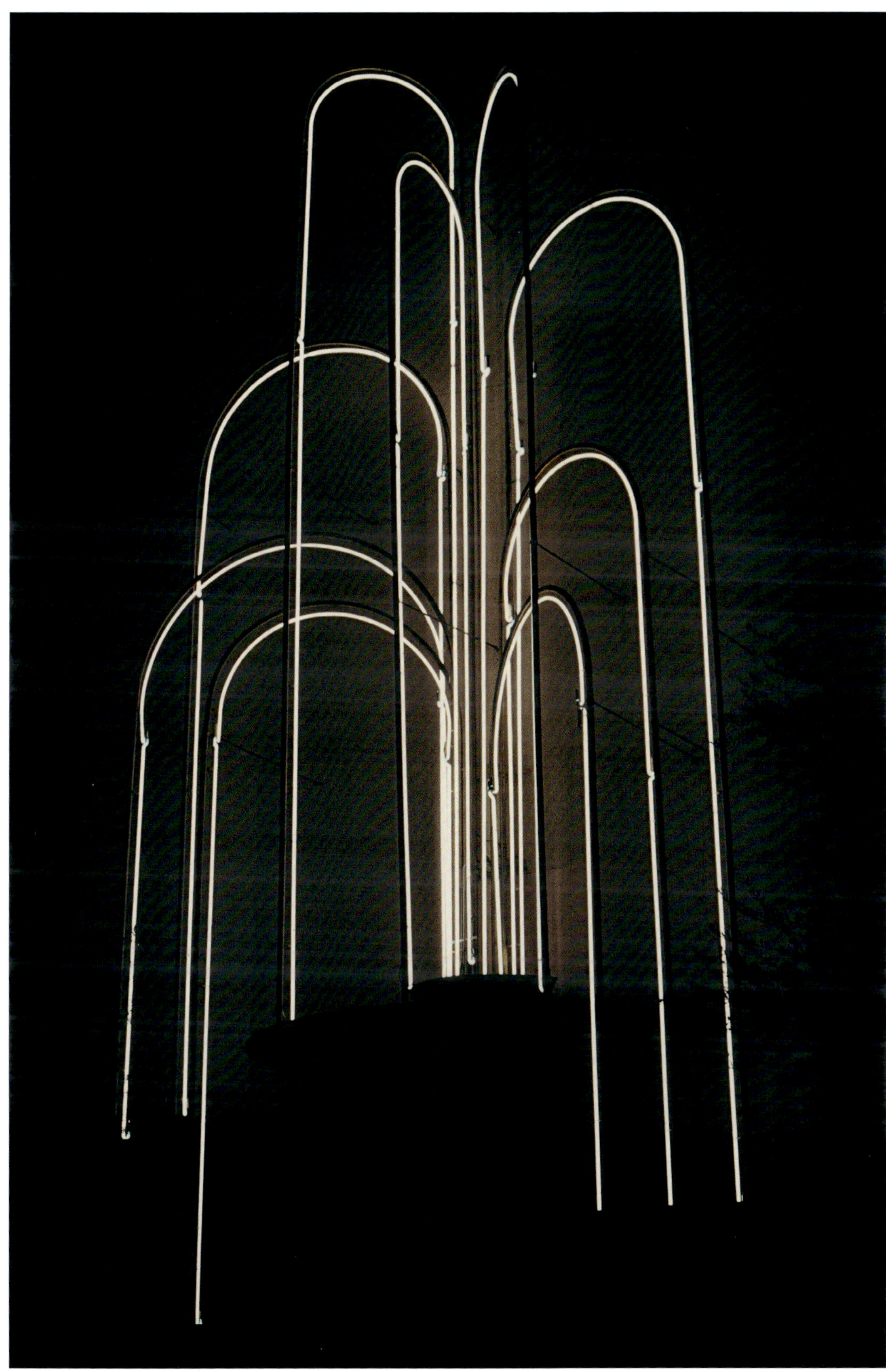

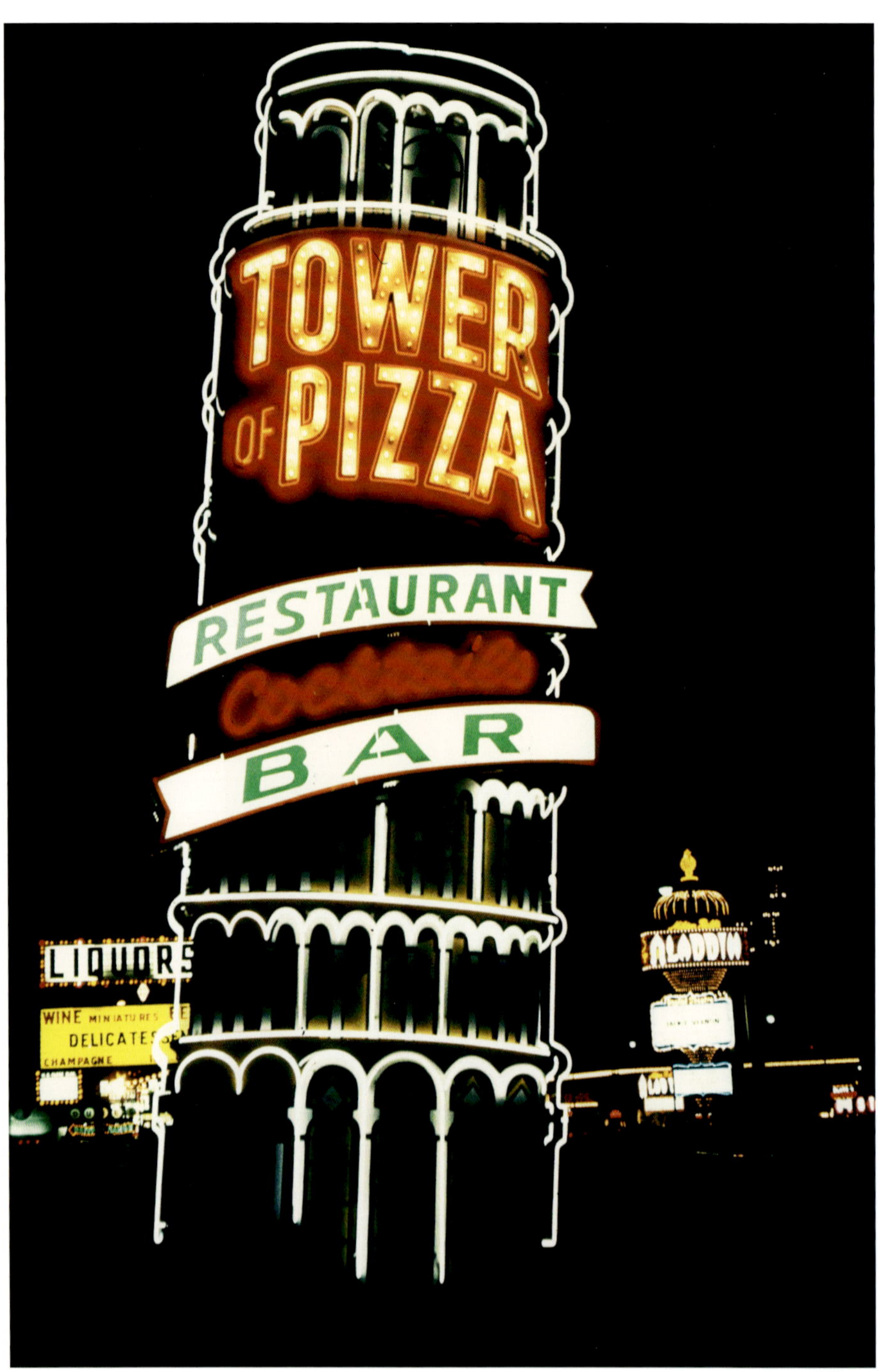
TOWER OF PIZZA
RESTAURANT
BAR
LIQUORS
WINE MINIATURES
DELICATES
CHAMPAGNE
ALADDIN

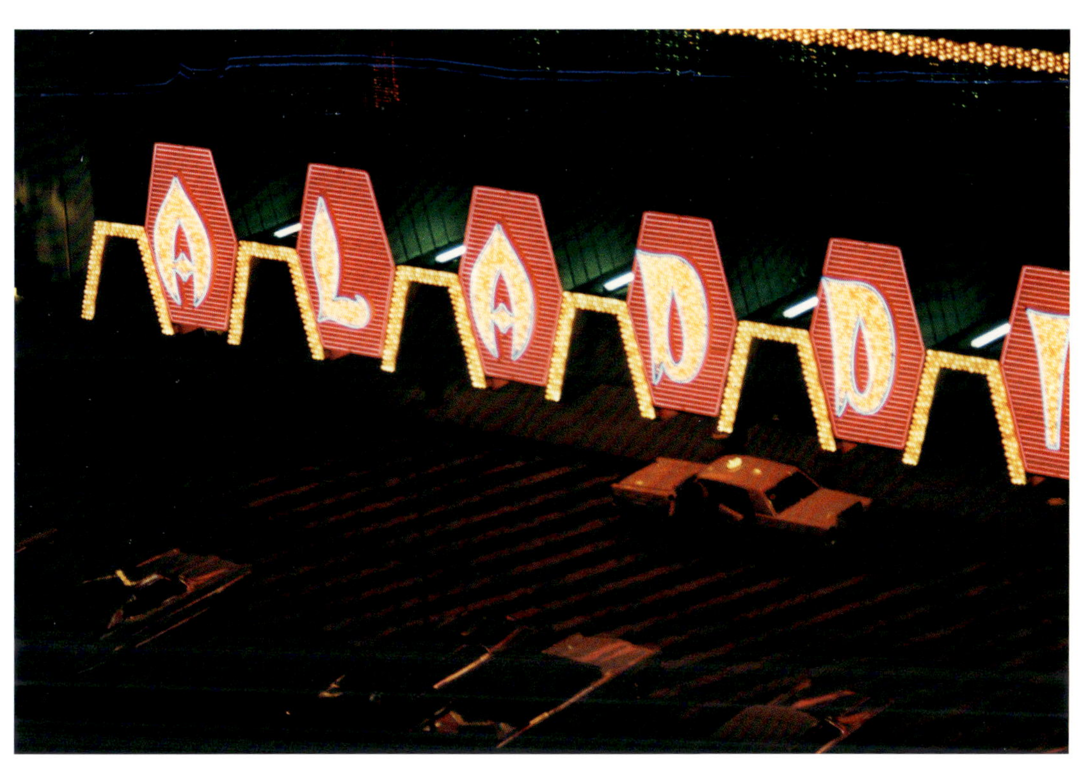
ALADD

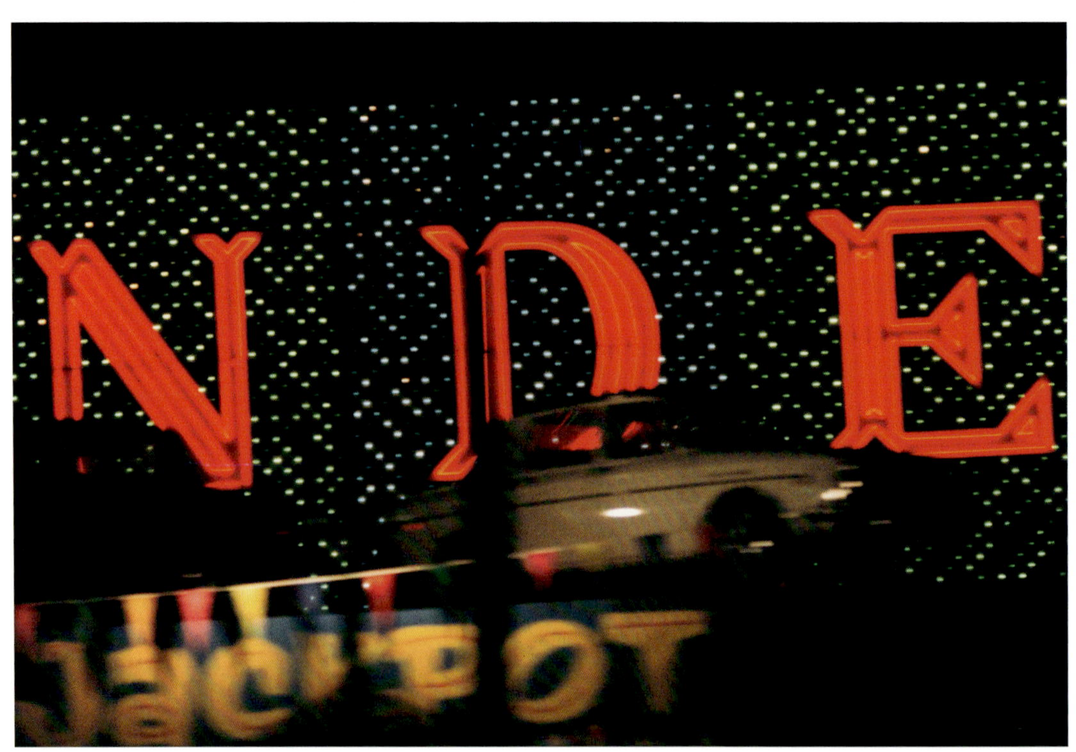

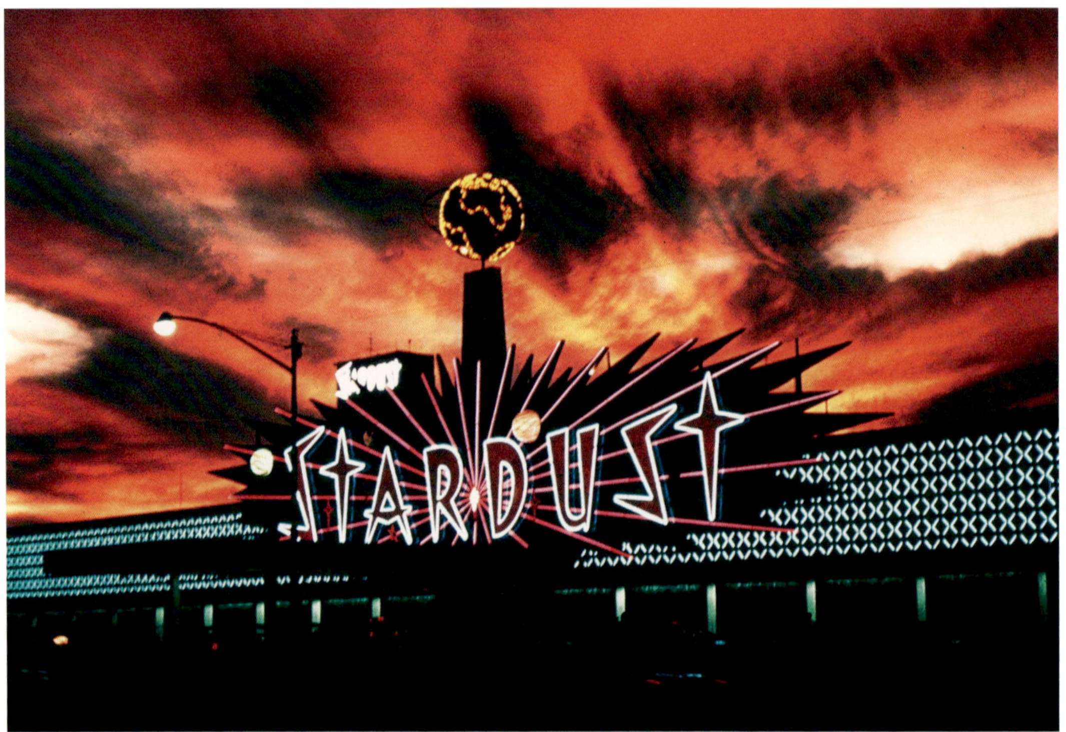
STARDUST

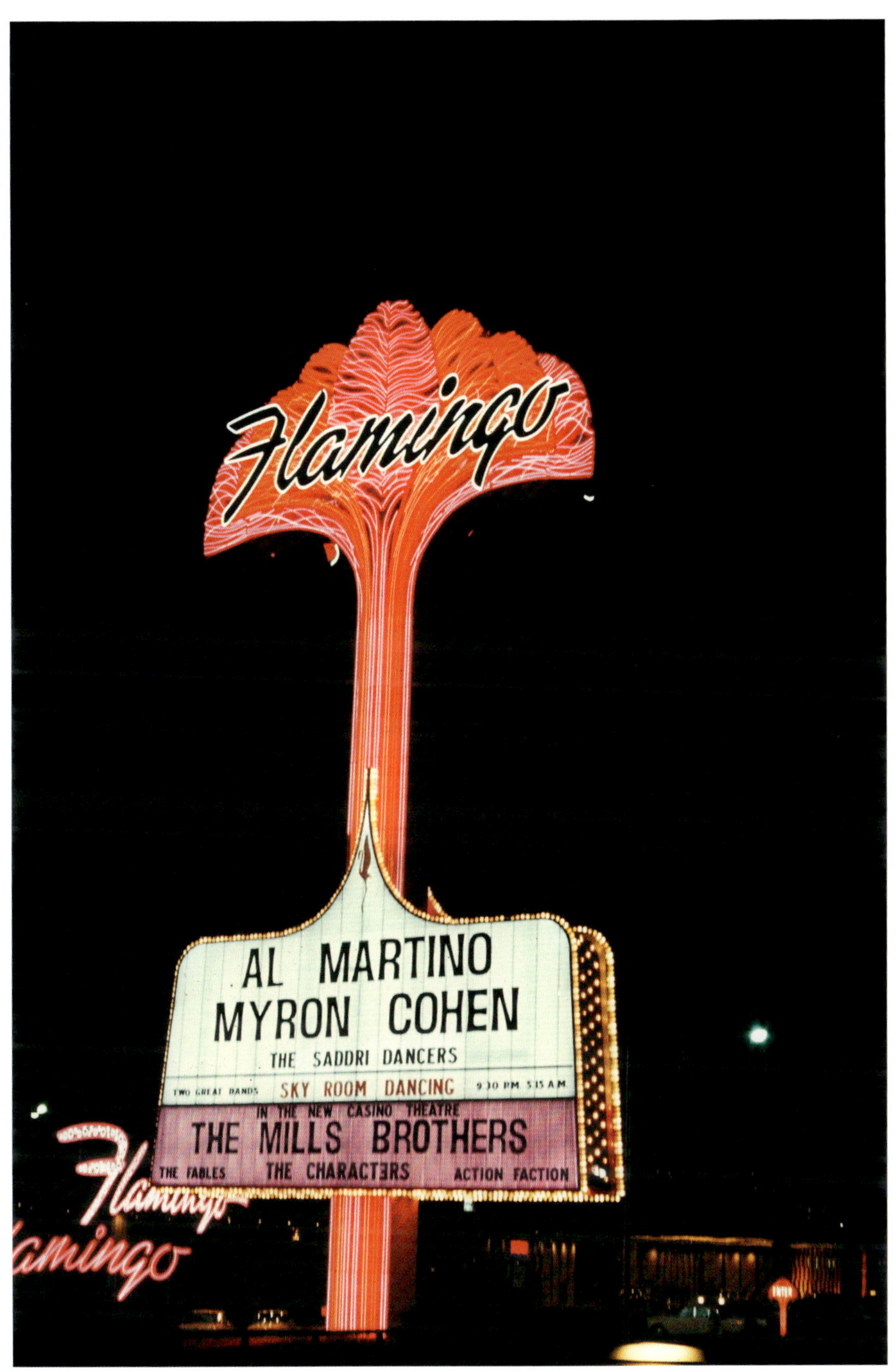
Flamingo
AL MARTINO
MYRON COHEN
THE SADDRI DANCERS
TWO GREAT BANDS
SKY ROOM DANCING
IN THE NEW CASINO THEATRE
THE MILLS BROTHERS
THE FABLES
THE CHARACTERS
ACTION FACTION
Flamingo

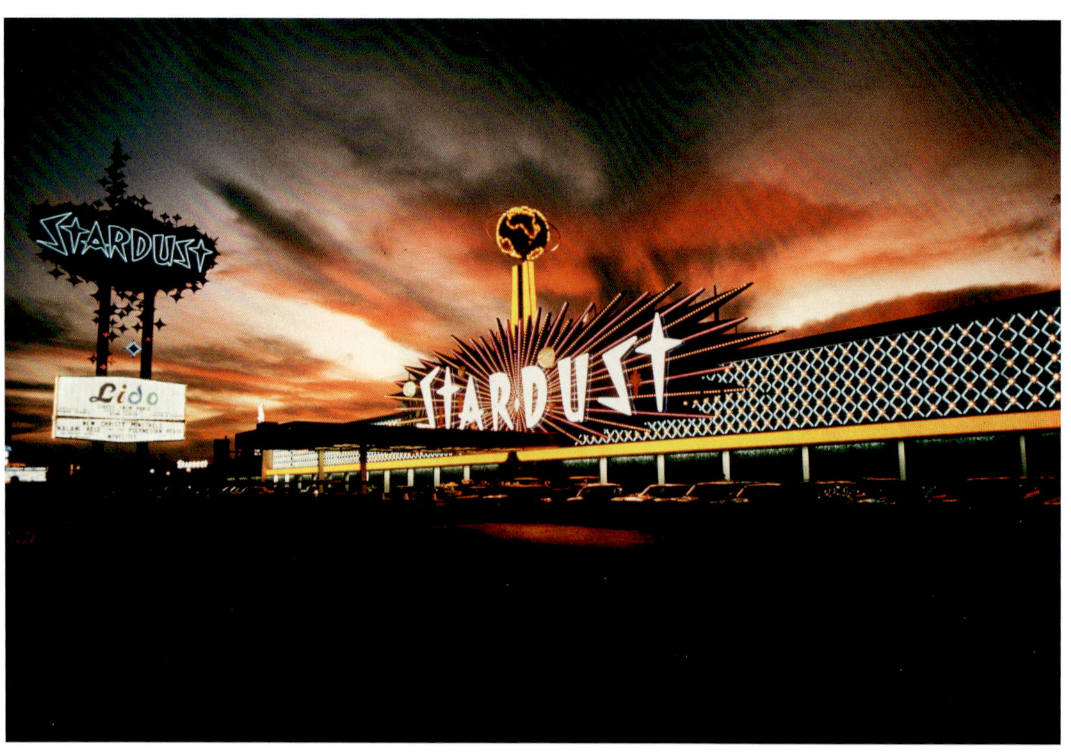
STARDUST
Lido
STARDUST

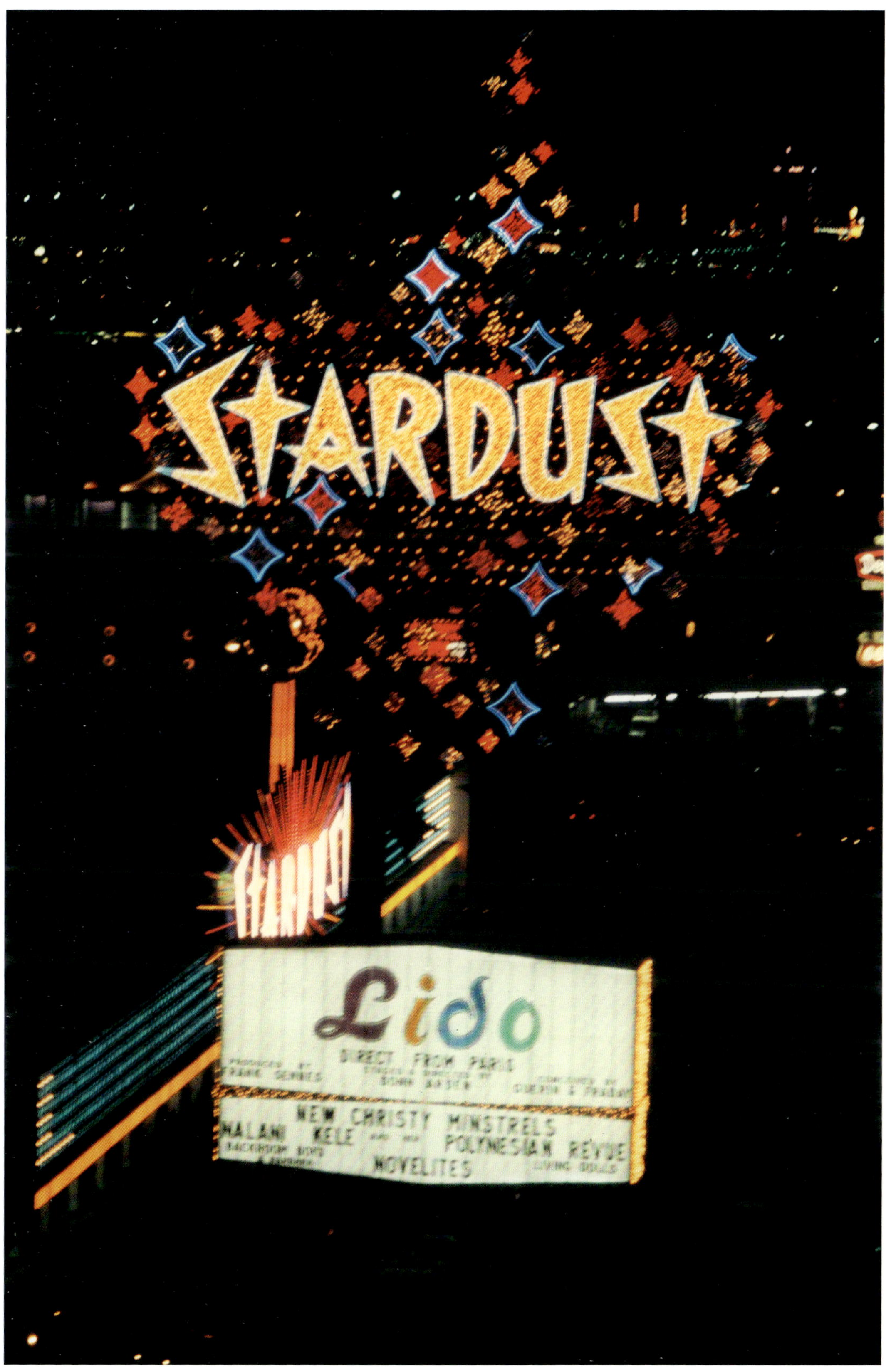
STARDUST
Lido
DIRECT FROM PARIS
NEW CHRISTY MINSTRELS
MALANI KELE
POLYNESIAN REVUE
NOVELITES

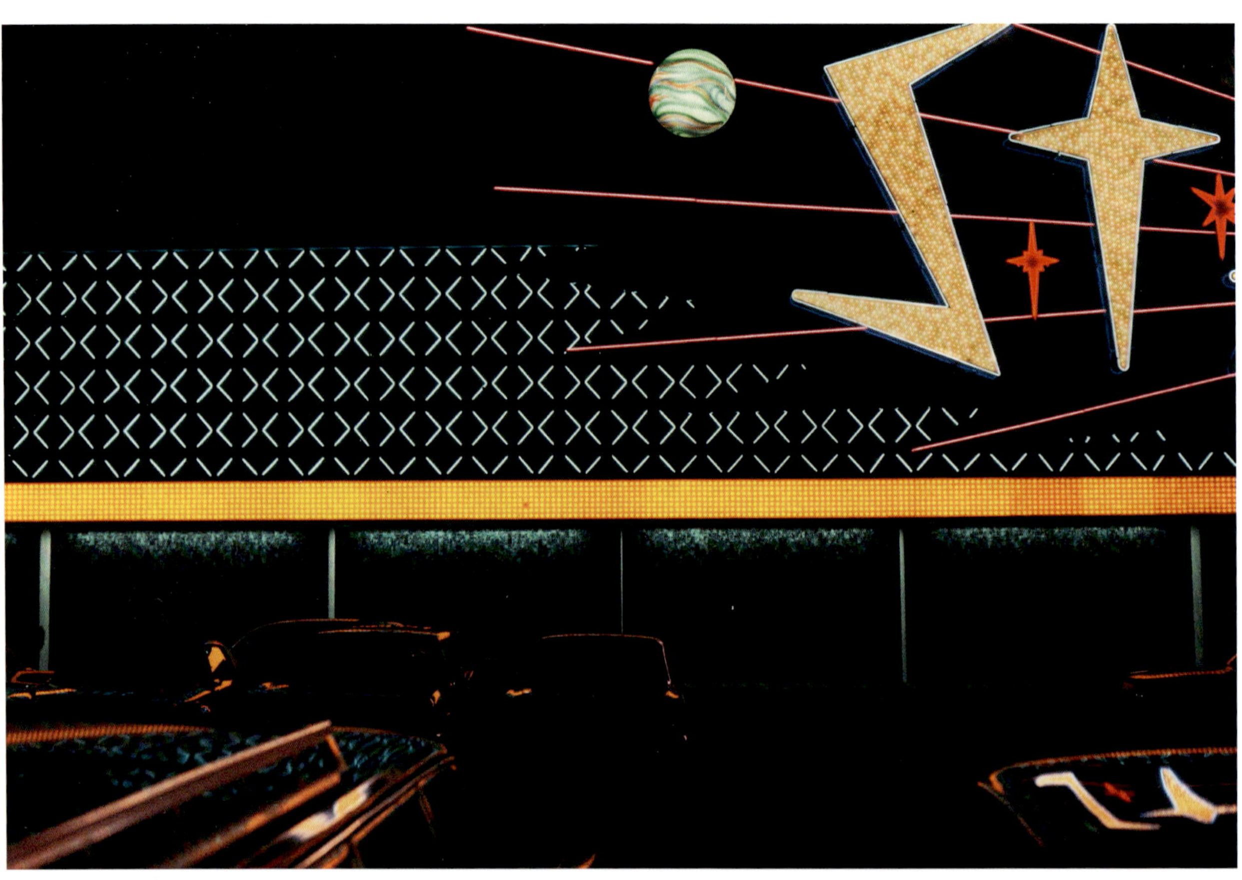

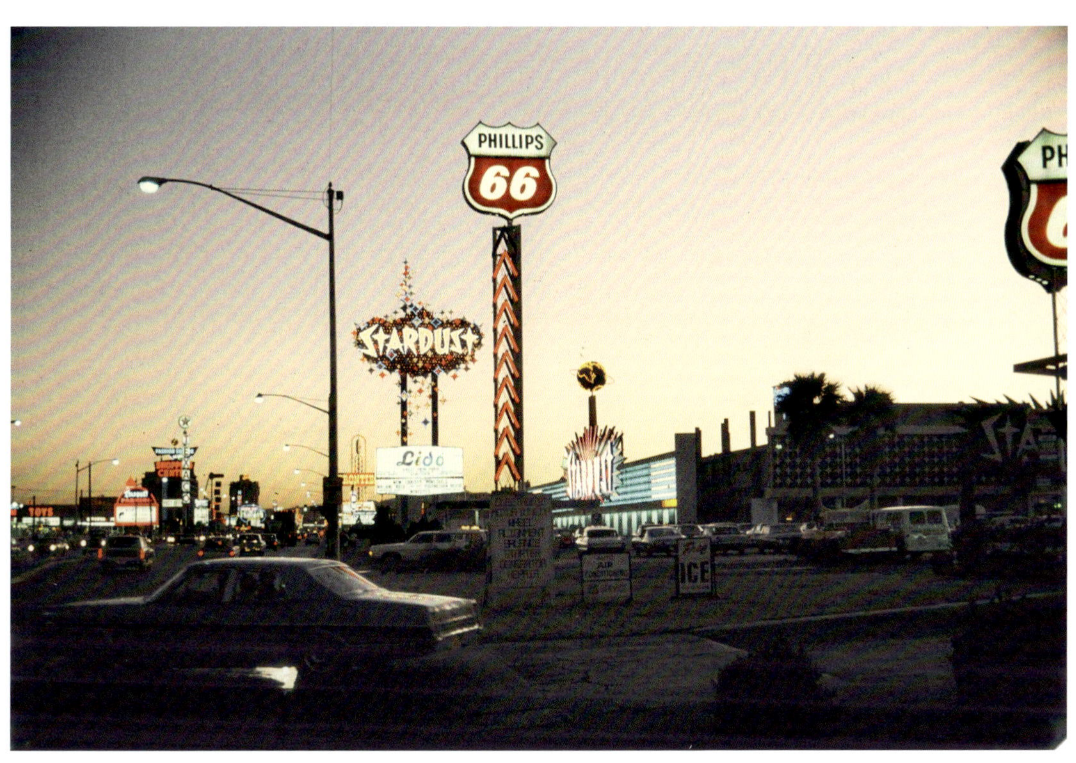
PHILLIPS
66
STARDUST
Lido
ICE

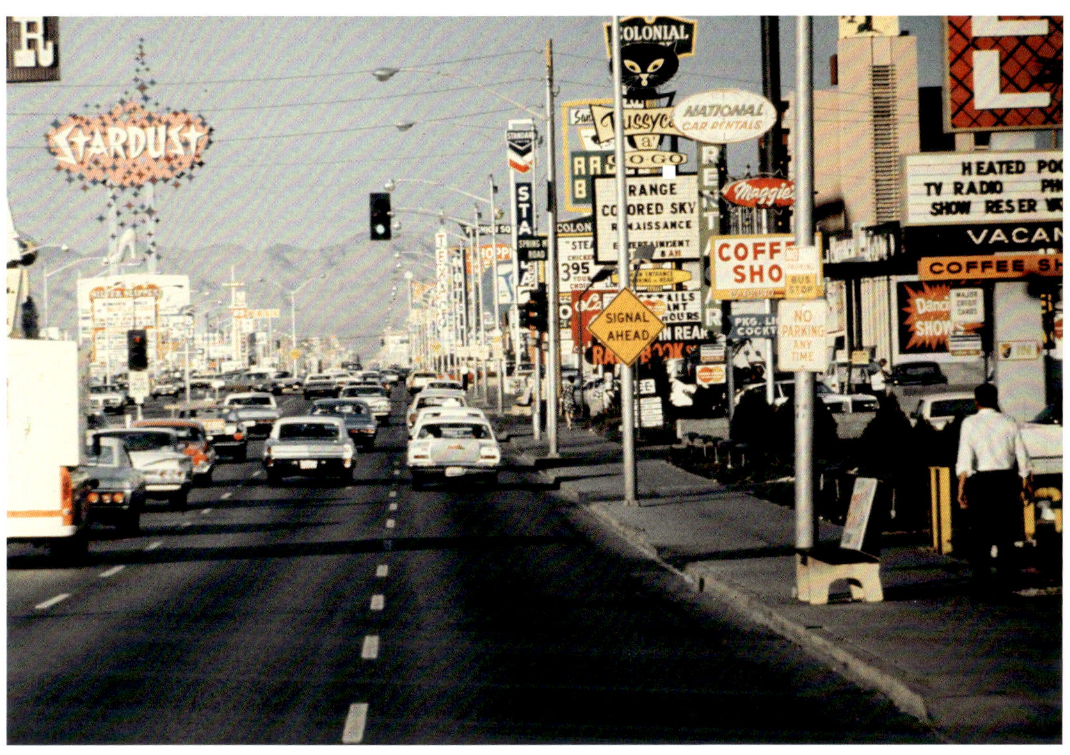
STARDUST
COLONIAL
NATIONAL
CAR RENTALS
SIGNAL
AHEAD
NO
PARKING
ANY
TIME
HEATED
TV RADIO
SHOW
BUS
STOP

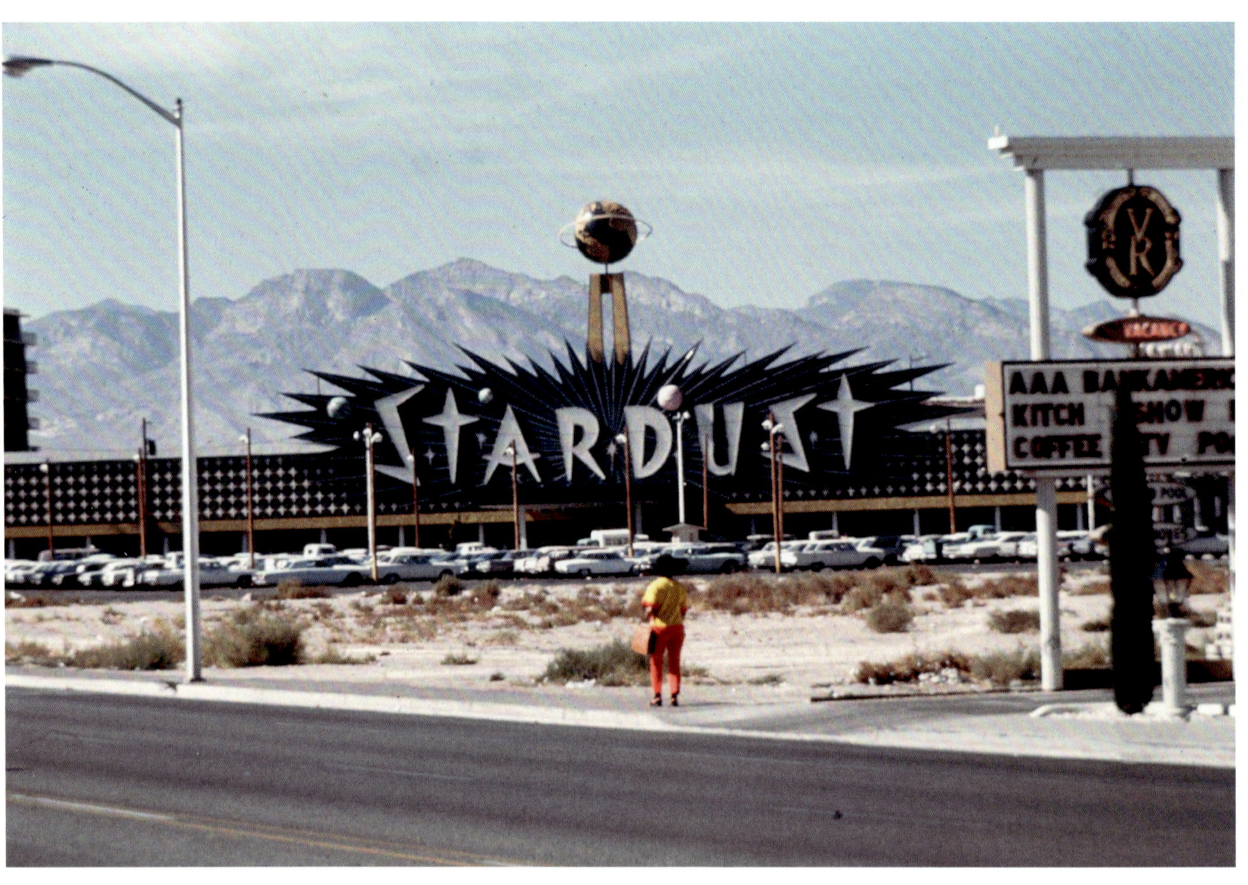
STARDUST

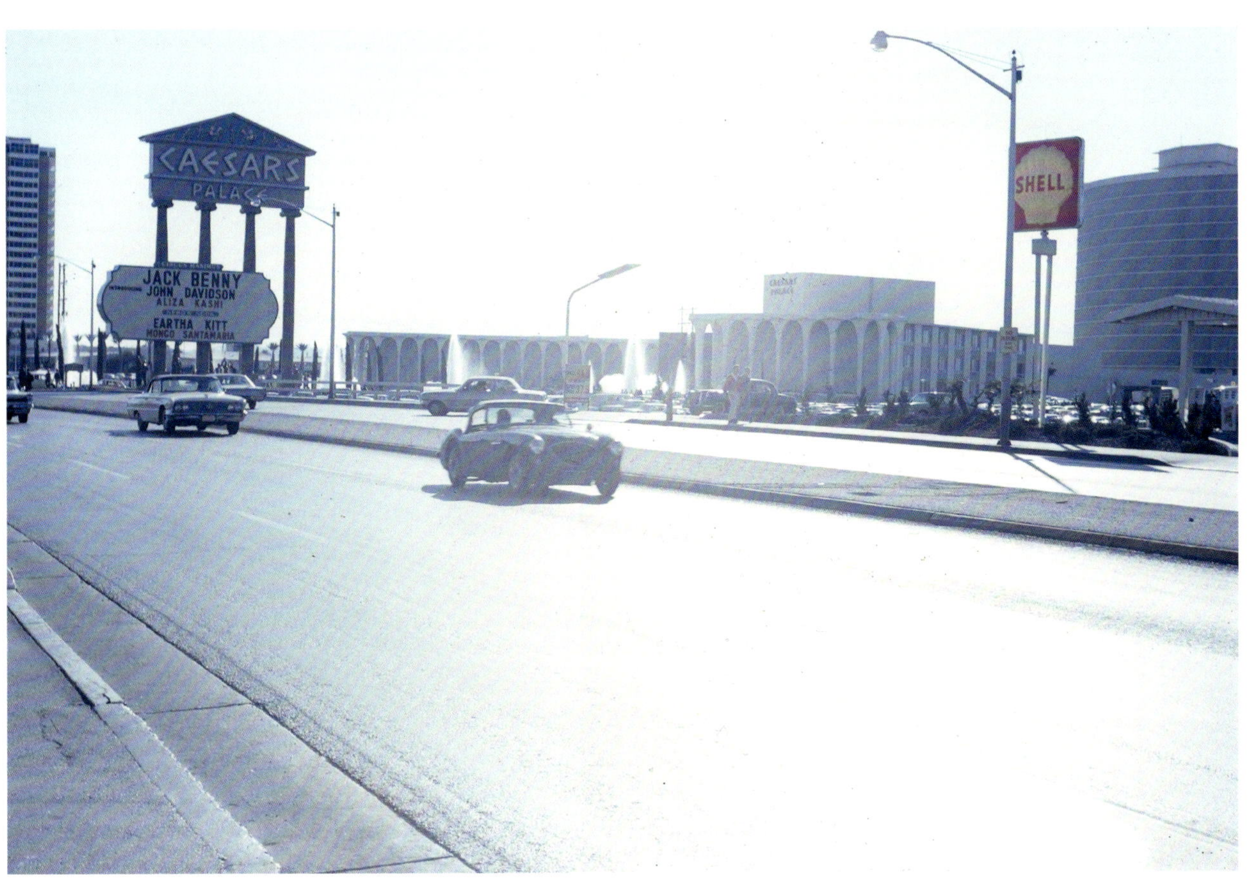
CAESARS
PALACE
JACK BENNY
JOHN DAVIDSON
ALIZA KASHI
EARTHA KITT
MONGO SANTAMARIA
SHELL

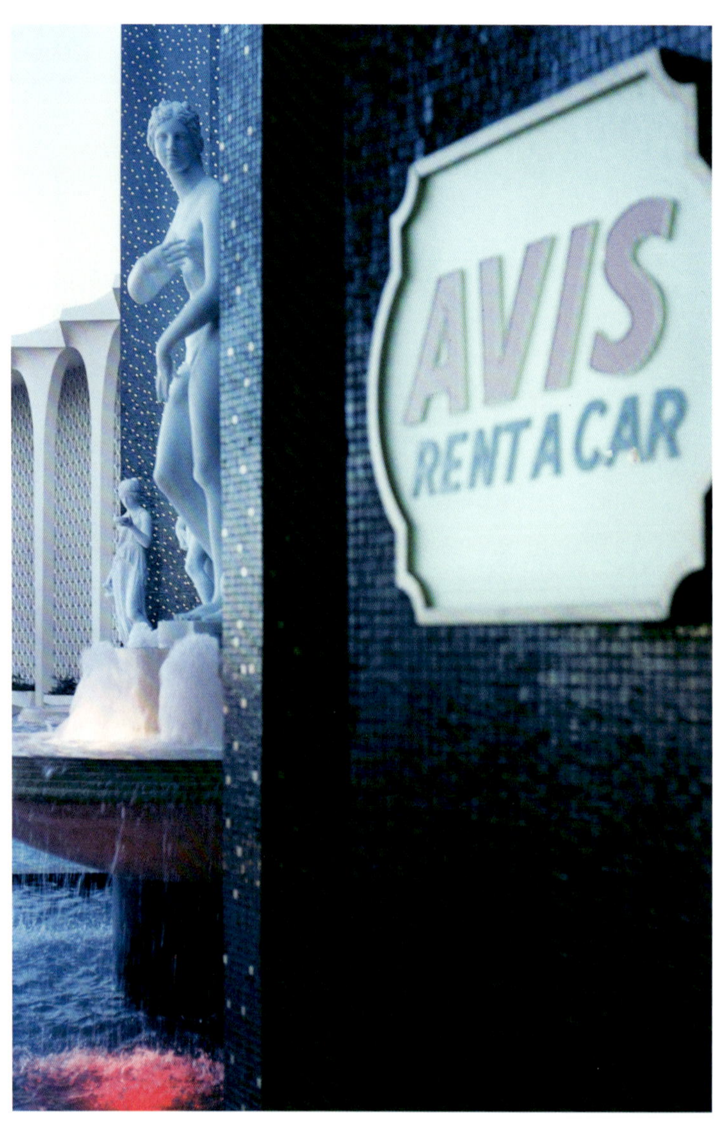
AVIS
RENT A CAR

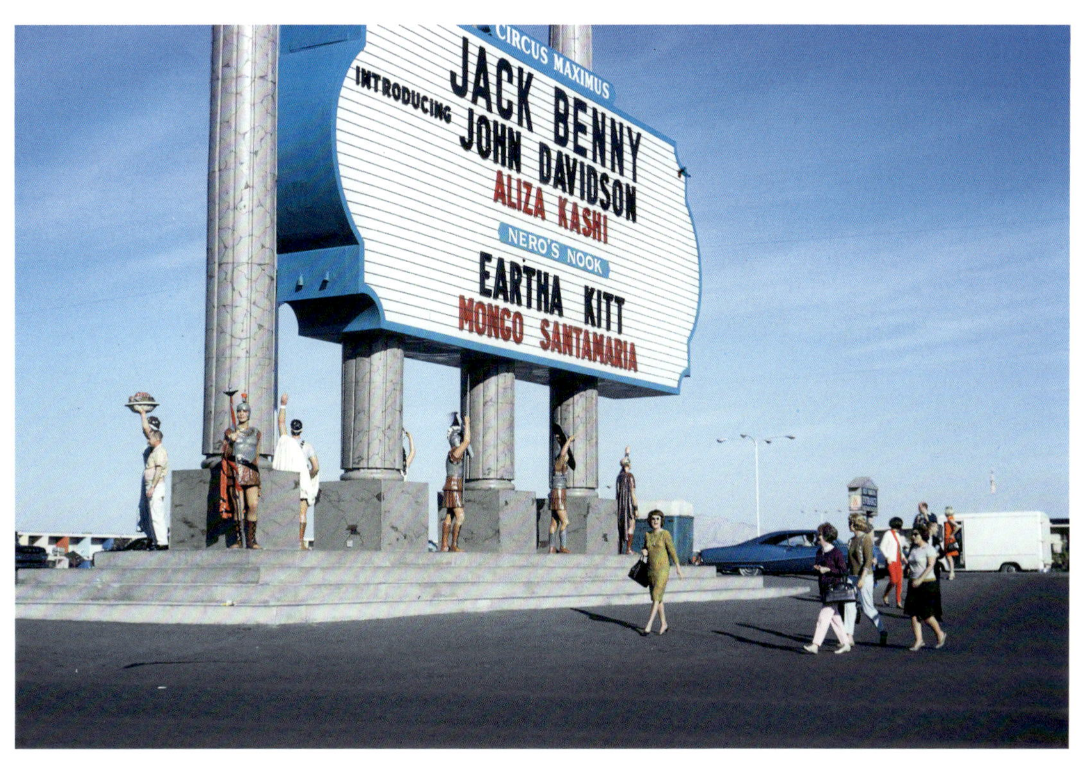
CIRCUS MAXIMUS
JACK BENNY
INTRODUCING JOHN DAVIDSON
ALIZA KASHI
NERO'S NOOK
EARTHA KITT
MONGO SANTAMARIA

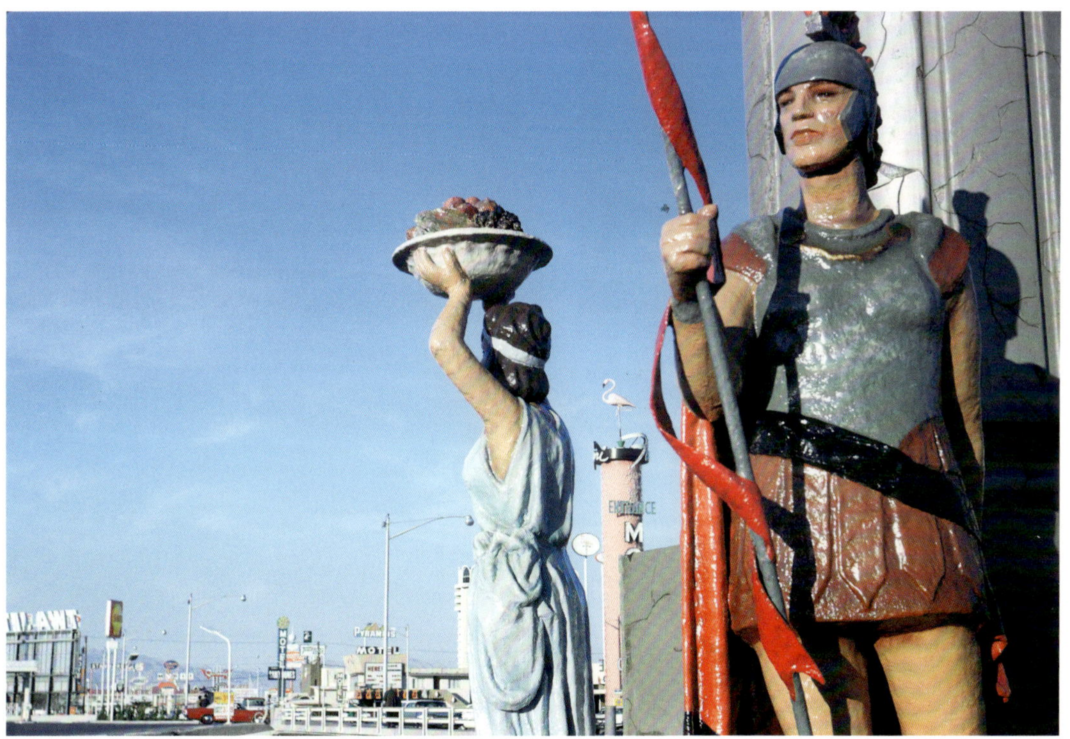
MOTEL

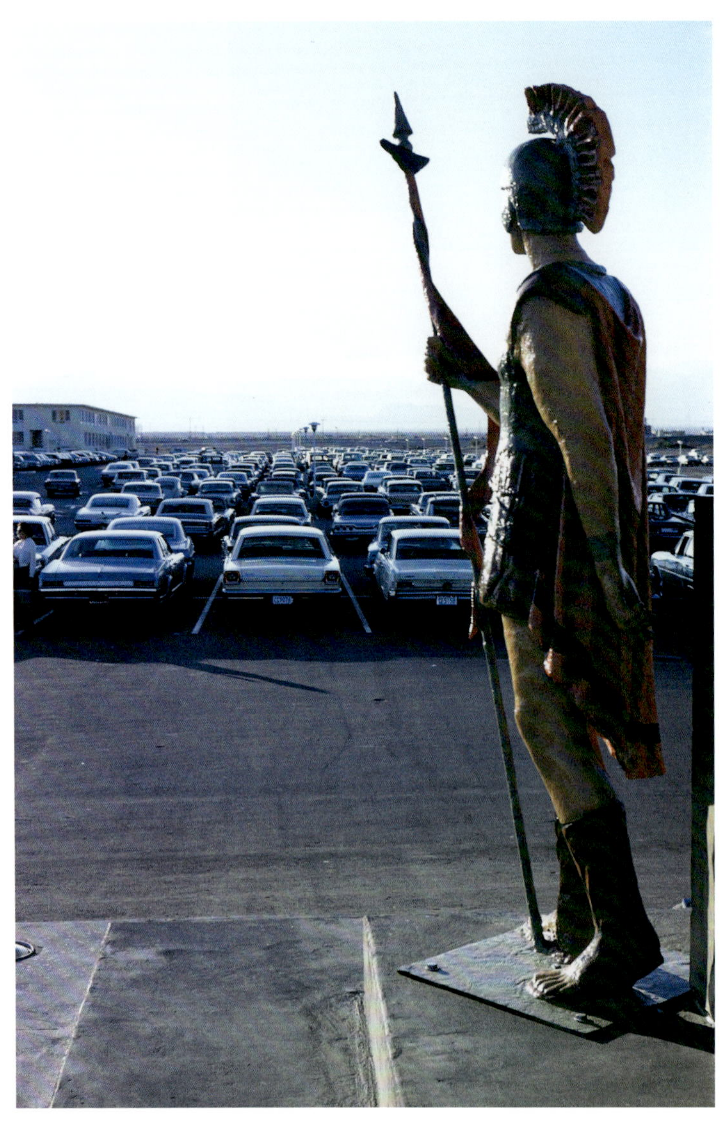

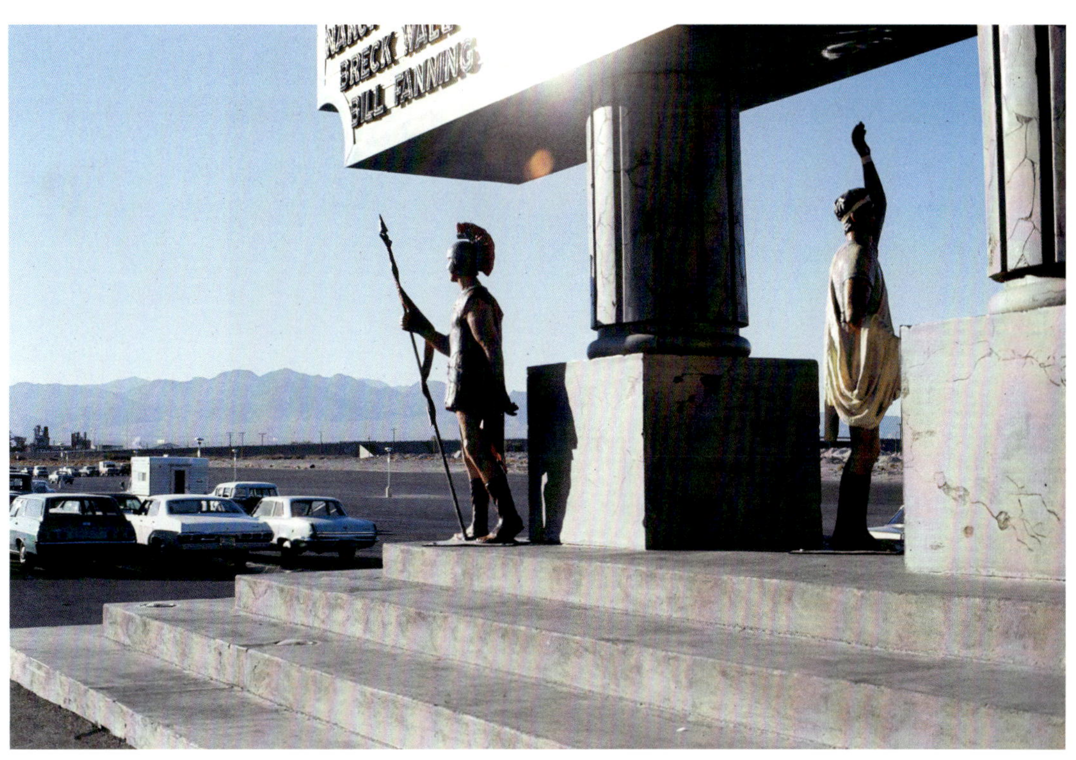
BRECK
BILL FANNING

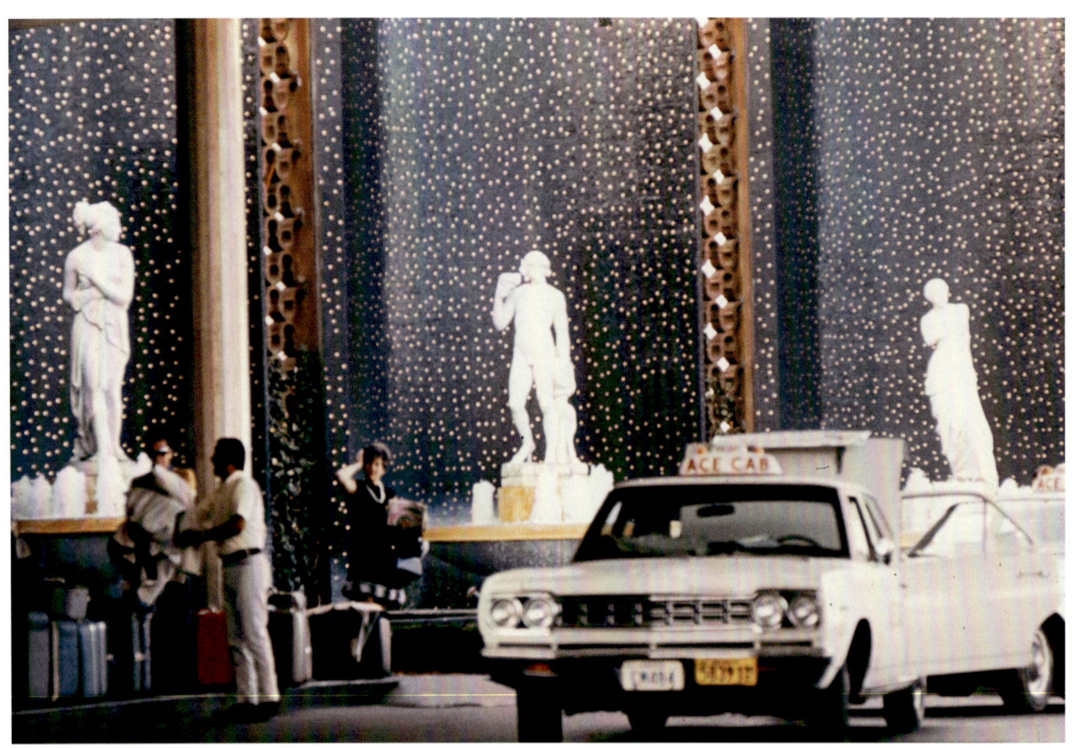
ACE CAB

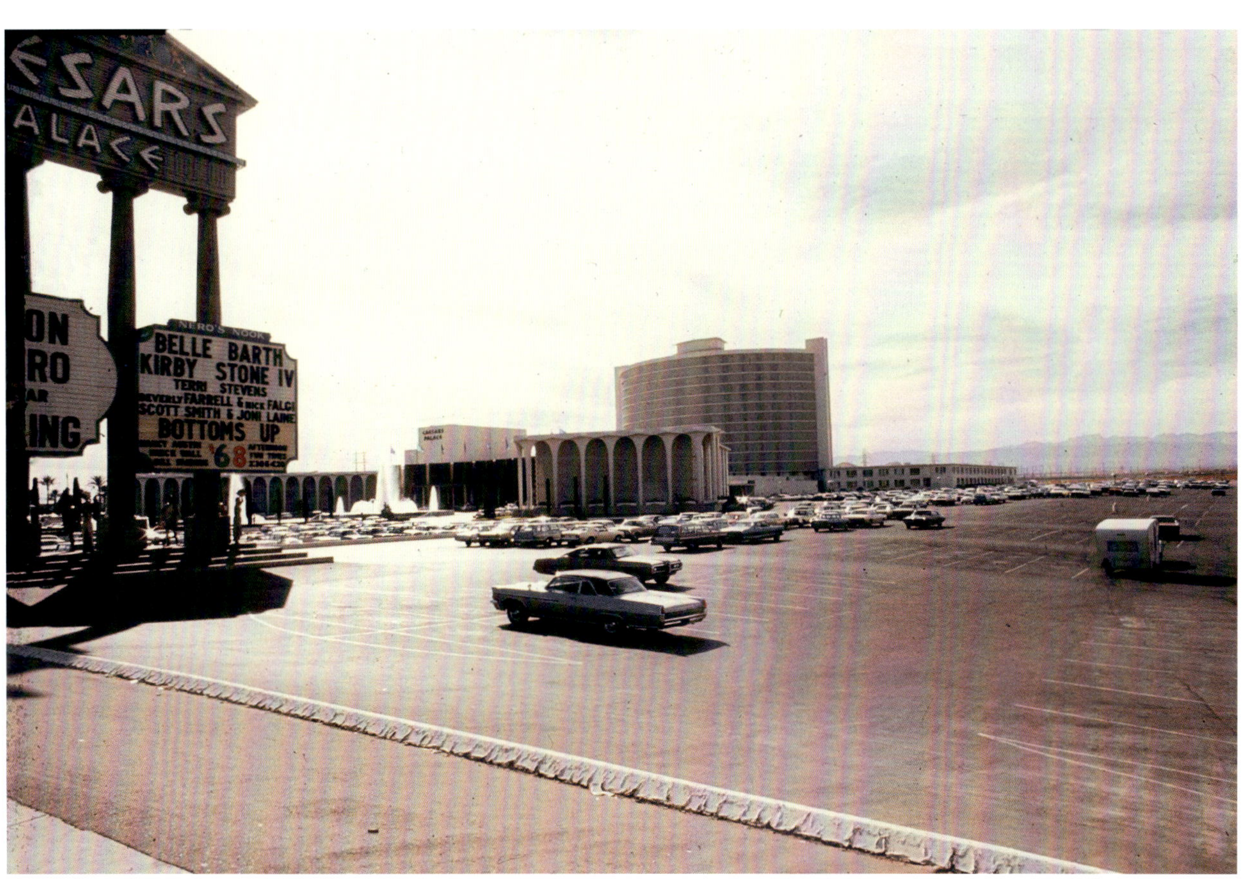
ESARS
ALACE
NERO'S NOOK
BELLE BARTH
KIRBY STONE IV
TERRI STEVENS
FARRELL
SCOTT SMITH & JONI LAINE
BOTTOMS UP
'68

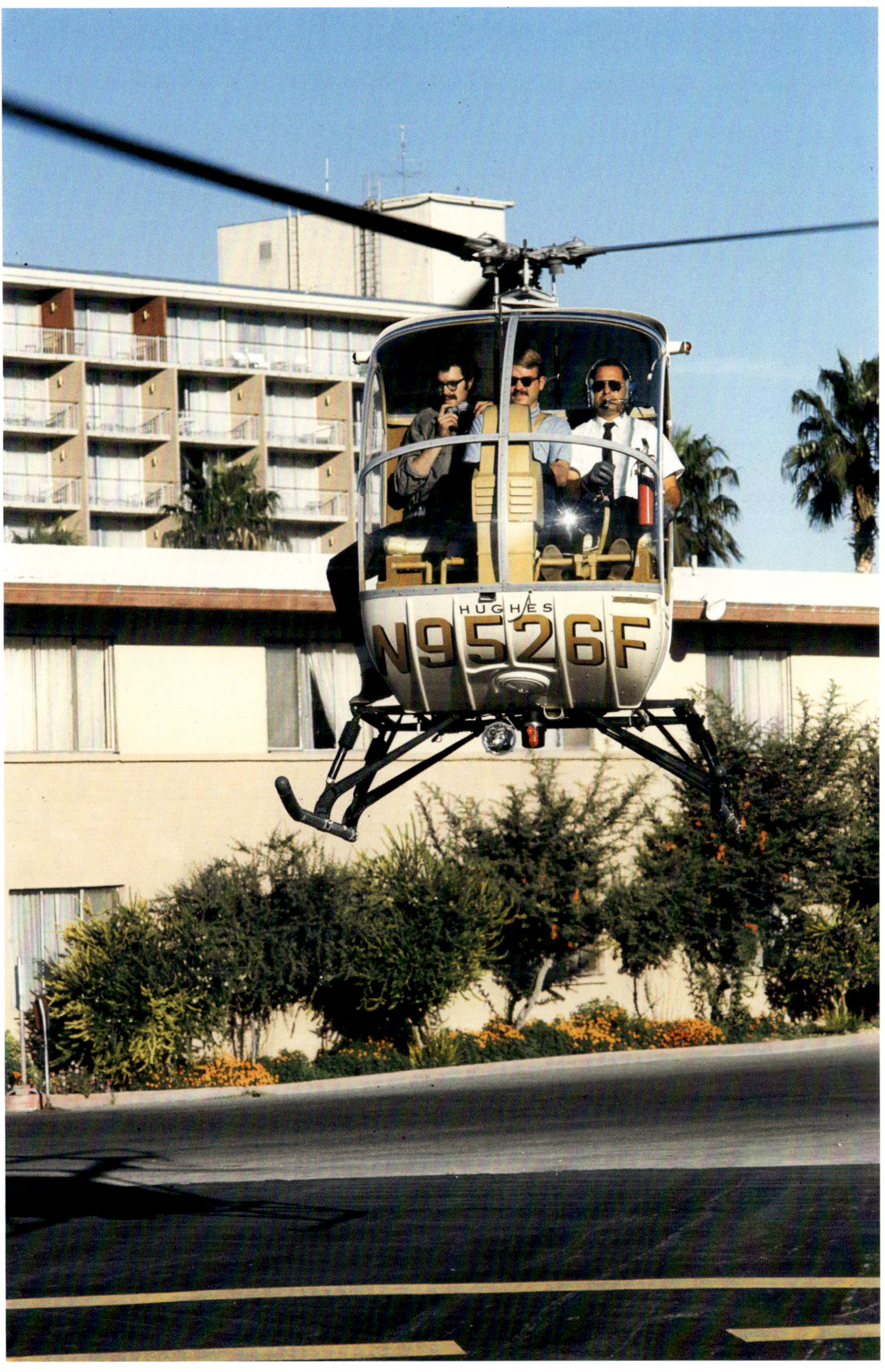
HUGHES
N9526F

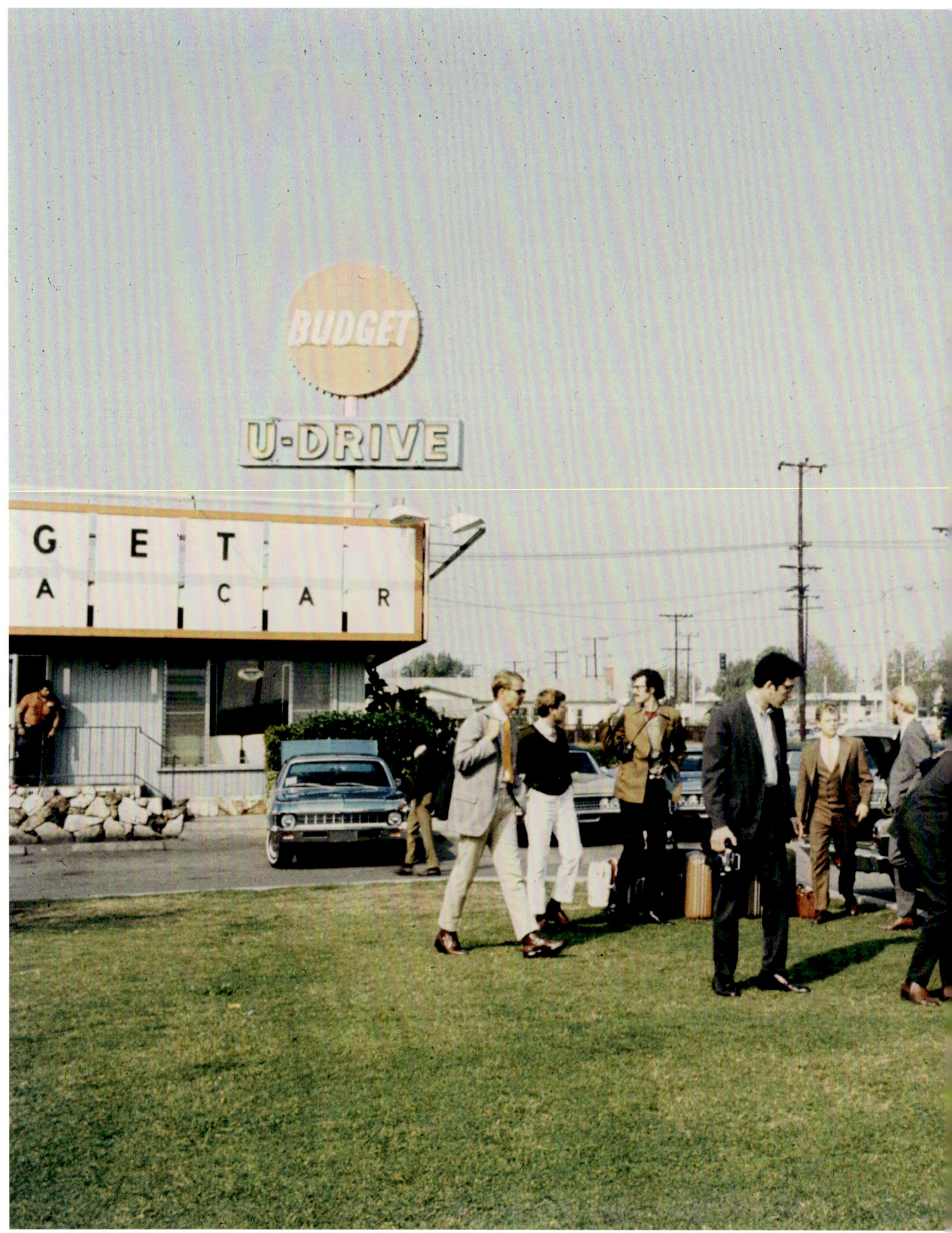
BUDGET
U-DRIVE
G E T
A C A R

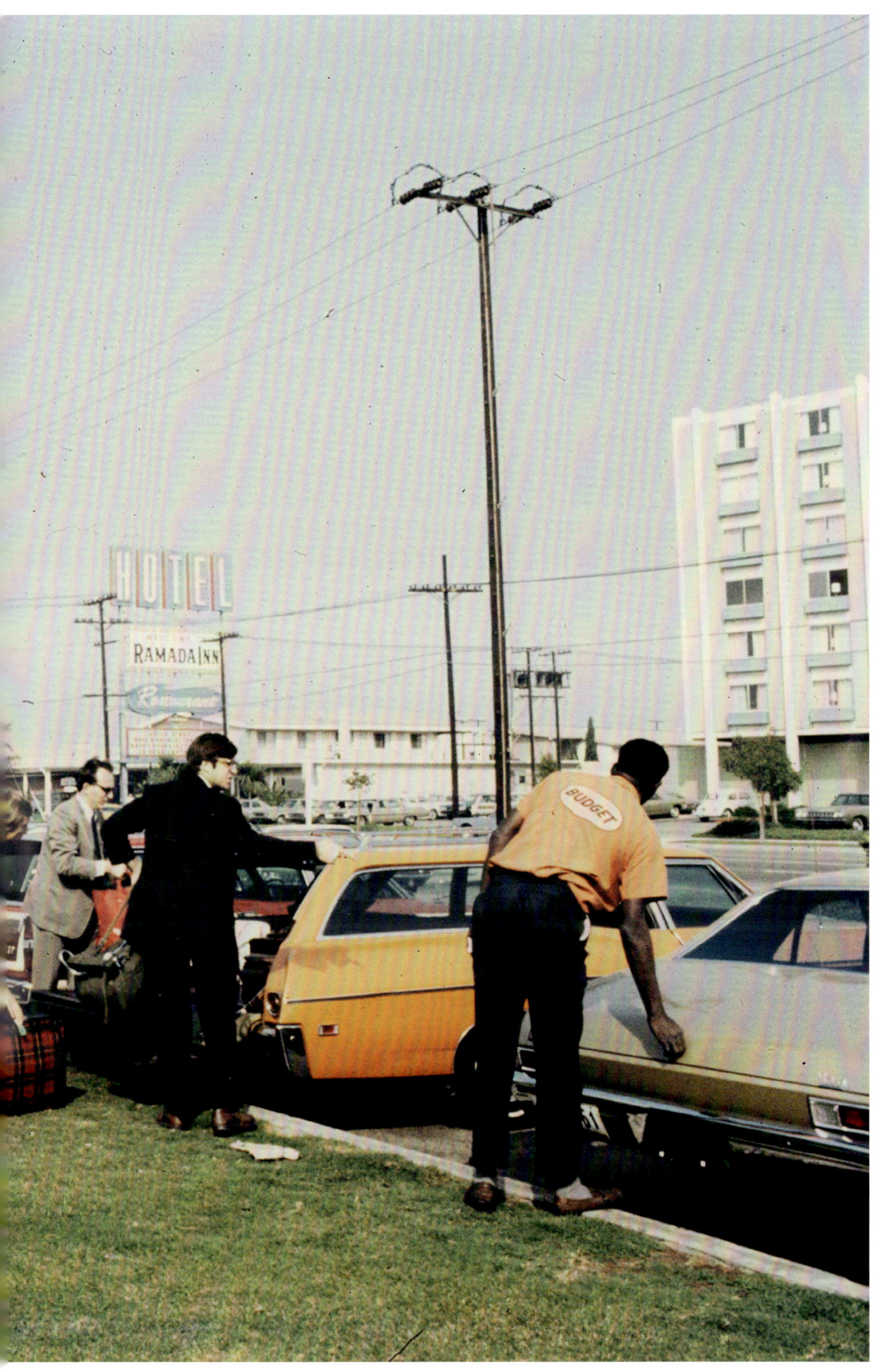
HOTEL
RAMADA INN
Restaurant
BUDGET

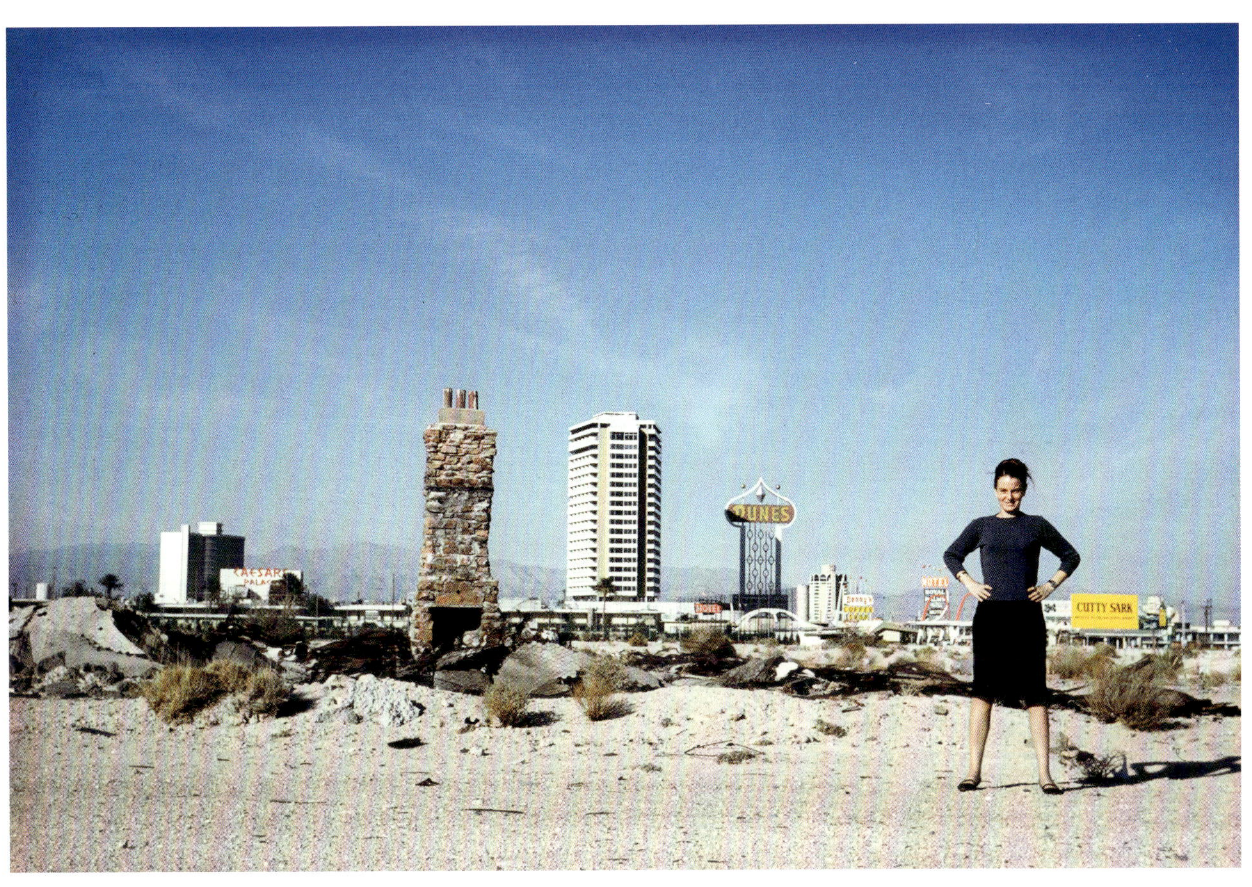
DUNES
CUTTY SARK

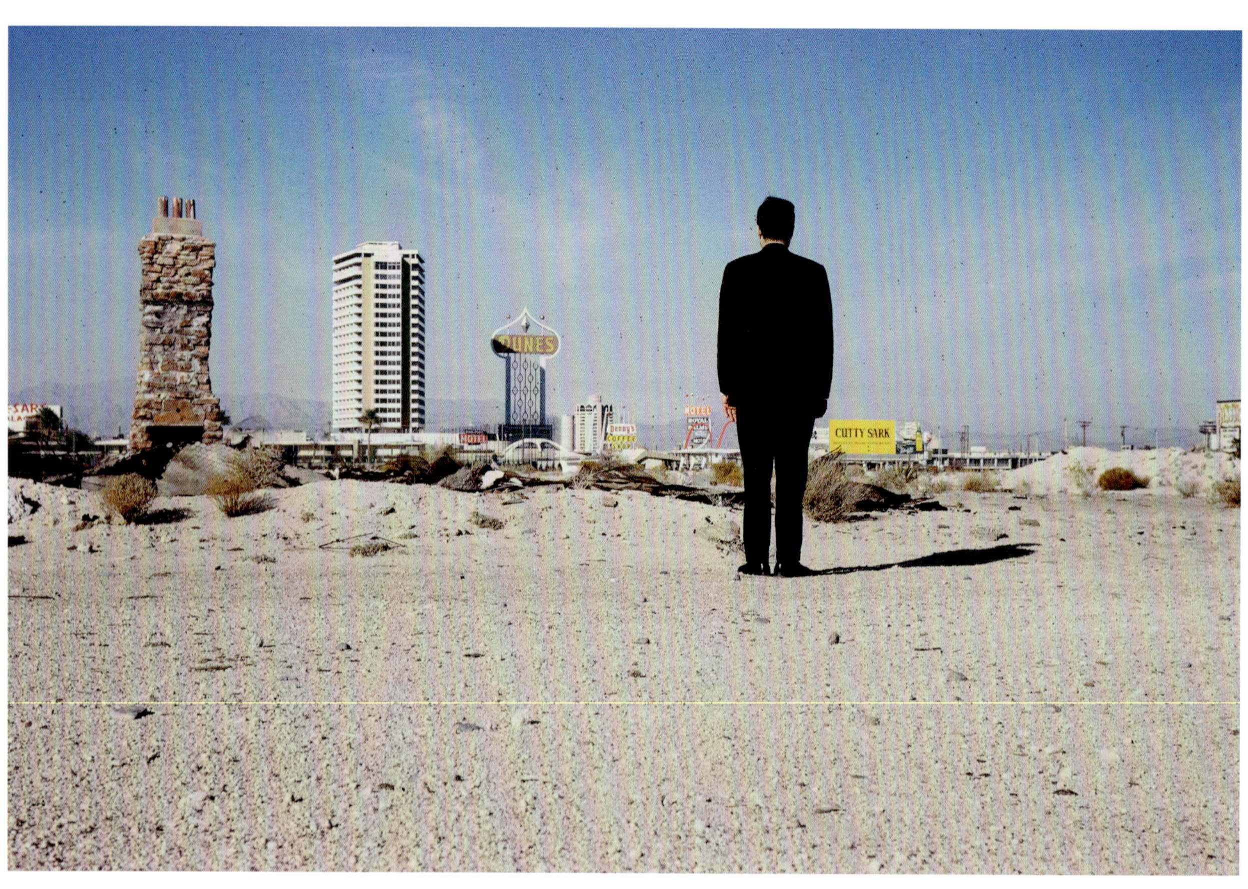
DUNES
CUTTY SARK

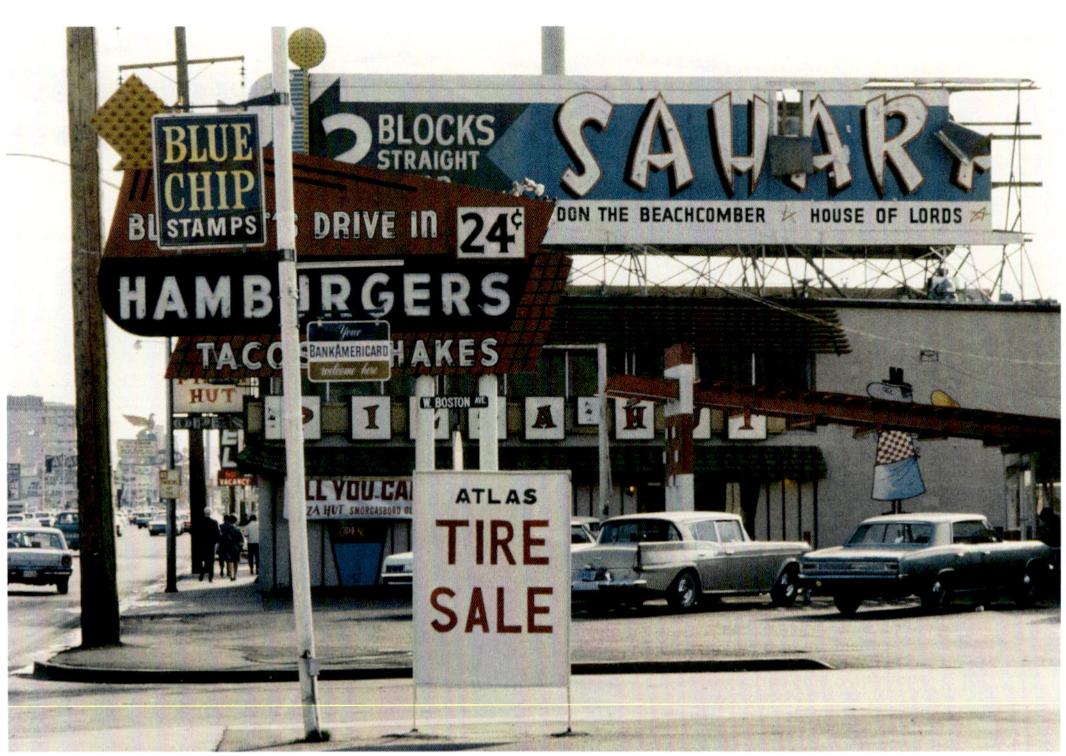
BLUE CHIP STAMPS
BLOCKS STRAIGHT
DON THE BEACHCOMBER
HOUSE OF LORDS
DRIVE IN
24¢
Your BankAmericard welcome here
W. BOSTON AVE
ATLAS
TIRE SALE

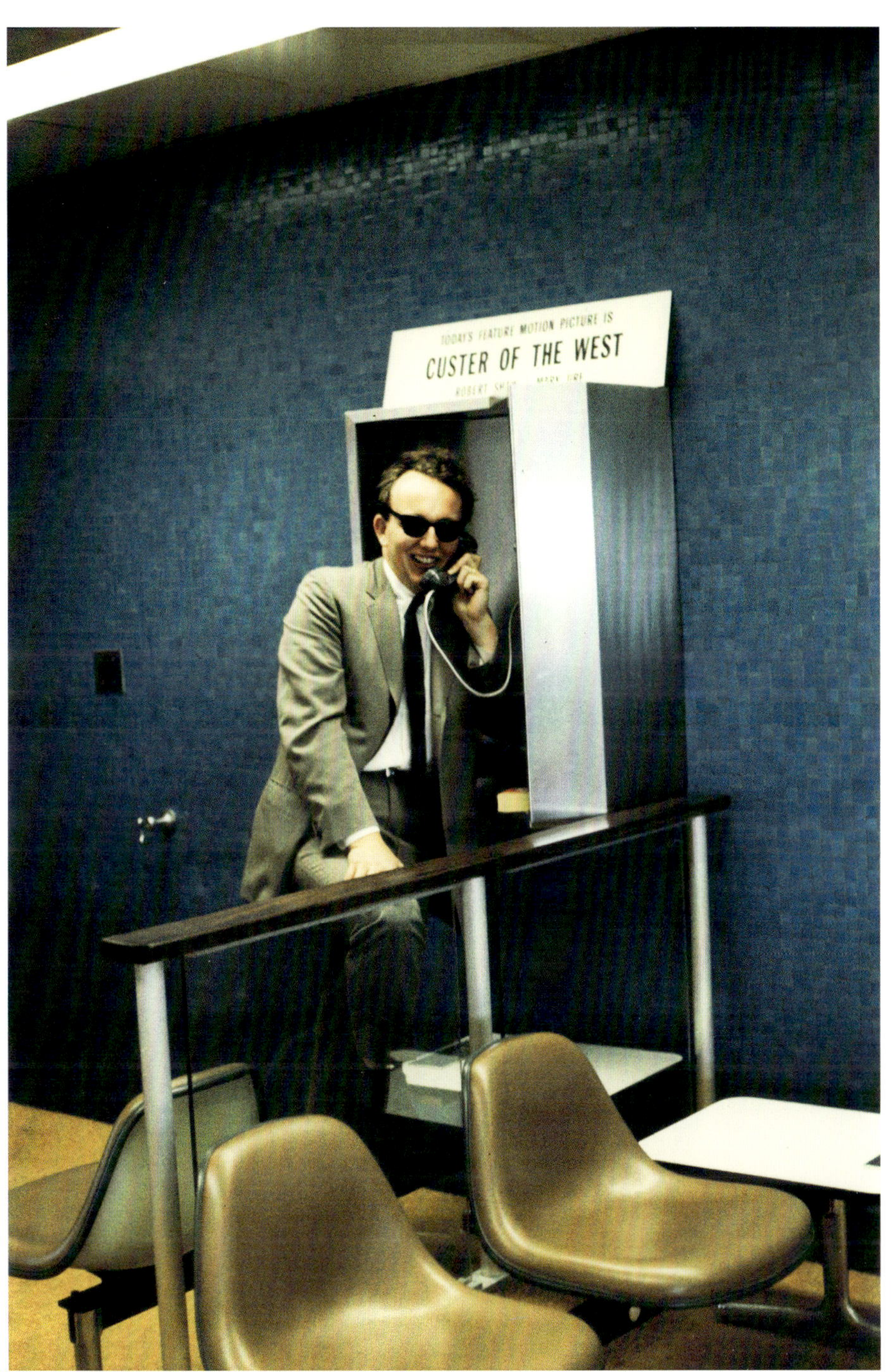
TODAY'S FEATURE MOTION PICTURE IS
CUSTER OF THE WEST

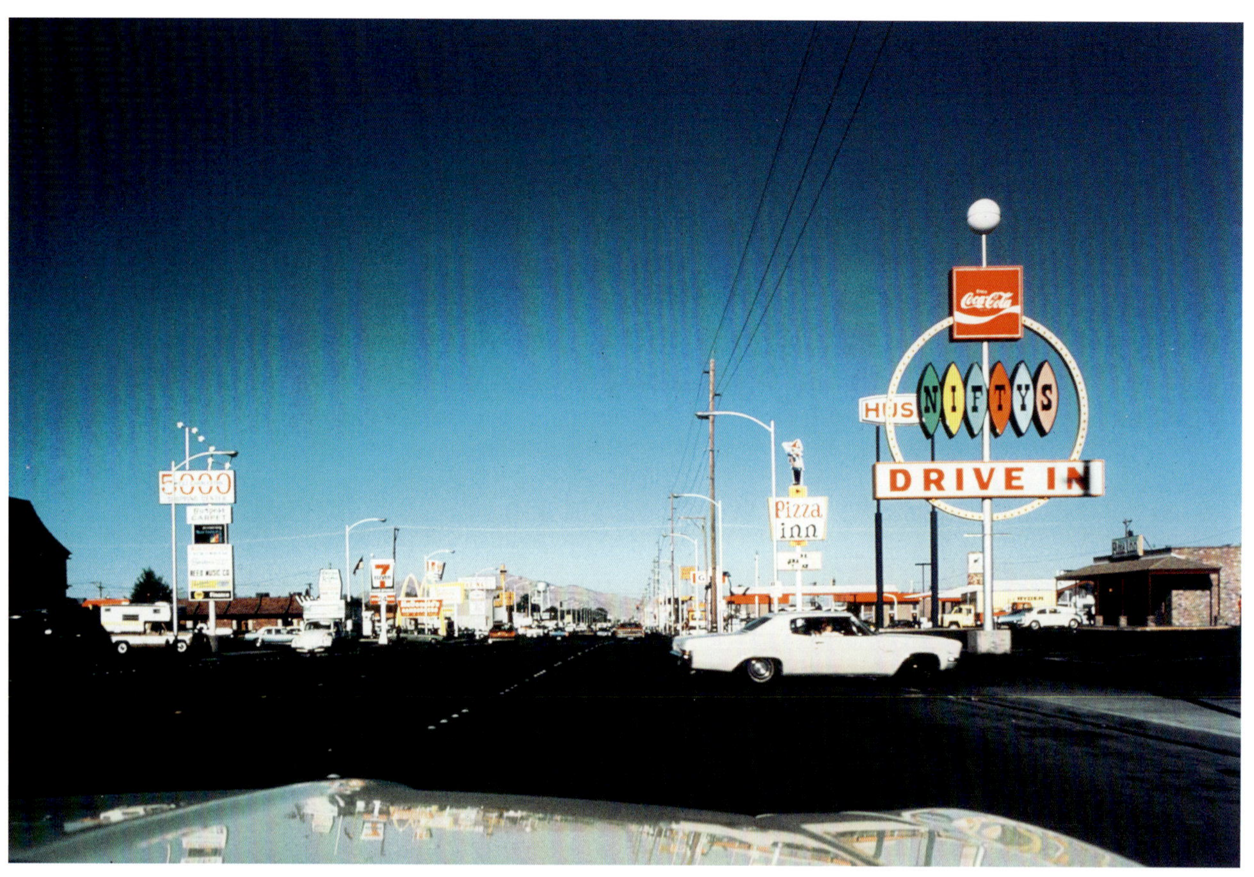
Coca-Cola
HUS
NIFTYS
DRIVE IN
Pizza inn
5000

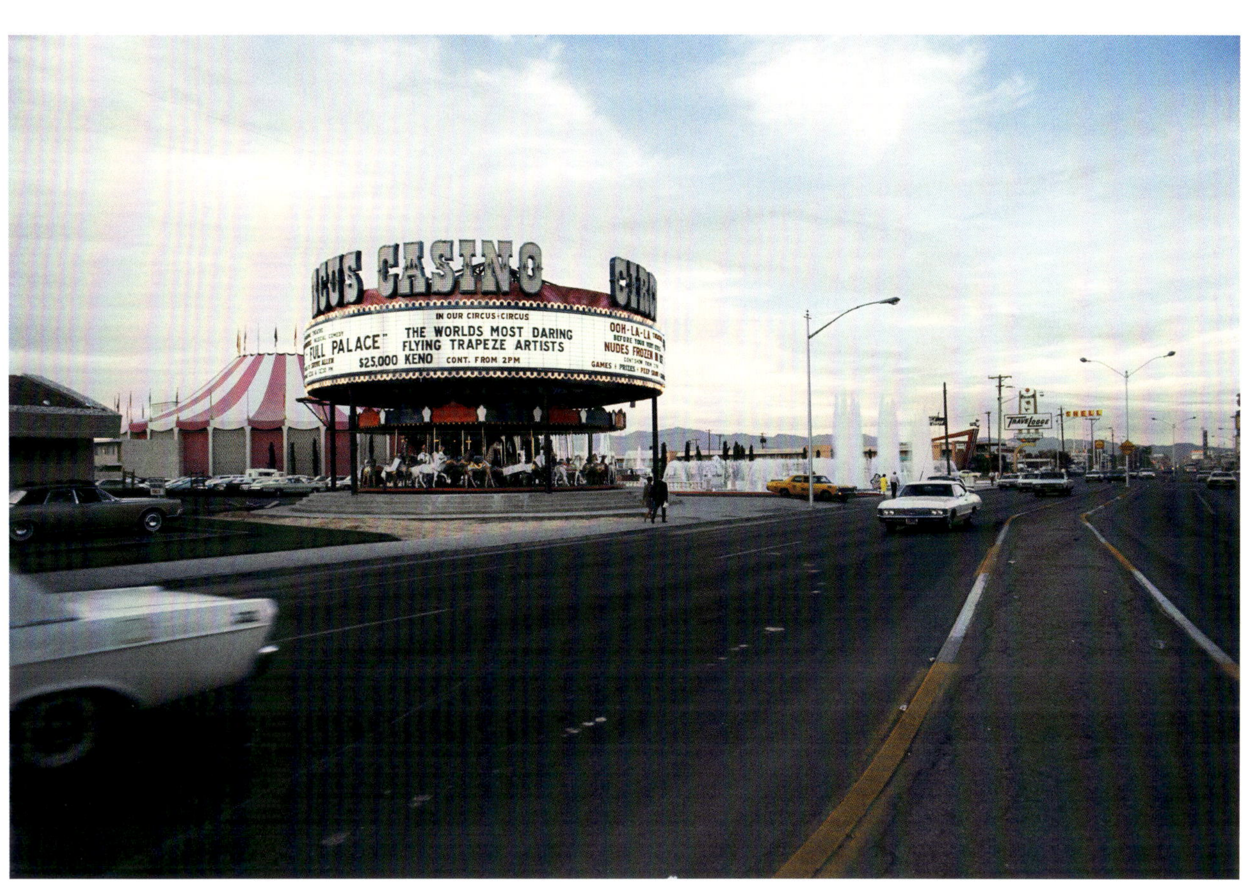
CASINO
IN OUR CIRCUS+CIRCUS
FULL PALACE"
THE WORLDS MOST DARING
FLYING TRAPEZE ARTISTS
$25,000 KENO
CONT. FROM 2PM
OOH-LA-LA
NUDES FROZEN
GAMES + PRIZES

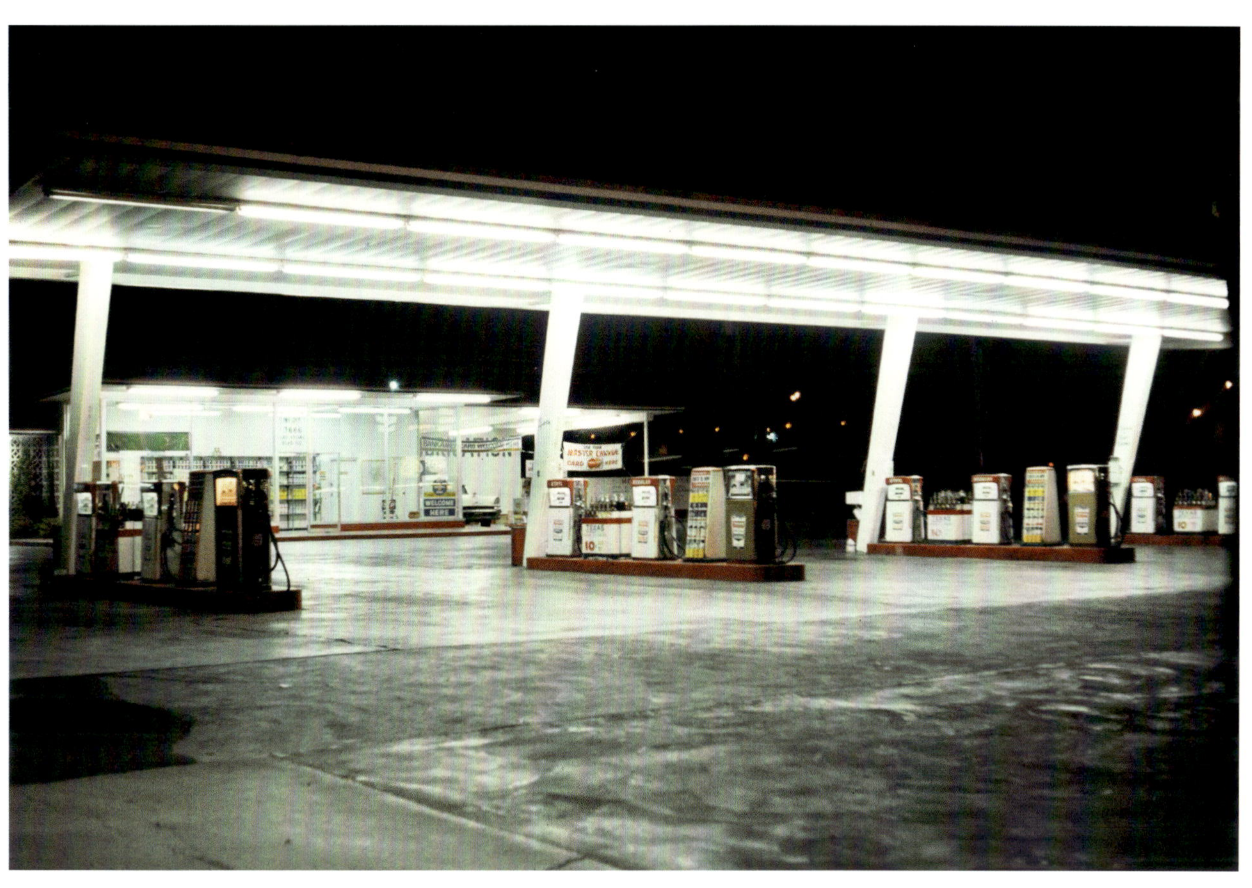
WELCOME
HERE
TEXAS

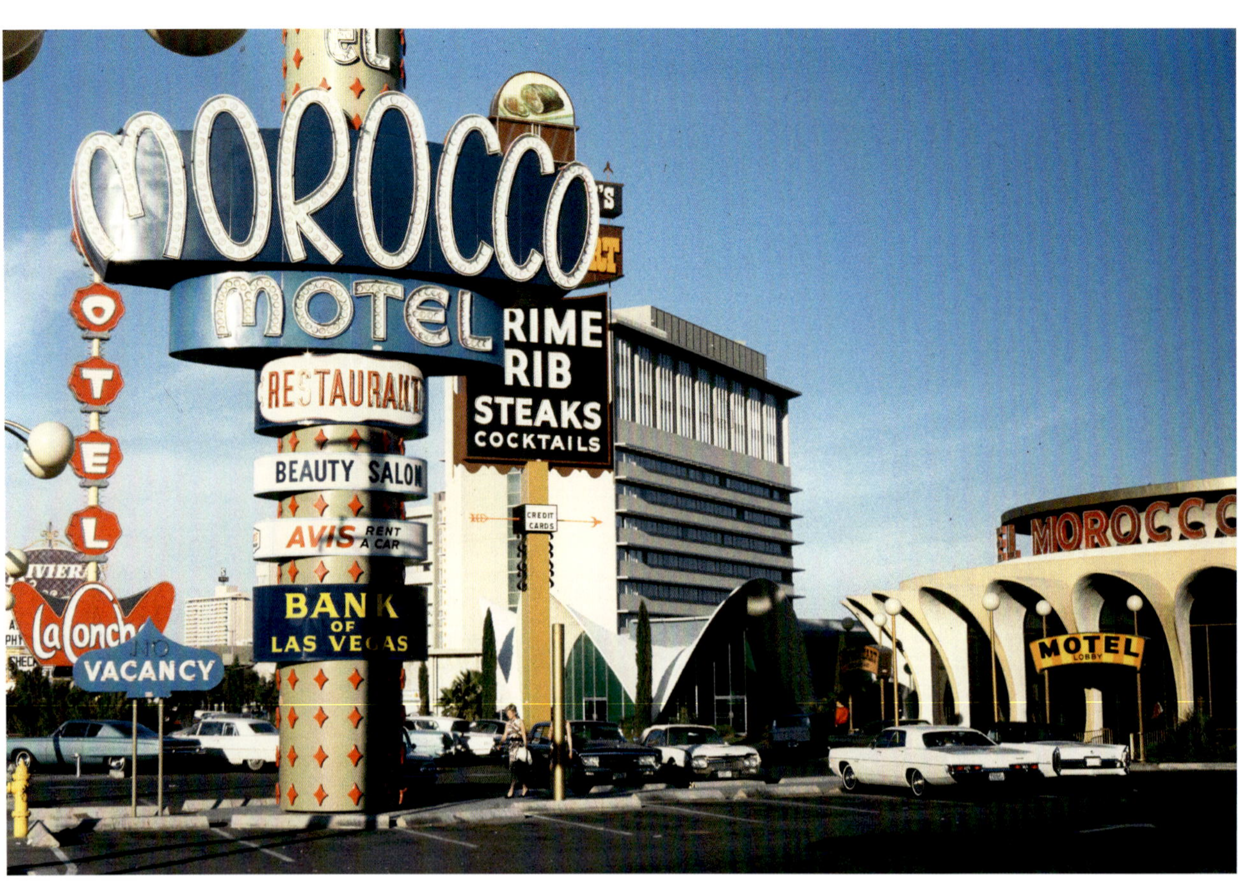
MOROCCO
MOTEL
RESTAURANT
BEAUTY SALON
AVIS RENT A CAR
BANK OF LAS VEGAS
RIME RIB
STEAKS
COCKTAILS
CREDIT CARDS
O T E L
NO VACANCY
EL MOROCCO
MOTEL
LOBBY

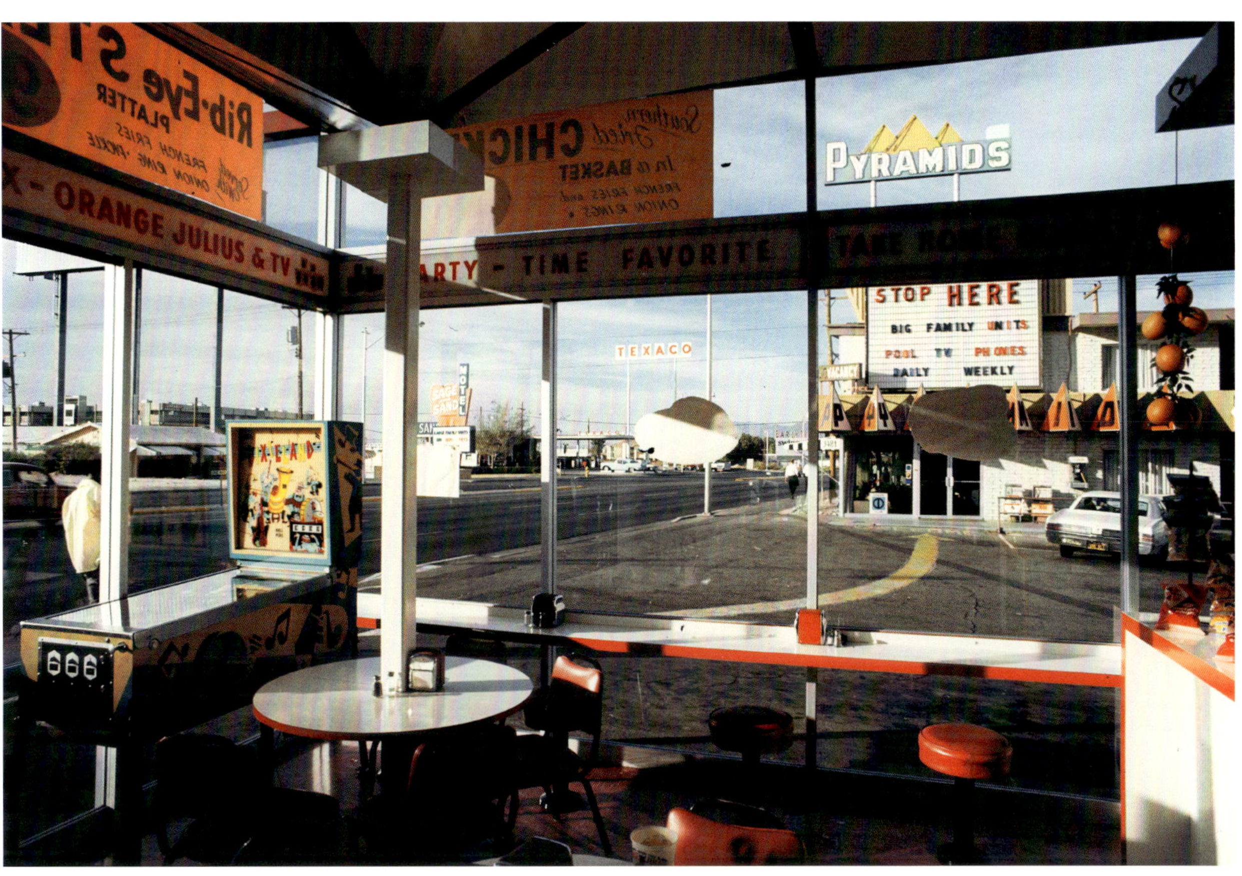
PYRAMIDS
ORANGE JULIUS & TV
TIME FAVORITE
STOP HERE
BIG FAMILY UNITS
POOL TV PHONES
DAILY WEEKLY
TEXACO
666

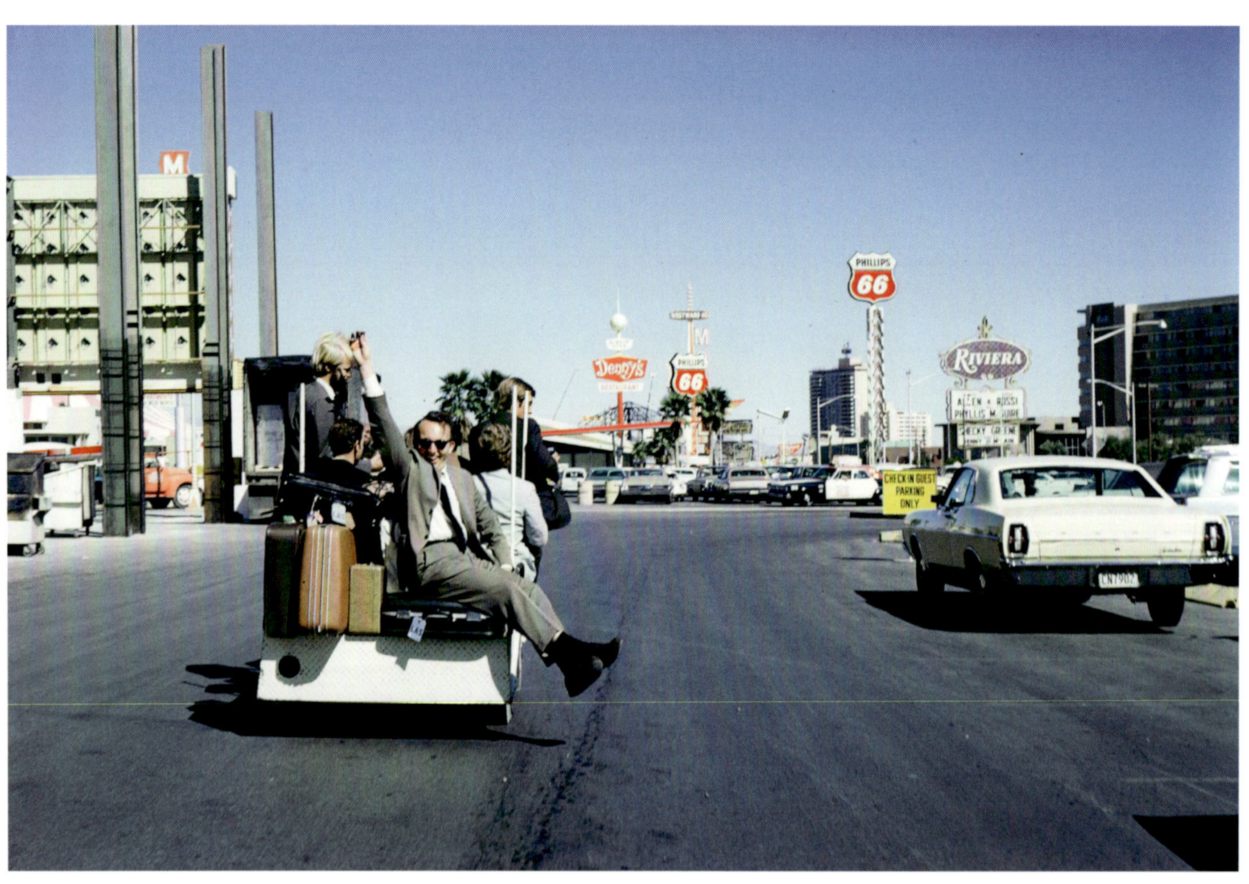
M
PHILLIPS
66
Denny's
PHILLIPS
66
RIVIERA
CHECK IN GUEST
PARKING
ONLY

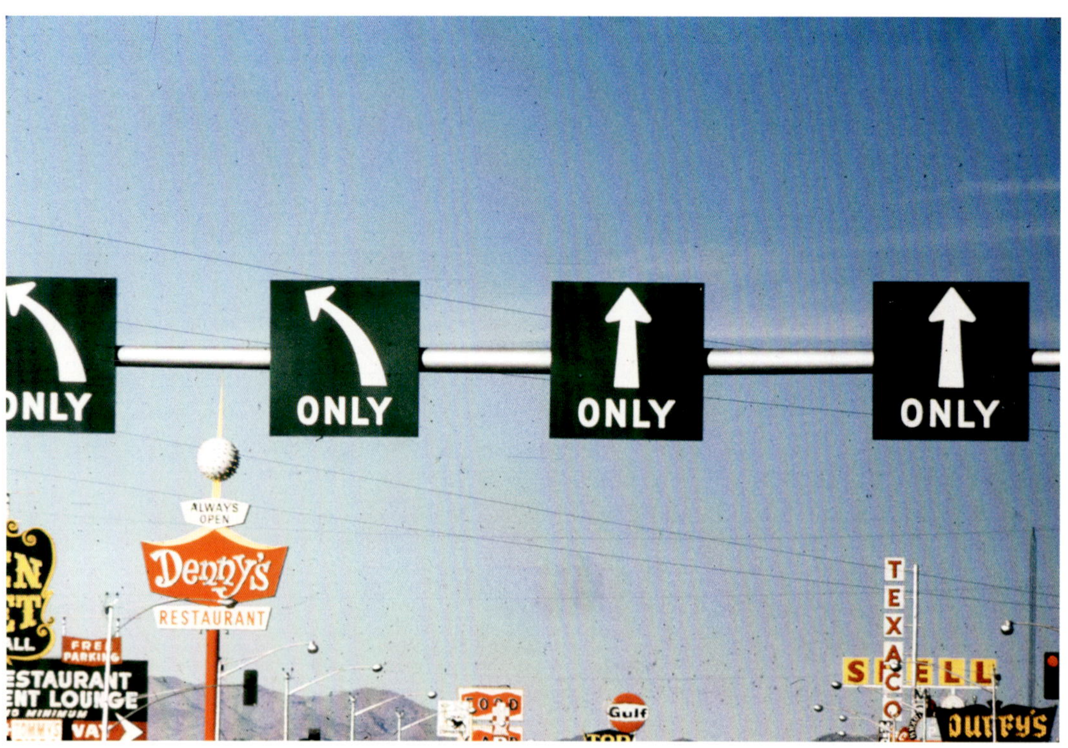
ONLY
ONLY
ONLY
ALWAYS OPEN
Denny's
RESTAURANT
TEXACO
Gulf

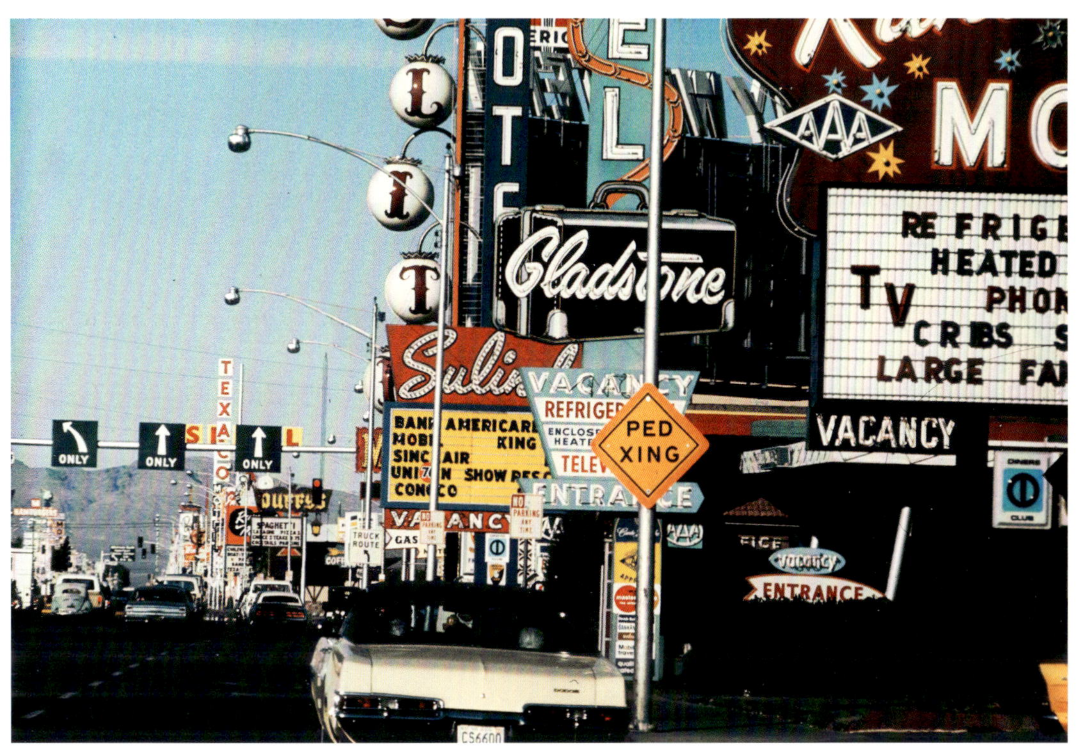

ONLY
ONLY
ONLY
TEXACO
Gladstone
VACANCY
PED
XING
AAA
HEATED
TV
CRIBS
LARGE
VACANCY
ENTRANCE
TRUCK ROUTE
GAS

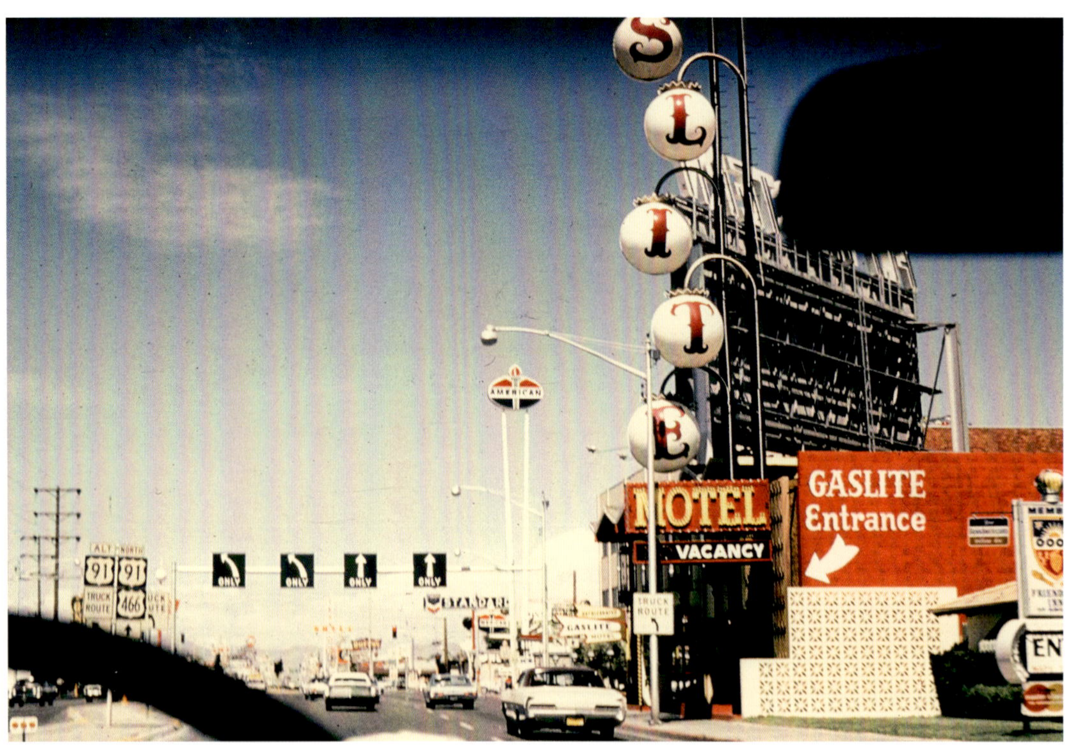
MOTEL
VACANCY
GASLITE
Entrance
STANDARD
AMERICAN
TRUCK ROUTE
ONLY
ONLY
ONLY
ONLY

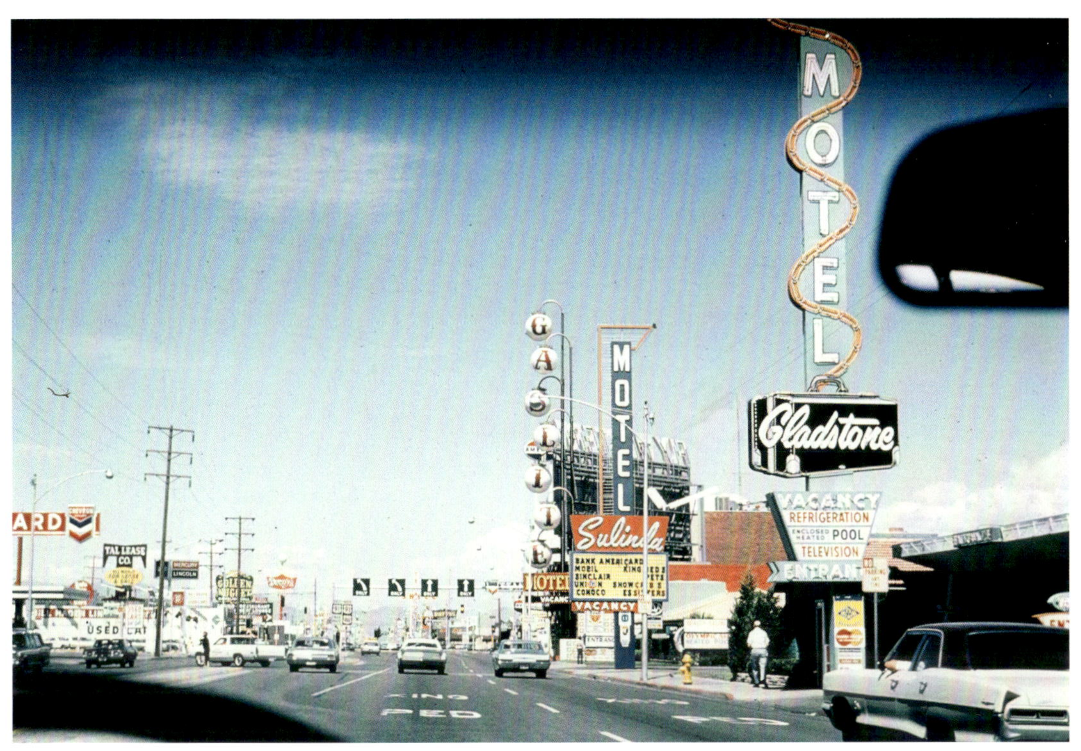
MOTEL
Gladstone
VACANCY
REFRIGERATION
ENCLOSED HEATED POOL
TELEVISION
MOTEL
Sulinda
VACANCY
TAL LEASE CO.
LINCOLN

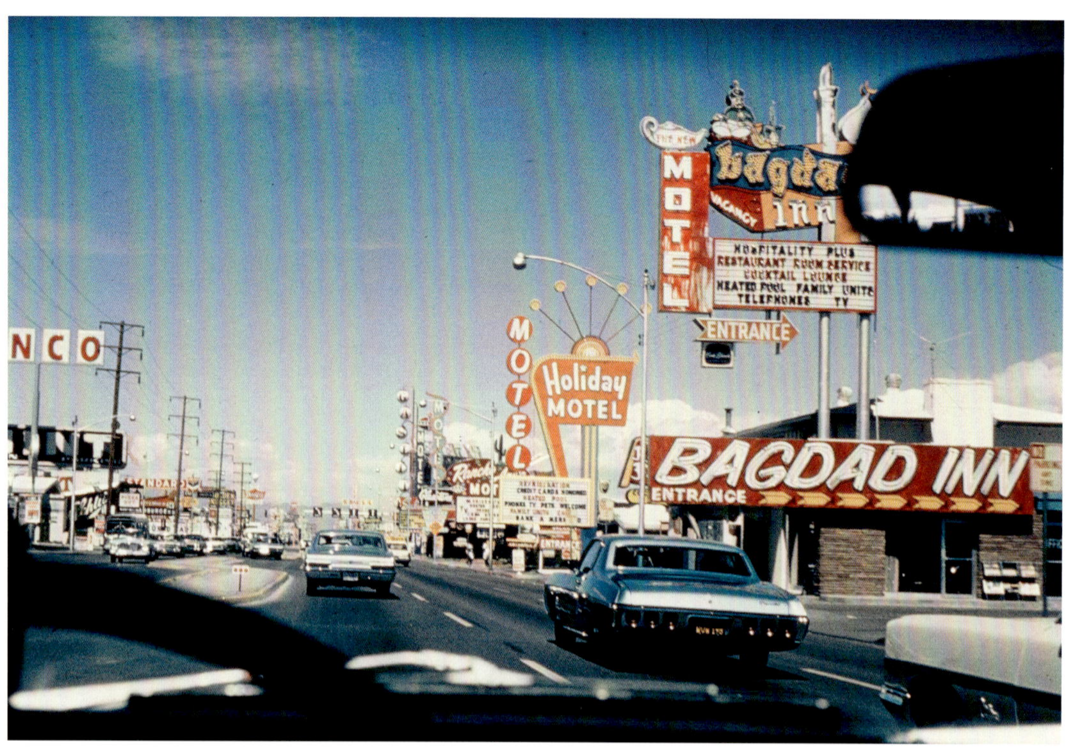
MOTEL
inn
HOSPITALITY PLUS
RESTAURANT ROOM SERVICE
COCKTAIL LOUNGE
HEATED POOL FAMILY UNITS
TELEPHONES TV
ENTRANCE
NCO
MOTEL
Holiday MOTEL
BAGDAD INN
ENTRANCE

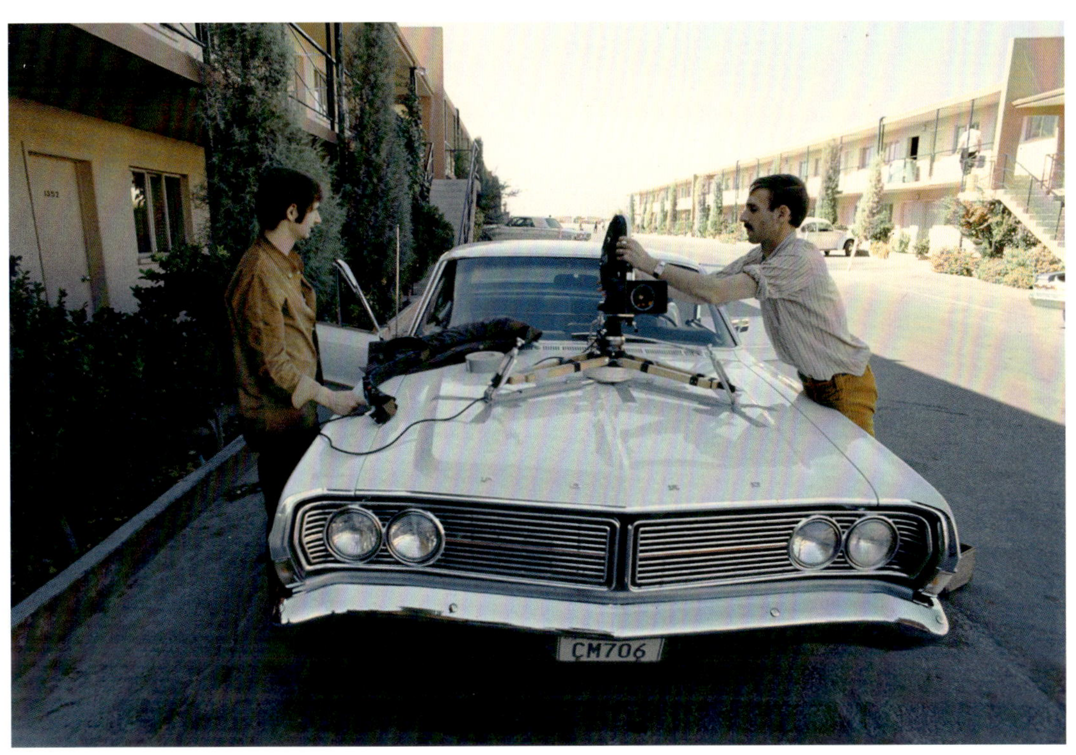
CM706

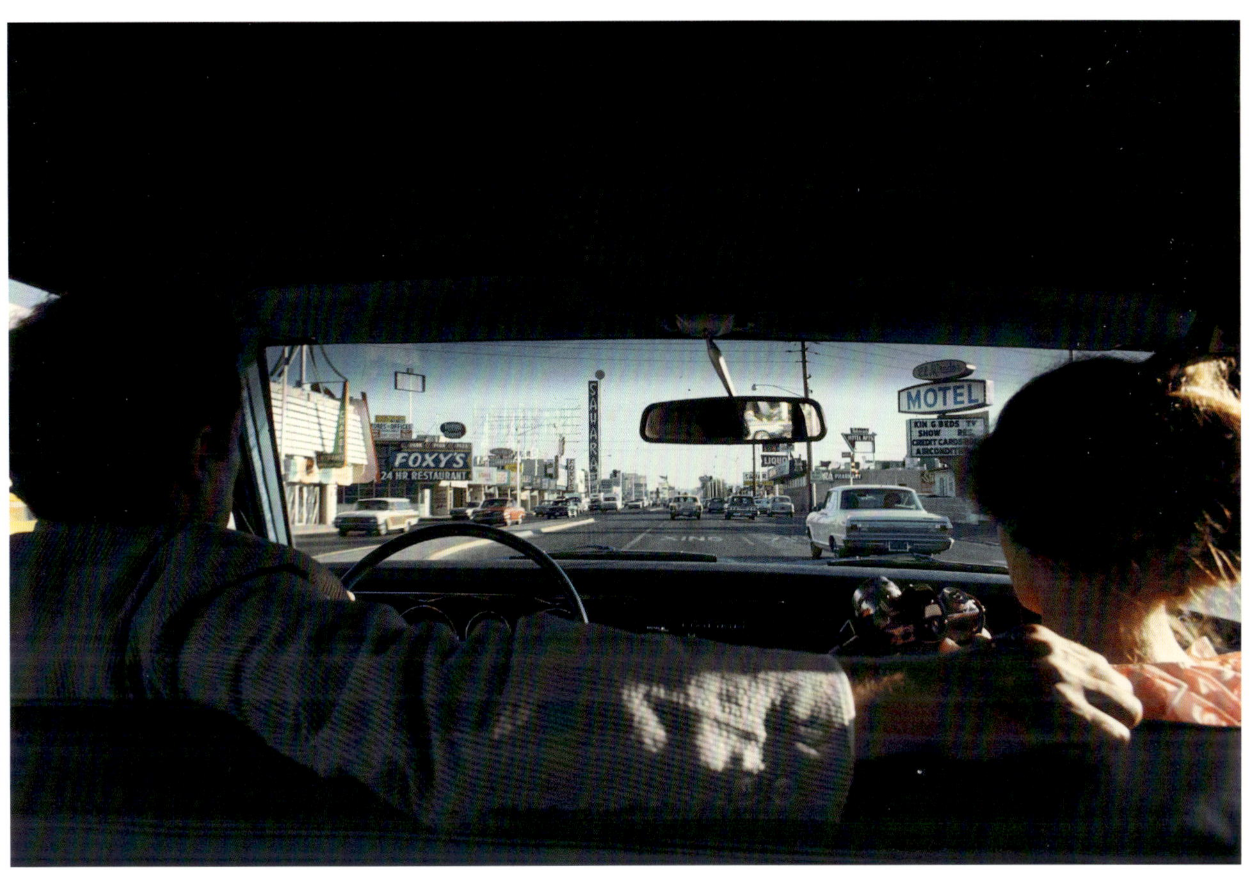
FOXY'S
24 HR RESTAURANT
SAHARA
MOTEL

Flâneurs in Automobiles

A conversation between

Peter Fischli
Rem Koolhaas
Hans Ulrich Obrist

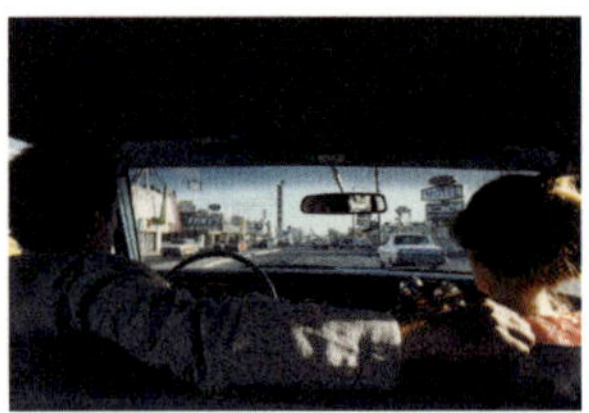

1)

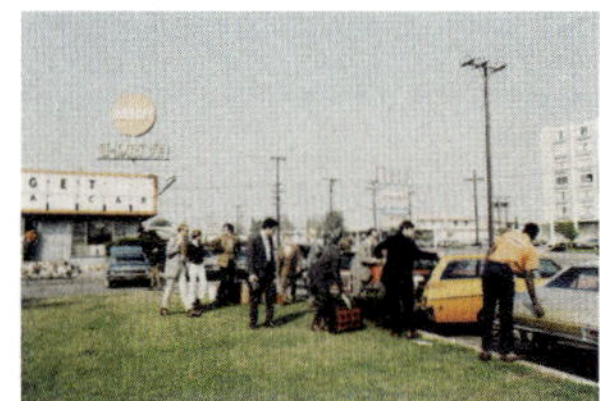

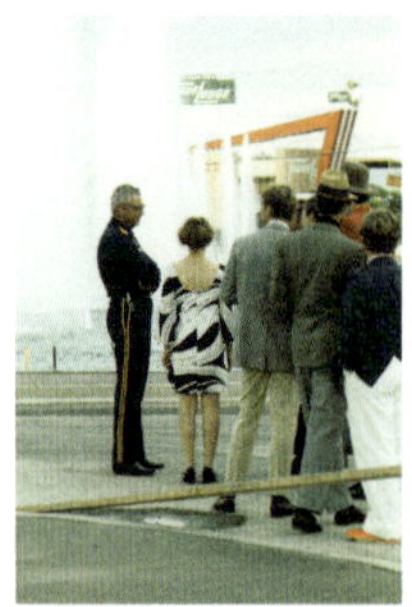

2)

F I've brought along a selection of photographs from the archives of Robert Venturi and Denise Scott Brown and would like to talk about them with you. Besides the already well-known motifs, I was very interested in the photographic "side-products" of their research in Las Vegas. Some of the images were not included in the book *Learning from Las Vegas.*

1)

K It's interesting that many of the pictures that were taken did not make it into the book. That must have required enormous self-restraint. These newly discovered pictures are a kind of incredible rewriting. Because it's not two intellectuals I see on this photograph, but two lovers. It's a romantic couple.

F On this image, the sun shines on Denise Scott Brown's neck, as if the guardian angel of Las Vegas was kissing her on the neck in order to thank her for seeing the city in a new light.

K Compared to their display of remoteness in the book, this image is almost hot. I think one should compare it to Antonioni, for instance. *Blow Up* (1966) was more or less from the same time. And Bob and Denise were also this type of fashionable icon in American culture.

O That's an interesting thought. When I visited Ed Ruscha's studio in Los Angeles, the artist told me that Venturi, Scott Brown, Izenour, and their students had visited him on their way to Las Vegas. It's fascinating that Ruscha's work changed and influenced architecture; so it went back into architecture. That obviously had to do with his books that they had seen. As Ed told me in our interviews: "I think I met them in the late 1960s or maybe mid-1970s when I had my studios in Hollywood, and also I seem to remember studio visits from them and not having exactly that much to exchange with one another except that we were just curious about each other. I recall at the same time Michelangelo Antonioni coming to my studio —not the same day, but in that period of time—and I could see somehow that all these people were connected. Even the world of film had some vital part in my actions as an artist, so architecture, film; it's all sort of tied in together."

K That's astonishing. These pictures so clearly emanated from the same inspiration. It actually looks like a honeymoon.... A honeymoon with students! When did they meet, how long did they know each other at this point?

O They had already known each other for several years. They met at a faculty meeting at the University of Pennsylvania in 1960. Two years later, they co-taught a course there. In November 1966, they visited Las Vegas for the first time together. And they were married in 1967 in Santa Monica.

F Possibly that's why the photograph looks so relaxed, because, besides their scientific project, I guess they had a good time together. Often this helps to see things in a fresh way.

2)

F It's important to talk about appearances in connection with Denise Scott Brown and her students from Yale. They are very well dressed and sophisticated. Denise has so much elegance and style. The participants in the Las Vegas research studio were aliens in Las Vegas. The appreciation was clearly coming from a sophisticated point of view. They were coming from and represented high culture. Normally, in the 1960s a lot of students would wear jeans.

K No, absolutely not! That's a very widespread misunderstanding. There were two ways of being in the 1960s. One was to be extremely well dressed, in a very modern way, defined by Antonioni's movies, for

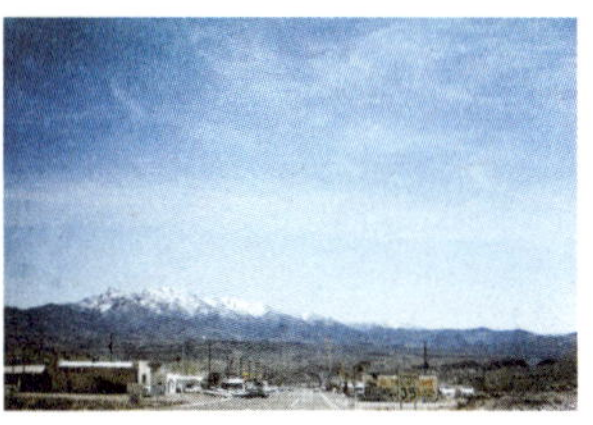

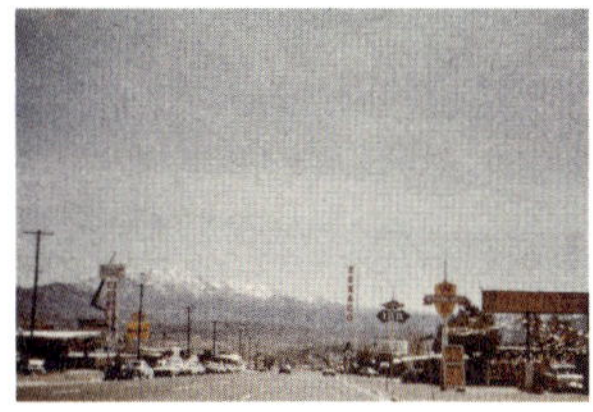

3)

instance. And the other type would be to look like a mess, to look like a hippie. But this well-dressed style we can see here was also normal! They look like fashion icons of the times. I used to look like that!

O They were participants and yet they remained foreigners in the realm of commercial culture at the same time.

K I think that is really a different issue. At that point there was still a more elegant form of mass culture. That's perhaps the great thing about the 1960s. It had that kind of perfection not only in high culture, but also in low culture. If you look at the interiors of the largest restaurants, the largest casinos or hotels from that time, they looked exactly like this. It was before the arrival of populism as we know it.

O When did you go to Las Vegas for the first time?

F In the early 1980s. In 1982, I guess. I bought a car in New York and drove across America for four months. It's a completely astonishing experience when you drive for three days through the desert and then come to Las Vegas. You see this "thing" in the middle of just dry stones and nothing. And when you arrive there, it starts with one sign, then two signs, and more and more.... So that big empty space around Las Vegas was always something important to me. The "fata morgana" moment. It wasn't the Las Vegas as we know it today, of course.

K I did the same thing in 1973, ten years earlier.

O You drove through the desert to Las Vegas. This all sounds very much like today's Dubai to me, this idea of the desert, of a city in the desert. And as much as it was taboo to work in Las Vegas at that time, it is now taboo to work in Dubai. So I see a connection there.

3)

K Badly photographed, but beautiful. It's the 1960s in color. Sixties color is Technicolor. That refers to that perfect moment when everything was coherent.

F There is a very relaxed negligence in these pictures in terms of the quality. They obviously didn't want to make "great pictures," that's why they all look so fresh. There was this unintentional quality with regard to the photography itself. It still looks rigidly composed, but it wasn't their goal to make good compositions. They have a special "non-style" in doing photographs. There is no such thing as a super-controlling of the framing of the image. It is not a photographic way of seeing the world. It is more the "Being John Malkovitch" effect. You see things through their eyes and their perception.

K It is rather that the photograph and the environment are one. It's not that you're looking at something strange, but you are participating in it.

F This picture gives the impression of a small roadside town in the middle of the desert, which is basically just an awful amount of almost nothing. Only very deep down scattered on this earth's crust, there are a few houses.

K Venturi and Scott Brown discovered the lightness of Las Vegas and how architecture could be provisional. But in the meantime this has become the heaviest, ugliest, harshest city in the world. This contrast between the early and the late Las Vegas is very important. Now the shimmering lightness is completely gone, and it's just heavy. Las Vegas as it is now is the opposite of the theories they extracted from it. Massiveness prevails, and maybe always has to prevail in cities.

O There is a difference between what you just said and what they said then. You mentioned that

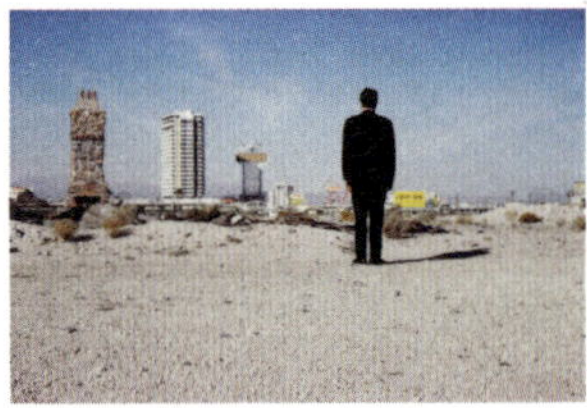

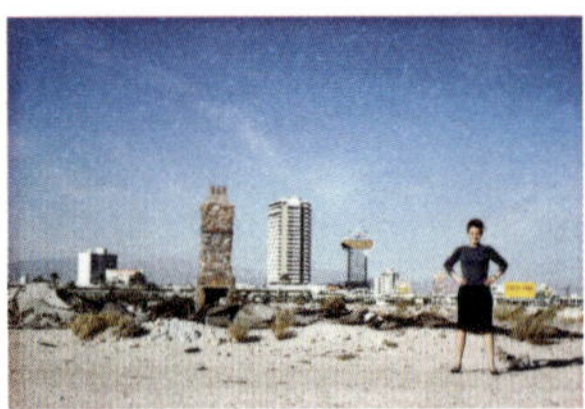

4)

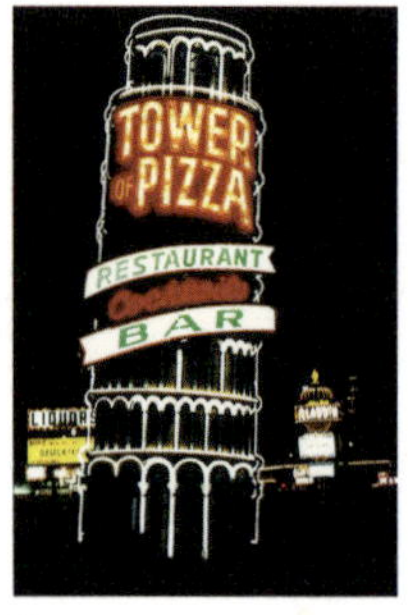

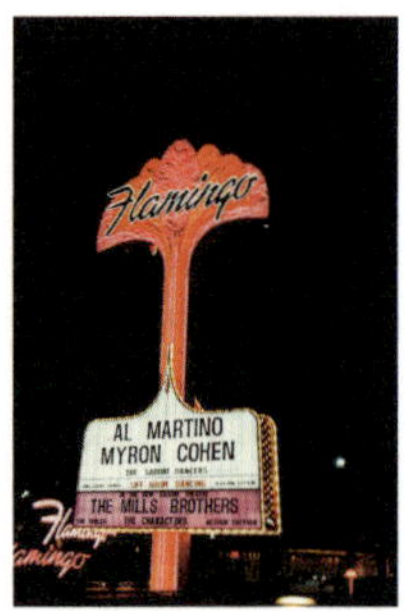

5)

Venturi and Scott Brown moved from sign to mass; however, Venturi and Scott Brown themselves said they were more interested in the development from sign to electronic billboard. They were very convinced of this whole idea that the signs would become electronic. They weren't so focused on mass.

4)

F In this picture, the figure of Robert Venturi becomes the fourth building, an additional landmark in the skyline.

K He's like Hitchcock, inserting himself into his own movies. But it's also possible that they would have thought of Magritte, the man with the bowler hat. This very generic man, in a black suit, inserted into the picture. This is a totally bizarre picture. But I don't understand the chimney. It looks old, a ruin. There were no ruins in Las Vegas.

F There was an old house there. Or, as regards Las Vegas, you immediately become doubtful and think "a fake old house."

K It's not really related, but there is an interesting chimney anecdote from that same time. This was also the time when people discovered that Philip Johnson had been in a German tank, during the Blitzkrieg when it moved into Poland. Peter Eisenman has written a kind of defense of Johnson. He said: If Johnson really marched into Poland with the Germans and destroyed everything there, then he must remember that only the chimneys remain from destroyed houses. And his own Glass House, as you probably know, is basically only a glass cube with a chimney. So, the Glass House must be the monument of this memory.

5)

K These two things on this picture have become very iconic, but maybe Venturi and Scott Brown didn't make the right distinction, or any distinction at all. I would say: On the one hand we have popular culture, popular icons, and on the other hand we have popular culture producing icons without knowing it. So it is about populism, but also about a new sublime. This is really a sublime. Only an artist can do a thing like this.

F As an artist, when you start doing something, you sometimes have a concept and an idea in your mind, but at the same time, unconsciously or not, you do more, you don't just implement the idea. That's the interesting thing about doing things. That's why we have to follow our ideas, because something more than the original idea comes out of it. That would describe what happened with these images.

K That's a very generous way of expressing it… You have an idea and you want to prove it, then you reveal and you suppress things… (laughter). But I like your explanation. I really remember from doing field work that, sometimes, you make inconvenient discoveries. Things that don't fit.

F We recently did a book about a work from twenty years ago. At that time we had the idea to build these objects and we just used the ones that matched the ideas. Now, twenty years later, we see that we produced and photographed many objects that didn't match our ideas, but in a way they are nicer. It's not about judging quality, of course, but we also made these other objects. So we put many of the photographed objects into the book that we had originally discarded. They were displayed on the same level, because there would be different criteria for inclusion.

K People really think when editing.

6)

K This is a picture of the abject—not only beautiful, but also ugly, things falling apart, decay… How do you see it?

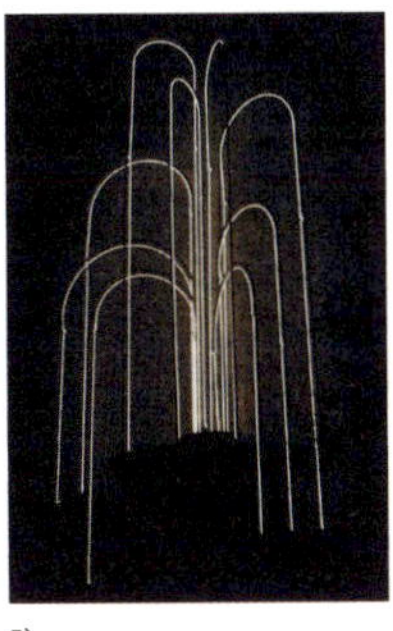

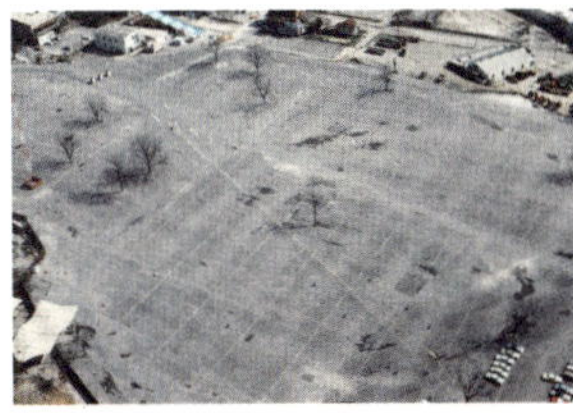

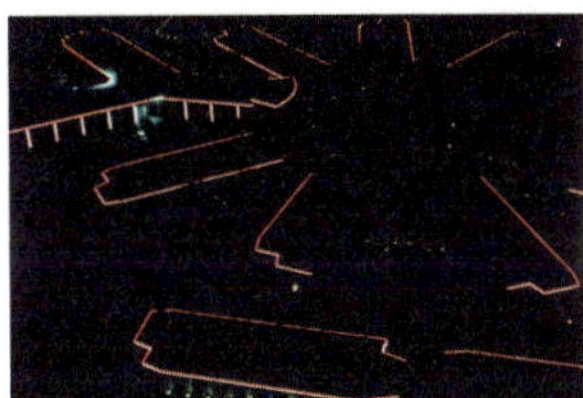

5)

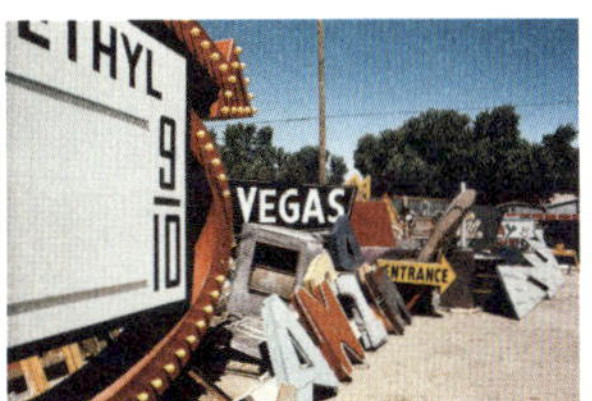

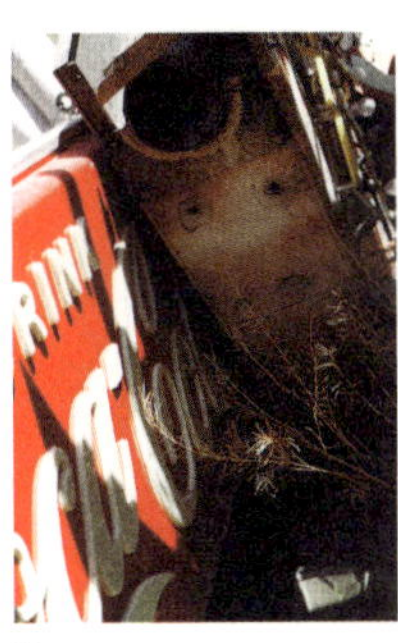

6)

F I see it in the context of another picture. This is basically the same, but it's a much more poetic depiction of the same topic. It's a graveyard of signs!

K And since this picture was not included in the book, it's a sign that it didn't fit into the theory. Venturi's theory of an architecture of signs and symbols makes it impossible to show the graveyard. The aftermath did not interest them that much.

F These pictures basically talk about the duration of architecture. Las Vegas is a city that has a much faster rate of change and turn-over than other cities. The "Stardust" sign or the cowboy on Fremont Street still exist. But I think, otherwise, most things in Las Vegas live for only twenty years, roughly. Or even less. These pictures tell this story. The whole city is like a stage with a storage area. You build a new stage-set and then you take it down again.

O Or there could be a contradiction in Venturi's theory, in the sense of what you said. That it was the revenge of the mass of the signs. Another thing I was puzzled by: It's not only that these pictures are not in the book, they're actually not even part of the archives that they have given to the University of Pennsylvania. They did not even valorize them enough to put them into the archives. So, there's a double neglect and that's what's so interesting. Another idea is this link to cinema that Rem brought up earlier. These pictures almost look like a film set, an artificial setting in the desert, some Cinecittà in the desert. We already talked about Antonioni before. I spoke to Ken Adam, the world's greatest living production designer the other day and he told me this great story that he also saw himself as an architect. He had always thought that in order to be an architect in the 20th century it would be more effective go into cinema.

F When you look at the story of Las Vegas you see how they originally promoted the city with films. They made this Elvis movie, *Viva Las Vegas,* and many other films in the late 1950s, early 1960s in Las Vegas. So people knew the city above all through the media, through film and television. Which actually makes an interesting parallel to what happens with many buildings today—Rem's, or also the new stadium in Beijing by Herzog & de Meuron. Most people only know these buildings through a media image. One could say the image of the building is a much stronger reality than the building itself. In that respect, Las Vegas and its promotion was visionary.

O We talked about this in the sense of a different territory. There was this whole discussion about there being a peculiar non-material territory to architecture, next to the material territory of architecture. That of course has to do with the media.

K In terms of your question about the media… I think what Venturi and Scott Brown discovered is that signs could have a stronger presence than things, than objects. What we architects are now doing—and this is exactly what Venturi actually warned against—is, we're producing ducks. We make an extreme effort to turn signs back into things, into objects.

F Ironically, you could say: when you look at the Beijing stadium in an iconographic way, the nest is where the duck is coming from.

K …It is nest and duck at the same time…

7)

F Speaking of the duck. Peter Blake included a photograph of the duck in his book *God's Own Junkyard: The Planned Deterioration of America's Landscape* in which he discussed the American landscape and suburbia. He judged it all very negatively. It was

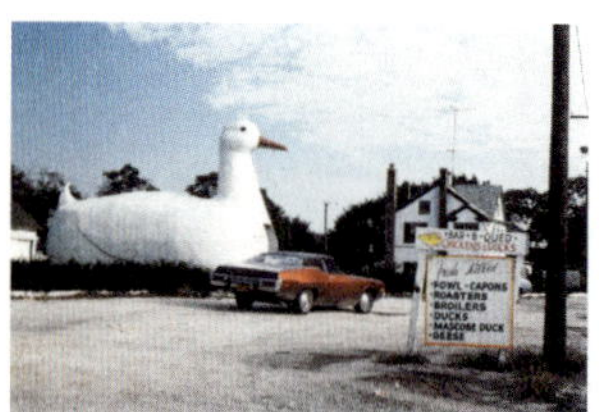

7)

an indictment. When Venturi and Scott Brown used this famous photo of the duck, it was—very ironically—a photograph by Peter Blake they were using. This photograph is one of the foundations of their theory, which functions as a powerful counter-argument to Blake's own, of course. In this "détournement" one can also see their wit. But to come back to what we discussed before, namely that architecture today is mainly perceived through images, is, as I said, also interesting in the context of Rem's building in Beijing, the China Central Television building. I haven't seen it in reality, but there seems to be this incredibly physical aspect to it, something almost grotesquely physical, this feeling that it's about to fall onto you when you stand in front of it. Has this something to do with the fact that next to the picturesque aspect you wanted to establish something else?

K Absolutely. What has been important to me for some time now is to do something that cannot be defined by one gaze, one shot, one position. And you only realize this when you actually stand there. This is a building with four hundred different identities, and this instability of identity is the most important aspect of the whole building. It's the opposite of this massive shape, this exaggerated geometrical form, it can be light, weak, even shapeless.

F Or it's both at the same time.

K Yes. But the instability is more essential than the other impression.

O I have seen it in reality. It was completely different from my expectations. No matter whether one is inside or outside, it's never the same building. Thus it's rather like a sculpture. And even if you move around just a few steps, it changes.

K Yes. This makes it impossible to pin it down permanently by one gaze or in one picture. There's an American, I don't know him, he is not even a photographer, who lives in Beijing and who does not like the building. But he felt obliged to photograph it. He took hundreds of pictures from different locations in the city, also from a great distance. Then it becomes beautiful.

F The question is, how do you get out of the duck dilemma?

K Is this a dilemma that you don't know at all in your work as an artist? Or is there also a dilemma there? What's your duck?

F Of course I know the dilemma. In some fields of contemporary art today, the spectacle is important if your target is a big audience. This starts with Christo's wrapped buildings. They have a great effect on a large audience. In that sense, the title of Guy Debord's book *Society of the Spectacle* (1967) was clearly visionary. His conclusions are debatable, but his diagnosis was correct. But there are more than two ways to deal with that. The question is not whether you can do something as an artist that is both successful and at the same time refuses to be a spectacle. Rather, the question is how to be both—one and the other—at the same time. But back to Venturi and Scott Brown. Where do you see the difference between a Pop attitude and the "as found" attitude in seeing Las Vegas?

K Pop is maybe a version of the "as found" attitude, but limited to whatever comes directly from the present and from Pop culture. It's about things without an author, without a history. In a way it was everything that was projected from this perfect bubble of completely integrated aesthetics that happened in the 1950s and 1960s, a kind of populist abstraction that attracted Venturi and Scott Brown to Las Vegas.

F ...and "as found," the spirit of "as found" was much broader...

K More nostalgic maybe, too. With Pop, everything was new. But "as found" could also be amazingly touching, or amazingly sad…. But there's nothing tragic to Pop. Whereas I would say that even Ed Ruscha's pictures of parking lots have something tragic about them.

O When I asked Ed Ruscha about "as found" and "Pop," he said that there were four rules: "Finding things in a world that are intriguing," that's rule number one. "Making note of them," rule number two. Third and very important: "Glorifying them." Fourth: "Assembling them in a collection." These are his four rules.

F I think it wasn't about "glorifying" Las Vegas, the "making note" of Las Vegas was much more important. What is also interesting is that Venturi wrote *Complexity and Contradiction* before he wrote *Learning from Las Vegas* together with Scott Brown and Izenour. It's important to see his perspective on Las Vegas through this first book. Because it's rather guided by this "as found" gaze and not by the "Pop" gaze. It has less to do with what, for instance, Susan Sontag describes as a pleasure for trash.

K No, it is a contemporary sublime rather than Pop. At the time of *Learning from Las Vegas,* the quality of the "spontaneous," "generic" architecture in America was quite intimidating, especially for "official" architects…

O Denise Scott Brown always said—and Venturi confirms this—how that sort of anthropological field research approach was very much driven by her. And that in some way this had something to do with her childhood in Africa. I'm not sure it's relevant, but it's definitely interesting. She had been looking at popular culture in Africa before she came to London —and later to Las Vegas.

K When we met them, we were totally astonished that Denise said it would never have happened without her growing up in Africa. Because that made her aware of being in a different culture and that had given her this kind of anthropological interest. Then she went to London and came to that leftist anthropology milieu of the Independent Group. You know that Venturi's father was also a leftist, a socialist. And related to all that, it was logical to make the trip to Las Vegas as a kind of anthropological exercise, not as a glorification of capitalism.

8)

Fischli: This is a very nice series. We're not sure whether this is in Las Vegas. We could talk about the fact that Las Vegas is not an ordinary, representative suburbia, and here we have the rather normal American suburbia. But this plays no role in their archives…

K Later, they wrote about suburbia in *Learning from Levittown* (1970). It's a different story for Venturi. He had to find a way to talk about normal people and their ways of living that was not condescending. That's a socialist story, guided by Scott Brown, to appreciate normal people's lives and housing, too. In a certain way, he was doing most of the learning, or, after *Complexity and Contradiction,* un-learning. What is very astonishing, particularly compared to the collapse of America today, how this downfall is already implied here. Everything is about bargains, half-price, shoe repair. These are the early signs of American demise. You can already see it right here. "Dry cleaning." Men have only one shirt, and they wear it all week. And there is also a certain sadness visible in these pictures.

F In contrast to Las Vegas and Venturi's view of Las Vegas, Ed Ruscha's *Every Building on the Sunset Strip* (1966) shows the Sunset Strip as more conventional suburbia. It doesn't have these extreme buildings, these

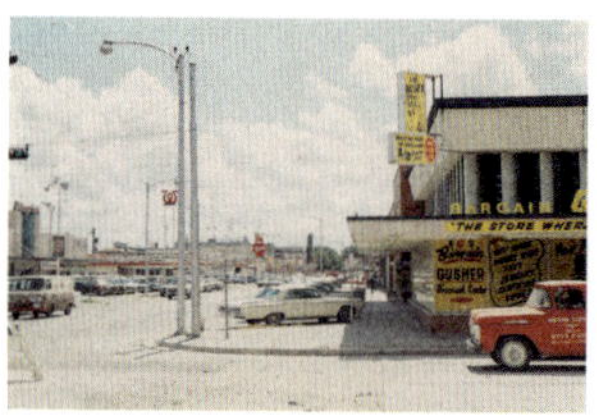

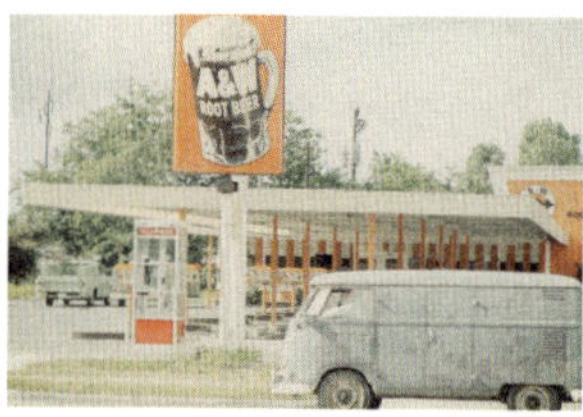

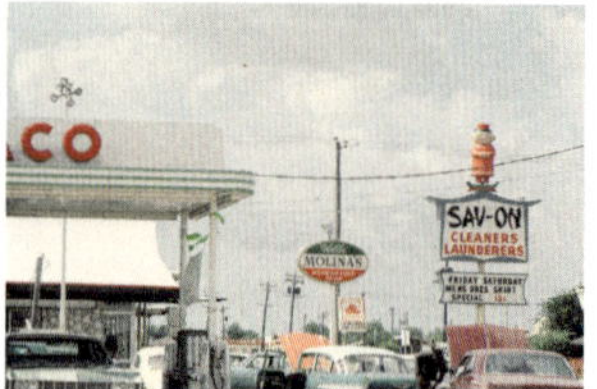

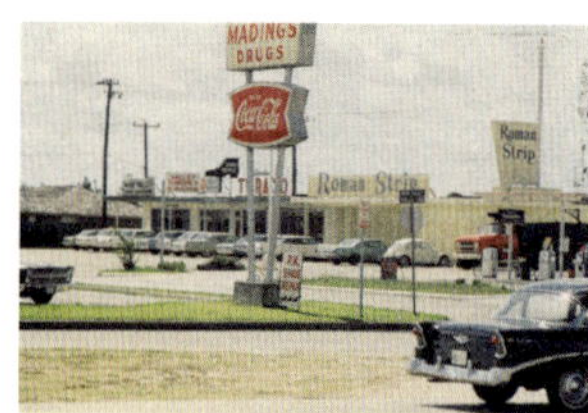

8)

extreme signs. It remains within the ordinary. Ruscha also calls his book "Every Building." The word "every" makes it clear for me. This seems to be important to him, this abolition of hierarchies, of the difference between "important" or "good" buildings and the less important ones. That's his statement. What the Venturis are doing is different. They choose certain things that they give value to. Others are just left out.

K It's the dialectics within this couple, Venturi and Scott Brown. It's also the dialectics of the architectural vs. the sociological…

F Exactly.

K And in this dialectic, the man represents the architectural, and the woman the sociological.

F That's a bold allegation! (laughter)
Another difference between Ed Ruscha and Venturi and Scott Brown is Ruscha's very consciously neutral look—which is a construct, of course. With Venturi and Scott Brown, it's rather the eye of the flâneur. They are driving through the city like a flâneur. They are flâneurs in automobiles.

O What also interests me is whether the Venturis also learned something from *Learning from Las Vegas?*

F It's great to look at it in that way. I assume that they also used the word "learning" in a slightly ironic way because I think their interest was exactly in the ambiguity of Las Vegas.

K Or did they learn what they thought they learned? That is the question.

F That's not the same thing.

K What they said they learned was that the American commercial vernacular is a never-ending source of modernity. A source of inspiration. In the interview we did with them we were trying to push them a little bit in the direction of what that means for the rest of the world, or for architecture in general. This is of course a real paradox for people with a leftist position, with an ideological past: Why the hell was it commercial American Pop culture of all things that became so important? That was the source. But when I lived in the States from 1972 to 1978, it was completely plausible. Back then, it was the most coherent, consistent and creative bubble you could possibly imagine.

O Maybe one should look at the Las Vegas project from the point of view of what it triggered. And it obviously triggered many other research projects. These other city research projects usually zoom in onto something and then zoom out again and move somewhere else. For instance, Rem's research in China. In your "Last Chance" text, you talk about Singapore in the 1980s, then about China in the 1990s. But they didn't do that. They didn't zoom in and then zoom out again.

K They were architects, and afterwards everything became so frenetic around them. They did so many architectural projects. Do you know how many buildings they actually built? By their own count, there exist over two hundred buildings by them, which is an astonishing number of realizations. So they simply didn't have the time to do another excursion. Another thing that I find really surprising when I see this is the question: Why did this research isolate them from the rest of the architectural profession? After that book, nobody for instance in New York wanted anything to do with them. I was working with Peter Eisenman at that time at the Institute for Architecture and Urban Studies and they were never invited, I guess because they were interested in issues other than architecture!

F So, when the book came out, the architectural world reacted very negatively?

K Maybe not negatively about the book itself; on the contrary. Nevertheless, I think it isolated them. It was also partly self-imposed. It's strange. They made a discovery and then shared it through their book, and the effect of it was that they were suddenly alone. Of course they had huge influence, but they were alone. Maybe this was also a consequence of being a couple, in architecture. Maybe.

O So you think, they were really isolated, to some extent?

K That's definitely my perception. In New York, people never spoke to them or about them. Peter Eisenman or my contemporaries rarely dealt with them either.

O You met them very late.

K The only reason I met them was because they came to a lecture of mine and I discovered them sitting in the audience. It was a lecture in Philadelphia. I was deeply touched that they came. That was the beginning of a respectful friendship.

F But for you, *Learning from Las Vegas* was a huge influence?

K A huge influence! Not necessarily because of the content but rather because of the book as an object, as a way of talking about a subject in architecture. It was seminal to see how and what they had done. They created a huge space. I also realized at that point—or it was the beginning of a realization—that you could no longer write manifestos, but that you could write about cities as if they themselves were a manifesto.

O So, *Complexity and Contradiction* is the last manifesto in architecture and from there we see a move to city manifestos.

F The city itself is the manifesto.

K Exactly. Or, the discovery of a city is a manifesto.

O When did you discover *Learning from Las Vegas?*

F I discovered it in the early 1980s. I knew the "as found" group, Pop Art, Ed Ruscha earlier. In the mid-1960s, it opened to me the whole field of bringing the ordinary and everyday things into art and transforming them by changing their size, for example. (To Koolhaas) Did you discuss the aspect of size with them?

K No, not really.... We tried to find out whether they still believed that what they say in their book was relevant. I was suggesting that at the time they wrote the book the symbol was dominant and that now the reality or the substance dominates. And to some extent this is connected to your question about size. First of all, you cannot establish the real size of all those buildings in early Las Vegas... they are mirages. You couldn't even tell whether they were real or not, whether they were big or not. Now you can. Now you know all these buildings on the Las Vegas Strip are forty stories high, for instance. They have now achieved reality. Basically, symbolism is no longer strong enough to dominate that discourse on size. Have you ever seen the really beautiful first edition of *Learning from Las Vegas?*

O You have the first edition?

K Yes. It was this big [he shows a huge rectangle with his hands]. And it was deliberately produced like a tablet book, like a kind of rare classic. The writing on the cover was as if engraved in stone. I remember where I first noticed it. It was my first year in America and it was lying next to underwear and white socks in the campus store. And I was beginning to think about *Delirious New York,* so I bought it immediately.

O This is really what Ed Ruscha says. That it was about glorifying the object. There is this famous quote by Venturi, "less is a bore." When I spoke to Peter Smithson about that statement, he was saying Charles and Ray Eames put so much data in their exhibitions, like a "forest of signs" (to quote a 1976 exhibition title of Venturi Scott Brown, *Signs of Life: Symbols in the American City*).

K One could say, the Eameses are at the beginning of this American bubble—and the Venturis would then be the end. And the bubble of this creativity was of course generated by the end of the war. It was the impulse after the war that gave birth to it. In Europe there was the equivalent "Wiederaufbau" (reconstruction) period. Suddenly, in the 1970s there was the question: what are we doing?

F But I can't see that *Learning from Las Vegas* is the end of something. I thought it was the start of postmodernism? I don't know that for sure, but it's clear to me that it offered a new language for architecture.

K I don't think the connection is so clear. They provided some of the arguments for postmodernism, but I'm sure the "postmoderns" were not really affected by that argument. I think postmodernism is more connected to a changing client base. Suddenly, everybody started working for developers ... and a new language was needed that everybody could speak.

F But with this book, just by breaking with the dogma of "form follows function," it surely opened up the possibility of postmodernism, don't you think? Or do you think the consequence is not postmodernism?

K Of course there's a relationship. But I seriously doubt that it had any influence on people like Michael Graves, who, I think, is much more responsible for postmodernism. The Venturis always had a hesitant relationship to postmodernism. They don't consider themselves postmodern. There's a reticence on their part, but also a real distance from actual postmodernism.

F So would you say their influence was not so much on their own generation, but rather on the next generation, the younger one?

K I have a feeling the book was both the apotheosis and the end of their influence—that's why, for me, it's a kind of waning. This is also connected to the isolation I mentioned. They repudiated the movement that they could have claimed to have invented. From that moment on, the whole issue of influence became very difficult to determine anyway.

Tableaux[1)]

Stanislaus von Moos

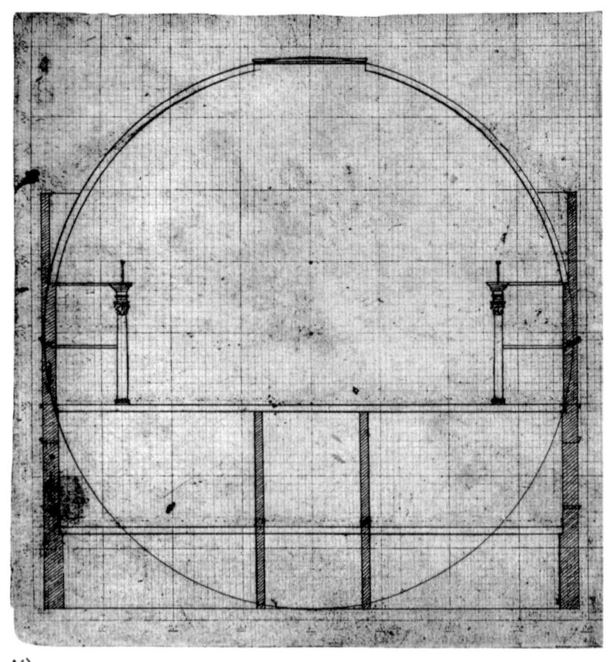

A1)

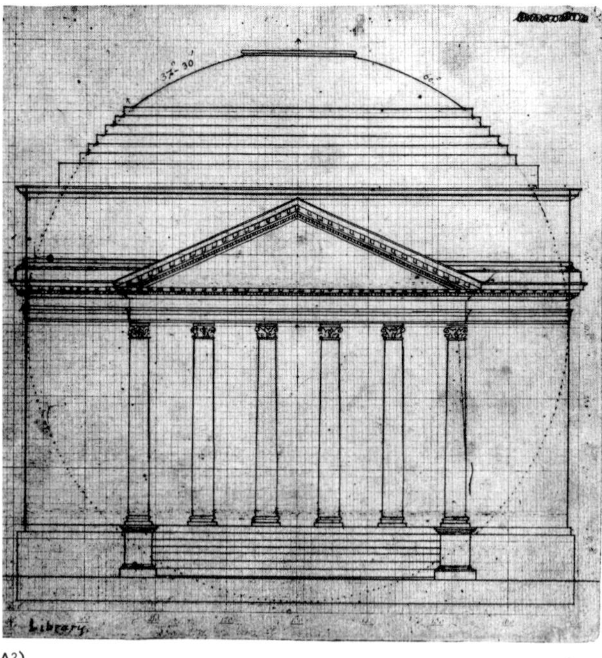

A2)

B)

A) Thomas Jefferson: University of Virginia, Charlottesville, ca. 1820, façade and cross section of the library rotunda

B) Giambattista Piranesi: View of the Pantheon in Rome, from *Vedute di Roma,* ca. 1745

1. Architecture and trompe-l'oeuil

Simulation or *Trompe l'oeuil* has always pursued two ends: to fool the eye, and at the same time to capture the mind through the elaborateness of the artifice. While the "naïf" is fooled, the sophisticate admires. The tension that exists between these two responses is inherent in any architectural revivalism from Hadrian's Villa in Tivoli to the themed shopping environments of today.

"Bastardy," an apparently innate obsession with "Replicated Replications," in short, an ingeniously pragmatic attitude towards de-materializing, propping up, and recycling the prototypes of historic architecture in altered circumstances and utilitarian contexts have often been discussed as characteristics of American building and mostly—from Le Corbusier to Umberto Eco—with a satirical bent.[2] George L. Hersey, in turn, takes a more detached view. Speaking of the University of Virginia at Charlottesville, and of the way the Pantheon in Rome with its massive walls is here reduced to a thin shell, superimposed upon a honeycomb of offices and corridors, he compares Thomas Jefferson's "sweetened restatement of the Pantheon" to "Fragonard adapting an antique Venus."[A)B)] American country houses of the 18th century, with their façades decked out with the "shrunken trappings of a much larger European prototype" (such as at Jefferson's Monticello or at Washington's Mount Vernon),[G)] appear to him characteristic of a constituent element of American architectural culture. If Hersey is correct, imitating larger prototypes on a smaller scale is as typically American as is the opposite procedure that gave us the campanile of St. Marks in Venice reproduced as the Metropolitan Life Tower in New York.[3]

Pragmatism and Pop sensibility

The work and research of Robert Venturi and Denise Scott Brown sits awkwardly between an ingenuous fascination which such procedures and a congenital passion towards acknowledging and exposing the contradictions involved. That they should have invested so much energy into the study of Las Vegas appears as almost natural given their interests. At least, Venturi's ironical question at the end of *Complexity and Contradiction in Architecture*, "Is not Main Street almost all right?," turned out to be programmatic in this context.[4] But how can architects of the late 20th century "learn" from Las Vegas?

Their work as designers offers only one possible answer to such a question, *their* answer. On the one hand, it is the answer of liberal (or Pop?) aesthetes both enthralled with, politically ambivalent about, and culturally detached from the mess of the commercial everyday that surrounds them. On the other, it is the answer of architectural pragmatists rooted in the tradition of functionalism. Many of their projects directly reflect this rather unique condition—which is why they generally follow the thought-pattern of the "decorated shed" as opposed to that of the "duck," which in turn has been adopted by most other architects ever since, admittedly or not.[5) D) L)] Like in Las Vegas, imagery appears to be projected upon generic buildings ("sheds") in various degrees of abstraction and in ways that at times seem casual and then again celebrate aggressive theatrical make-believe. In general, the imagery relates to the buildings' function, however metaphorically.[6] Often heraldic ornament or lettering is grotesquely enlarged and spread across an entire façade. Or then, architectural detail borrowed from some Elizabethan building is subjected to a metabolism

1) The present essay is based on the fourth chapter in Stanislaus von Moos, *Venturi, Scott Brown & Associates, 1986–1998: Buildings and Projects* (New York: Monacelli, 1999). As the title suggests, architecture is here approached from an angle that highlights conceptual links with the history of its sister arts, in particular, painting and photography. Pop Art as an important cultural context for the work has been discussed elsewhere (see Stanislaus von Moos, *Venturi, Rauch, Scott Brown: Buildings and Projects* [New York: Rizzoli, 1987]), pp. 47–73), but the perhaps most interesting aspect of this interdisciplinary dialogue, the relevance of Venturi's and Scott Brown's work in view of recent interests in the arts—art photography, installation art, site specific sculpture, virtual space, etc.—will be discussed in another context.

2) Chosen at random, Le Corbusier's *When the Cathedrals were White* (original ed. *Quand les cathédrales étaient blanches* [Paris: Plon, 1937]) and Umberto Eco's *Travels in Hyperreality* (San Diego, New York, and London: Harcourt Brace & Co., 1986) are treasures in this respect. See also footnote 3.

3) George L. Hersey, "Replication Replicated: Notes on American Bastardy," *Perspecta* 10 (1965), pp. 211–48, here pp. 215, 216, but see also Hersey's "J.C. Loudon and Architectural Associationism," *The Architectural Review* 144 (August 1968), pp. 88–92 which is among the art historical texts referred to in Robert Venturi, Denise Scott Brown and Steven Izenour, *Learning from Las Vegas* (Cambridge, MA: MIT Press, 1972), pp. xlv, 1.
Separating "true" and "false" in architecture has been of course a classic topic ever since John Ruskin's *Seven Lamps of Architecture* (1848). As to what degree the Ruskinian standards of architectural authenticity are applicable to contemporary production is another question. Among the recent contributions to this question, see Ada Louise Huxtable's fascinating yet rather moralizing study *The Unreal America: Architecture and Illusion* (New York: The New Press, 1997).

4) Robert Venturi, *Complexity and Contradiction in Architecture* (New York: Museum of Modern Art, 1966), p. 102.

5) On the concepts of "decorated shed" and "duck" see Venturi et al. 1972 (see note 3), pp. 65–80. Another question is whether the forecast (or the implication) that architecture will in the future follow the rule of the "decorated shed" as opposed to that of the "duck" has been verified or not by history since the 1970s. For some relative remarks see Stanislaus von Moos, *Nicht Disneyland und andere Aufsätze über Modernität und Nostalgie* (Zurich: Scheidegger & Spiess, 2004), pp. 157ff.

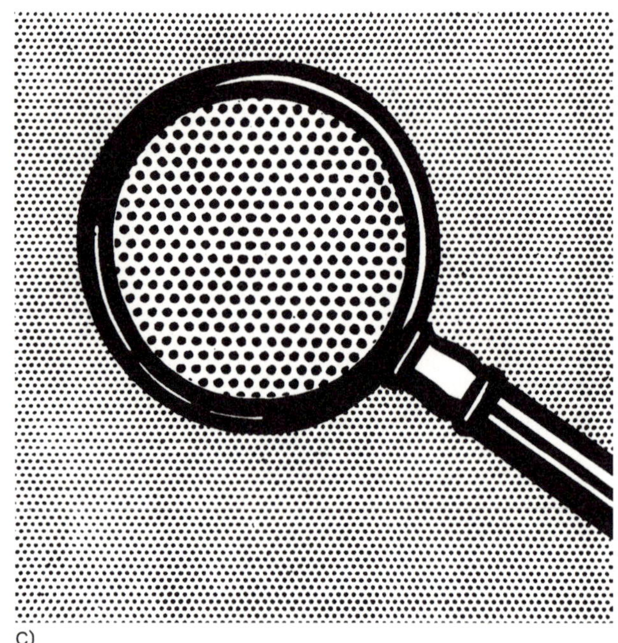

C)

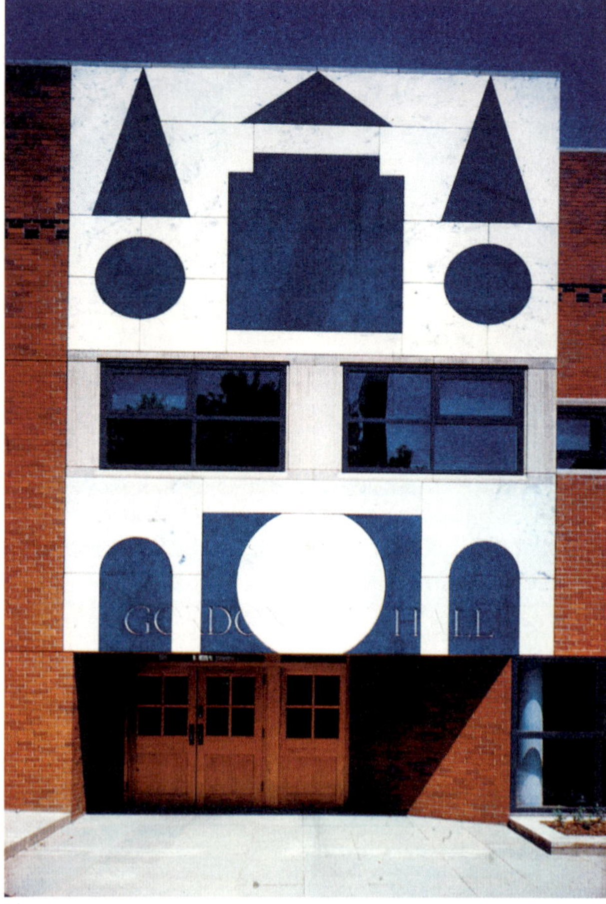

D)

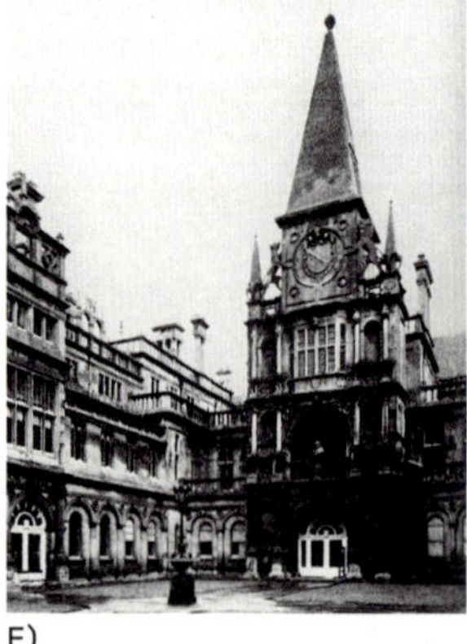

E)

C) Roy Lichtenstein: *Magnifying Glass* (oil on canvas), 1963

D) Venturi, Scott Brown & Associates: Gordon Wu Hall, Princeton University, Princeton, N. J., 1980, entrance panel

E) Burgley House, Northamptonshire, England, built 1585, view of courtyard gate

of abstraction, zooming in and blowing up before it is hung in front of a "modern" façade. [C) D) E)] Such extravagant manipulations of scale, space, and symbolism result in buildings that smack of what architects for a long time hated most: scenography and commercial kitsch. [7)]

More disturbing perhaps, some of Venturi's and Scott Brown's work is overtly historicist. At first sight, one would therefore expect the neo-conservative 1980s to have predestined them for *Grands travaux*. The convergence of interests was, to a large degree, merely apparent, however. In any case, it produced but a poor harvest. It is as if people sensed that they lack earnestness in their historicist borrowings and that they rather like to let us look into the gap that exists between the model chosen and its "replication" in the new building. In other words, there was just too much aesthetic nerve in these exercises to make them acceptable in contexts where "head-on" historicist reproduction or uncritical evocation is all that counts. With a "twisted smile" (Robert A.M. Stern), they like to make art from deconstructed architectural make-believe. An art that draws our attention not so much to the result of the "replacement" as to the mechanism of replacement as such. [8)]

Parody versus contextual accommodation

The history of Venturi's and Scott Brown's work is not at stake here. [9)] In the 1960s and 1970s, i.e., at the time of their "discovery" of Las Vegas, when their relation to both history and the everyday was to a significant degree driven by irony, historicist borrowings from "Classic" prototypes tended to take on the form of parody in their work. Venturi's re-interpretation of Mount Vernon, a national sanctuary (the estate was George Washington's residence on the shores of the Potomac in Virginia) is a good example. Its forced mannerism at the same time exacerbates the irregularities of the rather un-refined parti of the 18th century building as it exists and relieves it from the threat of colonial banality. [F) G)]

In recent decades, such often shrill distortions of historic models continued to be a theme in Venturi's and Scott Brown's more speculative projects. [10)] But in the category of built works these erudite mannerisms gave way to more relaxed appropriations. An example is the addition to the San Diego Museum of Contemporary Art in La Jolla, CA, which includes both the façade restoration of Irving Gill's Scripps House at the center of the complex as well as a quasi replica of the façade of Gill's Women's Club from across the street, a classic of Southern California early modernism (built 1914). [H) I)] At first sight, the irritating pastiche may look like a disillusioned accommodation to contextualist make-believe, or even an act of cowardice in front of the proverbial design review board. Given the presence of the authentic Gill building across the street, the resulting ambiguity as to what is original and what is not in the museum complex *is* heartbreaking. Yet the ribbon of ornamental letters on the beam of the pergola, most of the time illegible under the California sun, suggests that there must be a second, aesthetic level behind the "literal" contextualist accommodation. [I)] In fact, upon entering the small forecourt of the museum, the pastiche of the street façade gives away to the lofty International Style glass volume of the Museum lobby. Could it be that the theme of the building is not make-believe, after all, but the enacted dialogue, even clash, of historicist "envelope" and modernist "content"?

6) Note that among the built works by Venturi, Scott Brown & Associates there are only a few where "shed" and "decoration" are literally handled as separate components of a building. In most cases, it is the negotiation between the two concepts rather than their mere combination that is the crux of the design process. As a result, many of the firm's buildings turn out to be themselves more appropriately described as "ducks" than as "decorated sheds." On the theoretical implications of the term "decorated shed" see Deborah Fausch, "Towards 'An Architecture of Our Times': Scaffold and Drapery in the Work of Venturi, Scott Brown and Associates," in Deborah Fausch, Paulette Singley, and R. El-Koury (eds.), *Architecture in Fashion* (New York: Princeton Architectural Press, 1994), pp. 344–61.

7) Whereas "ducks," especially if configured according to the conventions of non-figurative sculpture, easily pass as "art." Scenography is obviously central to Venturi's and Scott Brown's architectural thinking, though it has been addressed as an issue by them only around 1993, in response to criticism. See Robert Venturi, "J'Adore St. Paul's," *AD Profile* 105 (Sept./Oct. 1993), pp. viii–xii; reprinted in Venturi, *Iconography and Electronics upon a Generic Architecture: A View from the Drafting Room* (Cambridge, MA: MIT Press, 1996), pp. 287–95. Cf. my own earlier discussion of scenography in von Moos 1987 (see note 1), pp. 60–69 ("The City as Stage").

8) Umberto Eco describes the full-scale model of the Oval Office in the Lyndon B. Johnson Library in Austin, Texas, as an example of the opposite procedure, where the "completely real" becomes identified with the "completely fake," i.e., where the "sign aims to be the thing, to abolish the distinction of the reference, the mechanism of replacement." Eco 1986 (see note 2), pp. 6f.

9) Cf. von Moos 1987 and von Moos 1999 (see note 1). The most complete diachronic survey of their careers is given in David Brownlee, David G. de Long and Kathryn B. Hiesinger (eds.), *Out of the Ordinary: Robert Venturi, Denise Scott Brown and Associates. Architecture, Urbanism, Design* (Philadelphia: Philadelphia Museum of Art, 2001).

10) Another example is the proposed monument for Marconi Plaza in Philadelphia, 1985. Apart from the transformation of the two highly sculptural façades into scenographic replicas, it is the distortion of the symmetrical façade of the Doge's Palace that underscores the parodying intent. See von Moos 1987 (see note 1), p. 144.

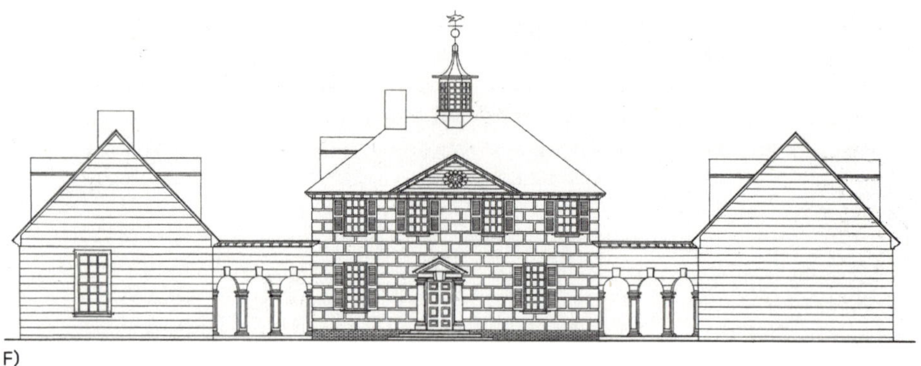

F)

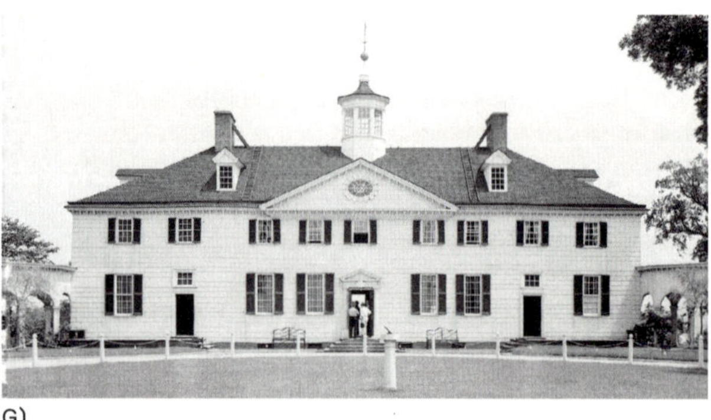

G)

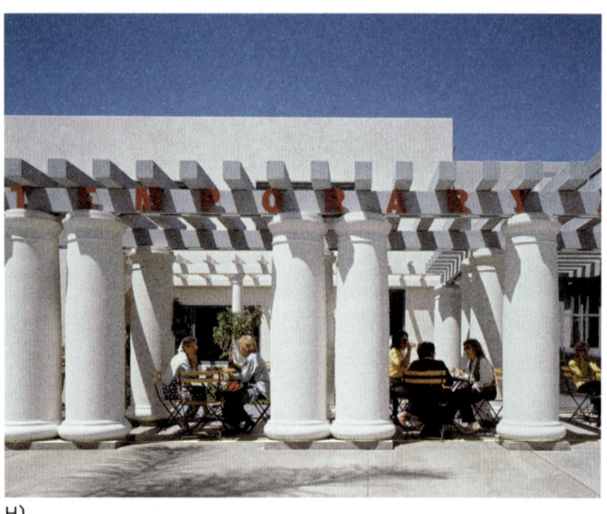

H)

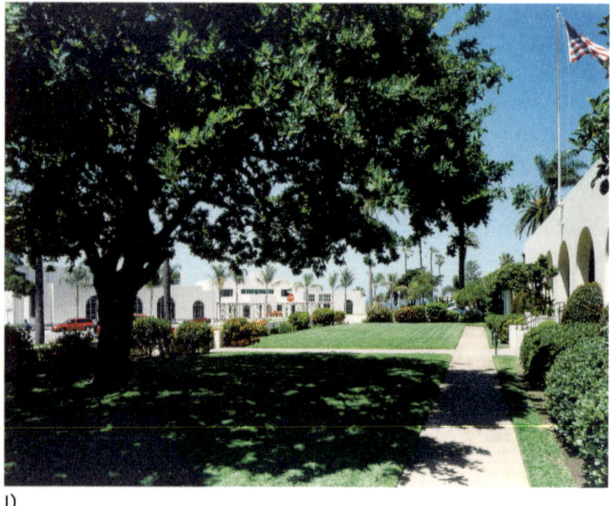

I)

F) Robert Venturi: unbuilt Mount Vernon House project to be realized in Greenwich, Connecticut, 1979, front elevation

G) Mount Vernon, George Washington's country estate, begun 1740, enlarged 1759

H) Venturi, Scott Brown & Associates: San Diego Museum of Contemporary Art, La Jolla, CA, 1986–96, entrance pergola

I) La Jolla, "Women's Club," built 1914 (at right; Irving Gill, architect) with the San Diego Museum of Contemporary Art (left)

Like Carlo Scarpa, whose remodeling of the Museo di Castelvecchio in Verona (1954–67) precedes them in its elegant play with historic evocation and modernist affirmation, Venturi and Scott Brown draw a special kind of energy from the juxtaposed layers of reconstructed memory and demonstratively shown modernity. [J)] [K)] Almost all of their projects done after 1975 are variations on that theme.

Built gaps, or: Architecture and "de-familiarization"

Although emphatically figurative and not abstract, the art of this kind of architecture is *about* abstraction in that it displays the procedure by which an original becomes its "duplicate." As Scott Brown puts it: "Contextual borrowings should never deceive; you should know what the real building consists of beneath the skin. For this reason our allusions are representations rather than copies of historic precedents. The deceit is only skin deep." [11)]

Bertolt Brecht has postulated a similar strategy for what he called the "epic theatre" of today. His aim was a rhetoric whereby the actor stands back from the role he performs, in order to allow the spectator not to be overwhelmed and "taken in" by the plot. [12)] Though Brecht has never been an explicit reference for Venturi and Scott Brown, their work could be said to have transferred his model to the field of architecture. What they refer to as their "irony" in the use of historic or Pop imagery could be said to be a counterpart to Brecht's strategy of "de-familiarization" ("Verfremdungs-Effekt"), by which he forces the spectator into a critical distance to the events on stage. Or should Venturi's and Scott Brown's understanding of historic or Pop iconography be seen as characteristic of the *flâneur*'s look at architecture as described by Walter Benjamin? If Benjamin is correct, a "filtrated," semantically defused theatricality of architectural form is already implicit in the distracted way in which the modern *flâneur* becomes aware of the buildings that surround him. [13)] Venturi's and Scott Brown's radically aesthetic vision of Las Vegas is doubtlessly related to this perceptive mode, as will be argued below. Yet as architects, they nevertheless act on stage, not facing it—which brings them closer to Brecht than to Benjamin.

The "ghost" house in Franklin Court is a case in point. Its purpose is emphatically not to act "as if" Franklin's House was still in place. Its theme is the gap that exists between the house that may have existed there at one time and its absence now. [14)] [J)] In a similar vein, the theme of the entrance façade of Gordon Wu Hall, a student center at Princeton University, is the gap—the difference—that exists between the obelisks and decorative panels drawn by Serlio or built in some Elizabethan mansion on the one hand and the use that is made here of such sources on the other. The impact and the meaning of this entrance panel result from the joint techniques of flattening out and blowing up, which generated the work. [15)] [C)] [D)] Similarly, the theme of the two flattened "columns" flanking the southwestern entrance to the Hôtel du Département de la Haute Garonne, in Toulouse, France, is the gap that exists between the three dimensional volumes of the two giant columns that had once marked the entry to the city in that location. [L)] [M)] In such a way, and set off against the hugely blown-up motif of a 17th century palatial gate that appears on the façade behind, the scenographic replicas evoke rather than reconstruct their Napoleonic models.

In the process of these ornamental recyclings of historic forms, symbolic reference in general evaporates with the widening gap between original and replica. [16)] The best example is the clock on the proposed Whitehall Ferry Terminal in Manhattan. [N)] Once again, the theme is the gap that exists between the "real" clock that might be built there (were it not obsolete at an age when everybody carries a wrist watch) and the colossal, electronically generated jumbotron-image of a

11) "Talking about the Context / A proposito del contesto," *Lotus* 74 (1992), pp. 125–28.

12) Among Bertolt Brecht's reflections on the theory of "Verfremdung," see in particular his "Kurze Beschreibung einer neuen Technik der Schauspielkunst, die einen Verfremdungseffekt hervorbringt," in Brecht, *Gesammelte Werke*, Bd. 15 (Frankfurt am Main: Suhrkamp, 1967), pp. 341–48.

13) Walter Benjamin, "Das Kunstwerk im Zeitalter seiner technischen Reproduzierbarkeit," in Benjamin, *Das Kunstwerk iom Zeitalter seiner technischen Reproduzierbarkeit* (Frankfurt am Main: Suhrkamp, 1963 [1936]), pp. 46f.

14) "Gap" is here intended not merely as the "gap between the building and its decoration (that) gets wider with each new technology of communication," as has been discussed by Mark Wigley (in "The Decorated Gap," *Ottagono* 94 [1990], pp. 36–47), but more generally as the "distance" that inevitably exists between a subject and its representation.

15) The technique had obviously been elaborated in earlier works, e.g., in the emblematic Fire Station Nr. 4 at Columbus, Indiana, 1966, specifically in the way its façade is made of two overlapping façades, both considerably bigger than the building behind: one real, built as a brick wall, one virtual, i.e., suggested by paint (see von Moos 1987 [see note 1], pp. 158f.). In a broader historical perspective, the principle can be said to relate to Palladio's church of S. Giorgio Maggiore in Venice, whose façade is defined as a flattened reproduction of the building behind.

Speaking of the "cardboard architecture" characteristic of what he refers to as the "neo-avant-garde," Robert E. Somol has described the visual strategy at hand as the technique of building structure "from the point of view of its reproduction" (in R. E. Somol, "'Les Liaisons Dangereuses,' or 'My Mother the House,'" *Fetish. The Princeton Architectural Journal*, 4 (1992), pp. 50–71, here p. 63.

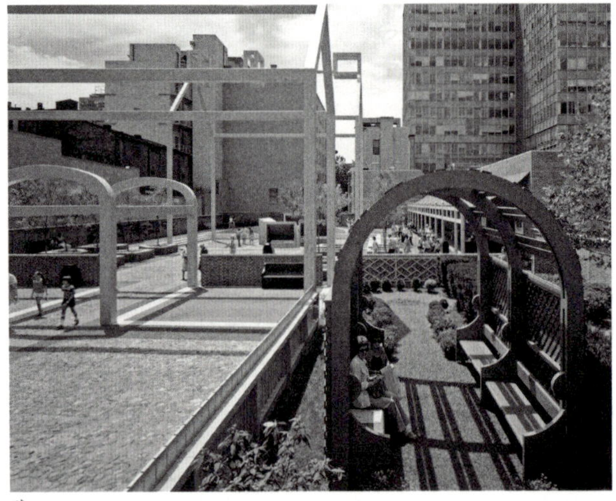

J)

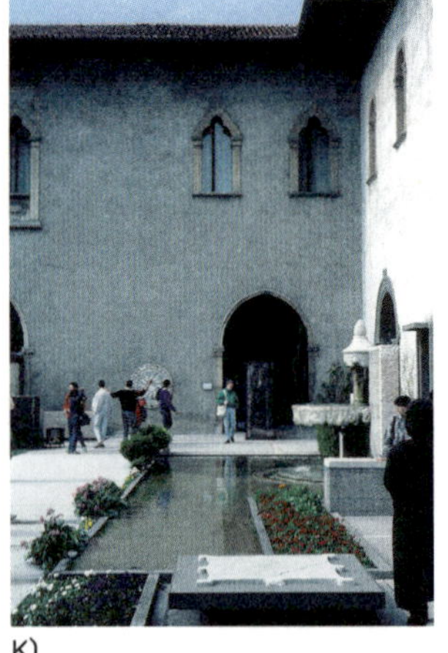

K)

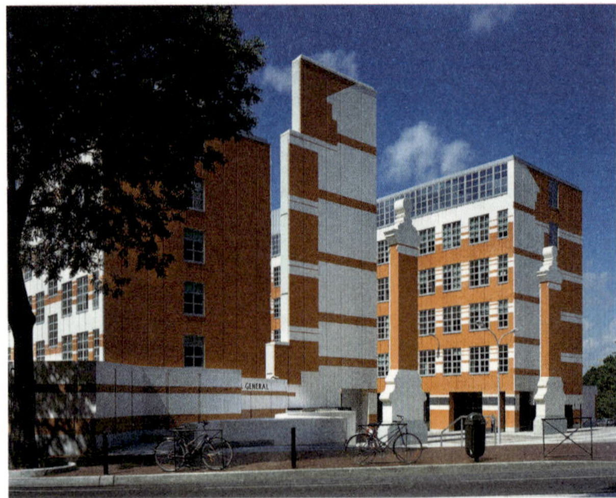

L)

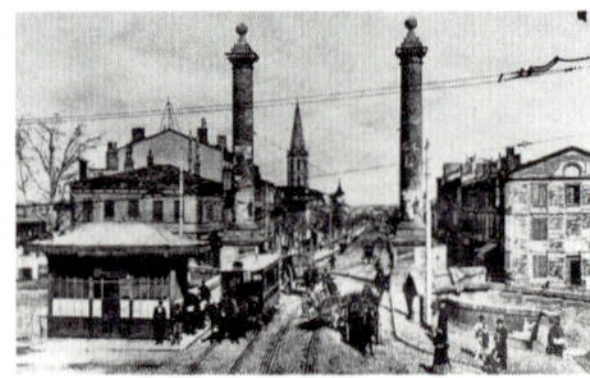

M)

J) Venturi, Scott Brown & Associates: Franklin Court, Philadelphia, PA, 1972–76, view of ghost reconstruction of Franklin's house and garden

K) Carlo Scarpa: Museo di Castelvecchio, Verona, 1954–67, view of entrance courtyard showing reconstructed medieval wing with "modern" entrance and window details (photo author)

L) Venturi, Scott Brown & Associates: Hôtel du Département de la Haute Garonne, Toulouse, France, 1992–99, view of north entrance with "symbolic" columns

M) Toulouse, "Colonnes des Minimes" as gateway to the city flanking the Route de Paris, early 19th century (no longer extant)

clock. Venturi and Scott Brown appear convinced that by virtue of the mere substitution of the real clock by its electronic surrogate the image's atavistic symbolism of authority and order—in short: of control by the "system"—will be neutralized.[17] They seem to believe that post-industrial publics will increasingly consume such "outdated" symbols as entertainment.

The tourists who today gather around the colossal mechanical clocks in Venice, Strasbourg, and Berne, deciphering the astronomical symbols displayed around them and awaiting the procession of the heraldic animals and folks generated by the clockwork at certain times, support their reasoning.[O] But the New York of the early 21st century either did not notice the irony of the intended "de-familiarization" or simply had no patience for this kind of joke. It rejected the clock and the façade remained unbuilt.

2. Architecture, photography, and "townscape"

Albeit more successfully as a camp comment about the real world rather than as a part of it (as with the New York clock), Venturi's and Scott Brown's negotiations of form and symbolism, history and modernity, popular iconography and Pop sensibility relate to the multi-cultural dialectics of urban space. More precisely, they rely on the means by which urban space is represented in the 20th century: photography, film, and the media at large. That Las Vegas as one of the world's most notorious suppliers of raw materials for photography, advertising, and the movies should have become a key reference in their undertakings as observers of *and* as designers in the United States is thus no coincidence.

In painting, photography, and film, architecture does not need to be "good" in order to look good. Venturi argues that architects should not forget the simple truth that a boring shed, a miserable hut, a ruin, rusting signs along the highway, or even "bad" architecture can be powerful *sujets*.[P] In *Complexity and Contradiction in Architecture*, speaking of Peter Blake's book *God's Own Junkyard*, he writes: "The pictures in this book that are supposed to be bad are often good. The seemingly chaotic juxtaposition of honky-tonk elements express an intriguing kind of vitality and validity, and they produce an unexpected approach to unity as well."

As if to limit potential damage of such aestheticizing "irony," he goes on to say: "It is true that an ironic interpretation such as this results partly from the change in scale of the subject matter in photographic form and the change in context within the frames of the photographs."[18]

The next step was *Learning from Las Vegas* (1972; written jointly with Denise Scott Brown and Steven Izenour), a study that frames the "seemingly chaotic juxtaposition of honky-tonk elements" in one of the world's flamboyant sites of greed and commercialized vice. Throughout, the "frames of the photograph" work as a means of redeeming aesthetically what everybody agrees to be "bad," commodifying in such a way "the experience of everyday life for a high cultural market."[19] In that respect, *Learning from Las Vegas* explicitly draws on the tradition of Pop Art. Ed Ruscha, in particular, served as a direct reference.[20]

16) The changing nature of this "gap" has been the subject of Scott Brown's and Venturi's study of "hot" and "cool" borrowings in developer housing. Although the bulk of their "Learning from Levittown" study still awaits publication, see V. Carroll, Denise Scott Brown and Robert Venturi, "'Styling' or 'These Houses are exactly the same, they just look different,'" *Lotus International* 9 (1975), pp. 162–71, here pp. 234ff. For an excerpt from that study as well as more recently, Deborah Fausch: "Ugly and Ordinary. The Representation of the Everyday," in Steven Harris and Deborah Berke (eds.), *Architecture of the Everyday* (New York: Princeton Architectural Press/Yale Publications on Architecture, 1997), pp. 75–106.

17) Ever since the Middle Ages, public clocks have served atavistic class interests of organization and control of space and time. For some examples from Switzerland see Stanislaus von Moos, *Industrieästhetik*, Ars Helvetica, vol. XI (Disentis: Desertina, 1992), pp. 23–32. A history of the resistance against this symbolism of bourgeois law and order throughout the centuries would be an interesting subject. The painter Paul Klee, who was born in Berne in 1879, felt so strongly about the atavistic symbolism of the 16th century Berne clock tower ("Zytglogge") that he carefully avoided including it in any of his numerous early drawings of the city's skyline. See Osamu Okuda, "Reflektierender Blick auf Bern. Paul Klee und seine Heimatstadt," in *Georges Bloch-Jahrbuch des Kunstgeschichtlichen Seminars der Universität Zürich* 2 (1995), pp. 146–62.

18) Venturi 1966 (see note 4), p. 102.

19) Wigley 1990 (see note 14), pp. 38f. As to Wigley's interpretation of *Learning from Las Vegas* as "an artwork" offered to the "gaze of a traditional reader" (p. 38), it may be added that the design of the original edition, published in 1972, was not done by Venturi and Scott Brown. In fact, they declare that the "latter day Bauhaus design of the book," its "'interesting' Modern styling... belied our subject matter (etc.)." They appear to be happier with the "ordinary," paperback edition done a few years afterwards (Robert Venturi, Denise Scott Brown, and Steven Izenour, *Learning from Las Vegas: The Forgotten Symbolism of Architectural Form*, revised edition [Cambridge, MA/London: MIT Press, 1977], p. xv). The history of the book's production has been documented by Martino Stierli in his Ph.D. thesis (*Ins Bild gerückt. Aesthetik, Form und Diskurs der Stadt in Venturis und Scott Browns* Learning from Las Vegas, ETH Zurich, 2007; publication in preparation with gta Verlag, Zurich, 2009).

20) See Ed Ruscha, *Every Building on the Sunset Strip* (1966) —or others among his precious photo scrapbooks, such as *Twentysix Gasoline Stations* (1963) or *Nine Swimming Pools and a Broken Glass* (1968). For more details, see Martino Stierli's essay in the present book.

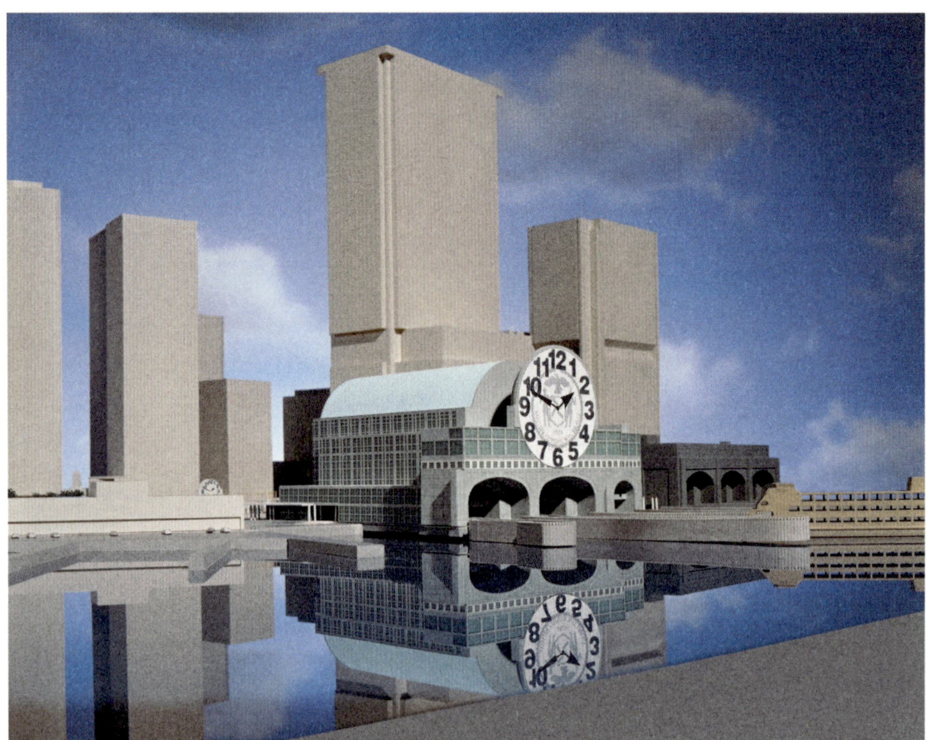

N)

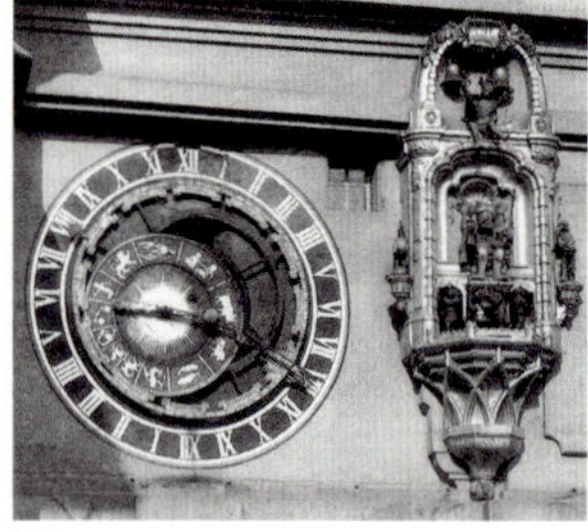

O)

N) Venturi, Scott Brown & Associates: proposed Whitehall Ferry Terminal with giant clock, New York, 1992, competition entry

O) Berne, Switzerland, east façade of "Zytglogge"-tower with mechanical clockwork and play clock dominating Berne's "Gerechtigkeitsgasse," 16th century with later additions

Photography, investigation, and documentation

Photography as a means of documenting and analyzing urban form is not limited, with Venturi and Scott Brown, to research and publication. It is also an aspect of the work in the studio. Photography is used both as a tool of investigation and as a support for design. Their projects are, in general, accompanied by renderings (more recently computer renderings) that show a culture of draftsmanship that makes one think of the Ecole des Beaux-Arts. In fact, the eclecticism of their graphic styles is a subject of its own. Some of their renderings, like the site elevations for Franklin Court, 1974, or those referring to the Westway Study, 1978–1985, are variations on the theme of Jacques Gréber's renderings of Benjamin Franklin Parkway (1917). [Q) R)] Others draw explicitly on graphic styles of fin-de-siècle-artists, such as Maxfield Parrish. [21)]

Once built, the Venturian projects were, up to his death in 2001, again subjected to meticulous photographic inventorization, in general, by a photographic crew headed by Steven Izenour.

What sense is to be made of this overpowering presence of photography? Today, such osmotic transfers between artistic genres (photography, the rendering, the elevation) are easily seen as characteristic of the postmodern culture industry. No doubt the scenic landscapes of Disneyland, some of them actually built as three dimensional illustrations of episodes from movies, come immediately to mind. [S)] Yet it would be too easy to leave it at that. Nor are Venturi and Scott Brown to be blamed for the boom of pictorial representation in the debilitating renderings of corporate architecture —a phenomenon that some elite schools now try to exorcise by banning perspective drawing altogether from their curriculum.

For centuries, architecture and landscape design have naturally drawn from concepts developed and imagery proposed in the visual arts. Perspective space, as it was first defined at the time of Masaccio and Brunelleschi, is the common conceptual base for painting *and* architecture. Centuries later, the picturesque garden was modeled on paintings by Claude Lorrain, Gaspard Dughet or Salvator Rosa. As Alexander Pope put it, "all gardening is landscape-painting. Just like a landscape hung up." [22)]

Modernism and "the picturesque"

With modern architecture, admittedly, the situation gets blurred. Le Corbusier rejected the pictorial concept of urban design he had inherited from Camillo Sitte, replacing it with a concept where "art" at first sight determines not so much the looks but the structural conception of the built artifact. On another level, however, he continues to use and develop it: First, by subjecting the building and the city to the logic of the "promenade architecturale." Second, by frequently abandoning or subverting classical formality in favor of irregular (=functional) arrangements. And third, by incorporating the landscape as a component of architectural form. [23)]

Modernism's ambiguity with respect to the "picturesque" is eloquently mirrored in the negative twist given to the term in Venturi's *Complexity and Contradiction in Architecture*. "I make no special attempt to relate architecture to other things," the author says. [24)] And in general, he locates "picturesqueness" at the opposite end of what complexity and contradiction is about. "An architecture of complexity and contradiction ... does not mean subjective expressionism," much less "an architecture of symmetrical picturesqueness which Minoru Yamasaki calls 'serene.'" [25)] (More recently, Venturi has suspected contemporary "Deconstructivism" to be infected by the virus of breaking orders not on the grounds of circumstance, as it should be, but "for ... picturesque or arty reasons." [26)])

21) On Jacques Gréber and the Franklin Parkway project see David Brownlee, *Building the City Beautiful: The Benjamin Franklin Parkway and the Philadelphia Museum of Art* (Philadelphia: Philadelphia Museum of Art, 1989), pp. 34 and passim. On the psychology of the rendering, see Denise Scott Brown, "Zeichnen für den Déco-Distrikt," *Archithese* 12 (1982) no. 3, pp. 17–21. On the relation between graphic and photographic image-making and design, cf. also Stanislaus von Moos, "Architektur als Bilderbogen. Graphik und Photo-Graphik bei Venturi and Rauch," in Heinrich Klotz (ed.), *Jahrbuch für Architektur* (Braunschweig and Wiesbaden: Vieweg, 1980), pp. 95–112.

22) Susanne Lang, "The Genesis of the English Landscape Garden," in Nikolaus Pevsner (ed.), *The Picturesque Garden and its Influence Outside the British Isles* (Washington, D.C.: Dumbarton Oaks, 1974), pp. 1–29. On the subject of the picturesque garden cf. Adrian von Buttlar, *Der Landschaftsgarten. Gartenbaukunst des Klassizismus und der Romantik* (Cologne: DuMont, 1989).

23) See Richard A. Etlin, *Frank Lloyd Wright and Le Corbusier: The Romantic Legacy* (Manchester and New York: Manchester University Press, 1994), pp. 112ff. ("Le Corbusier defines the architectural promenade"), pp. 143ff. ("The reasoned picturesque"), and passim. Many of these design procedures are, by the way, themselves related to Le Corbusier's techniques of manipulating photographic imagery. See Beatriz Colomina, *Privacy and Publicity: Modern Architecture as Mass Media* (Cambridge, MA: MIT Press, 1994).

24) Venturi 1966 (see note 4), p. 20.

25) Ibid., p. 25.

26) Robert Venturi, "Notes for a Lecture Celebrating the Centennial of the American Academy in Rome Delivered in Chicago," in Venturi 1996 (see note 7), pp. 47–56, here p. 51.

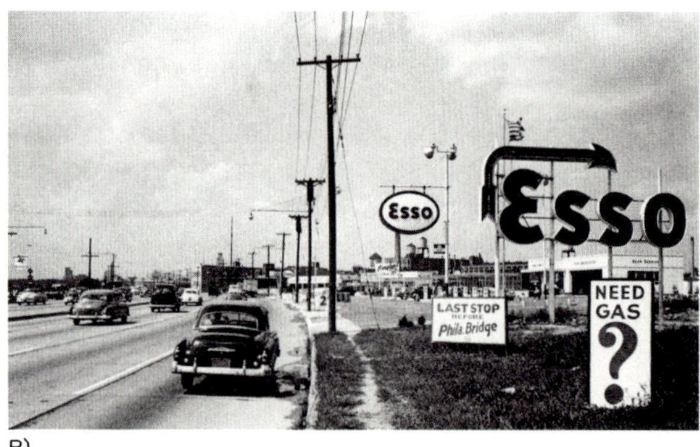

P)

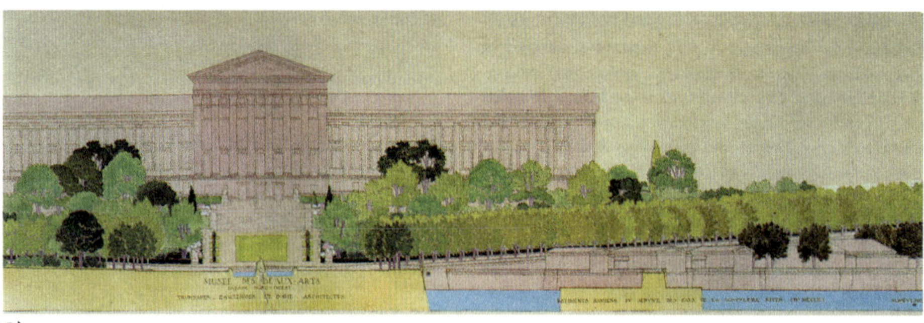

Q)

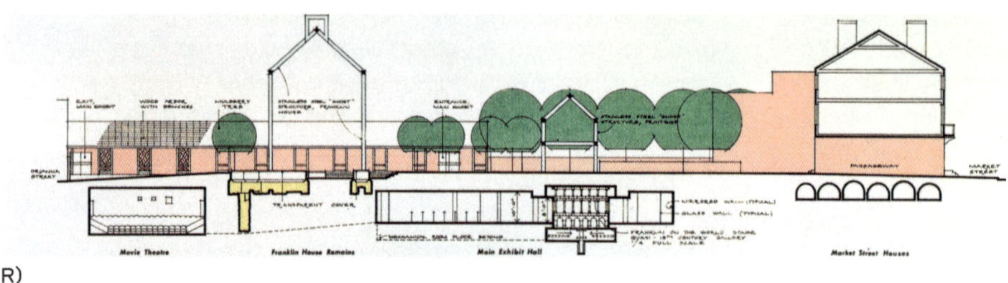

R)

P) "American Roadscape": Photograph from Peter Blake's *God's Own Junkyard*, 1964, "recycled" by Robert Venturi in his *Complexity and Contradiction in Architecture*, 1966

Q) Jacques Gréber: Franklin Parkway project, Philadelphia, 1917, view of the proposed landscaping around Philadelphia Museum of Art

R) Venturi, Scott Brown & Associates: Franklin Court, Philadelphia, 1972–76, section showing ghost reconstruction of Franklin's house, underground miniature reconstruction of and 1:1 reconstructed Market Street houses (right)

If even Venturi rejects the "picturesque" as spurious license as it might have been by any "straight" modernist, one is tempted to add that rejecting a concept is one way of learning from it. For at second glance, the analogies that link Venturi's and Scott Brown's position to the "Picturesque" appear to be stronger than the differences. [27] Many among their aesthetic concerns, their attitude to issues like contrast, variety, shifting scales, even to the issue of control (i.e., the idea that architects need to accept that there is a limit to their control) are closer to the Picturesque tradition than may appear. The principle of "mixture," of "abrupt variation," of "contrast"; the consideration of "things rough and careless in aesthetic matters," even "shifts of scale" have become central in their art. [28] Needless to insist that the mess of Las Vegas, i.e., its aesthetic transformation through the sheer logic of the picture frame, represents an inescapable challenge in the context of such interests.

The point may even be strengthened considering the roots of the picturesque aesthetic in rhetoric. For even though the "Picturesque" relates to pictures, painting is not its ultimate reference. Elements of the picturesque garden that serve diversion, variety, or even fun, relate also to the classical theory of the stage, as it is mirrored in Sebastiano Serlio's woodcuts depicting the "tragic," and, more important here, the "comic" scenes. [T] It is enough to recall that Serlio's views had had a profound impact on the theory of landscape painting by the 17th century Italian painter Lomazzo —which in turn serves as a link from Serlio to the 18th century concept of the Picturesque. [29]

The "townscape movement" and its legacy

Serlio may be long forgotten. Yet in the 1950s, with the hopes of social redemption once associated with modern architecture thoroughly compromised, traditional concepts of place and space have seen a *renaissance*. And slowly, this trend started to thoroughly subvert the doctrine of the Modern movement. With it came a reassessment of cities and neighborhoods that had resisted modernization. That architecture and urbanism have turned towards "pictorialism" is thus both a symptom and a consequence of a crisis of functionalism.

In England and America, such revivalist concerns, as well as the dogmatism that often comes along with them, are in part a legacy of the townscape movement, whose origins can be located in the pages of *The Architectural Review* in the late 1940s and early 1950s. Here is a description of its ingredients: "A perhaps wholly English taste for topography; a surely Bauhaus-inspired taste for the pregnant object of mass production—the hitherto unnoticed Victorian manhole, etc; a feeling for paint, the texture of decay, eighteenth century folly and nineteenth century graphics; representative titles of all this include: 'The Seeing Eye or How to Like Everything'; 'Eyes and Ears in East Anglia—a schoolboy's holiday tour by Archibald Abus aged 14 ½,' etc."

Colin Rowe and Fred Koetter, who wrote these lines, argue that "much of present-day activity is incomprehensible unless we are prepared to recognize the ramifications of townscape's influence"—including also what they refer to as "Pop-inspired appraisals of the strip at Las Vegas." [30]

Be that as it may, with the urban upheavals of the 1960s, with the Civil Rights Movement, the "Great Society" of the Johnson era, and with advocacy planning, the discourse of urban design turned towards pictorial and scenographic demonstrations, more or less

27) Venturi's and Scott Brown's theoretical antagonism to "picturesqueness" deserves a more thorough analysis than can be attempted here. In their theoretical statements, they emphasize the conflict that may exist between the "picturesque" and "function," such as when Scott Brown insists that qualities such as those just described are legitimate only if they emerge from the given problem or program, rather than as applications, adapted for the sake of being picturesque (communication to the author, 31 August 1997). While much current architecture may be characterized by such a conflict, the "picturesque" as a theoretical position in history also and primarily represents an attempt to give "function" its dignity and place in aesthetic theory. Seen in such a way, Venturi's and Scott Brown's own work is hardly imaginable outside the "picturesque" tradition.

28) Sidney K. Robinson, *Inquiry into the Picturesque* (Chicago and London: The University of Chicago Press, 1991), p. 1, 4. Robinson perhaps somewhat overstates the aspects of the picturesque tradition that would connect it to postmodernist sensibility. Stephen Copley and Peter Garside found it "disconcerting" to see how Robinson had stressed the proto-postmodern sides of the Picturesque: "... indeed, his presentation and celebration of the Picturesque movement's eclecticism, refusal of fixity, and authority, and exploitation of marginality, sometimes makes it sound disconcertingly like a program for architectural Postmodernism." Stephen Copley and Peter Garside (eds.), *The Politics of the Picturesque: Literature, Landscape and Aesthetics since 1770* (Cambridge: Cambridge University Press, 1994), p. 4.

29) Lang 1974 (see note 22). Serlio's woodcut of the "comic" stage is explicitly referred to in Colin Rowe and Fred Koetter, *Collage City* (Cambridge, MA: MIT Press, 1978), p. 14 and implicitly, as I have tried to argue, in Venturi's *Complexity and Contradiction in Architecture* (see von Moos 1987 [see note 1], pp. 60–9). More recently, M. Christine Boyer has challenged this interpretation, attributing the "failures of architecture as a narrative gesture," among other things, to the "false comparison" of the "tragic" and the "comic" scenes as drawn by Serlio. Cf. M. Christine Boyer, *The City of Collective Memory: Its Historical Imagery and Historical Entertainments* (Cambridge, MA / London: MIT Press, 1994), pp. 124ff.

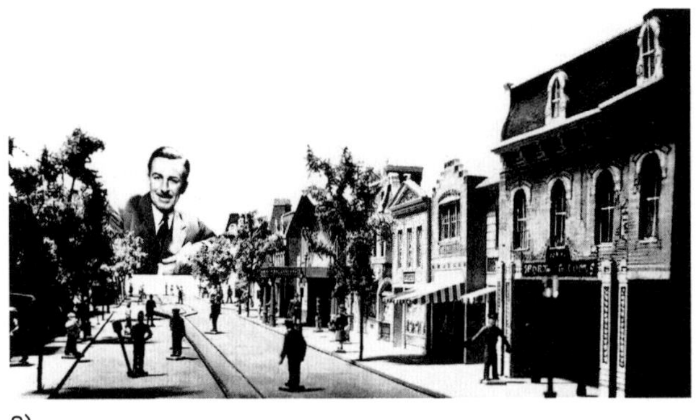

S)

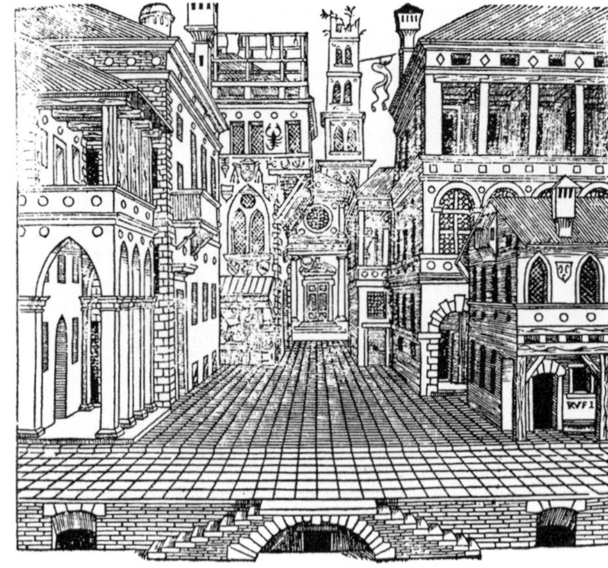

T)

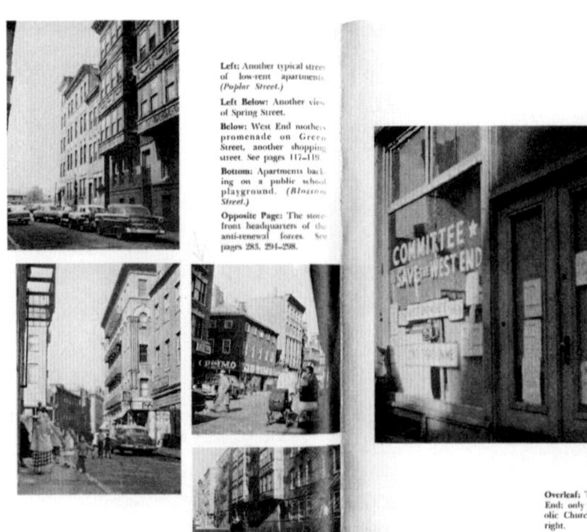

Left: Another typical street of low-rent apartments. *(Poplar Street.)*

Left Below: Another view of Spring Street.

Below: West End mothers promenade on Green Street, another shopping street. See pages 117–119.

Bottom: Apartments backing on a public school playground. *(Blossom Street.)*

Opposite Page: The storefront headquarters of the anti-renewal forces. See pages 283, 294–298.

Overleaf: This was the West End: only St. Joseph's Catholic Church remains at the right.

V)

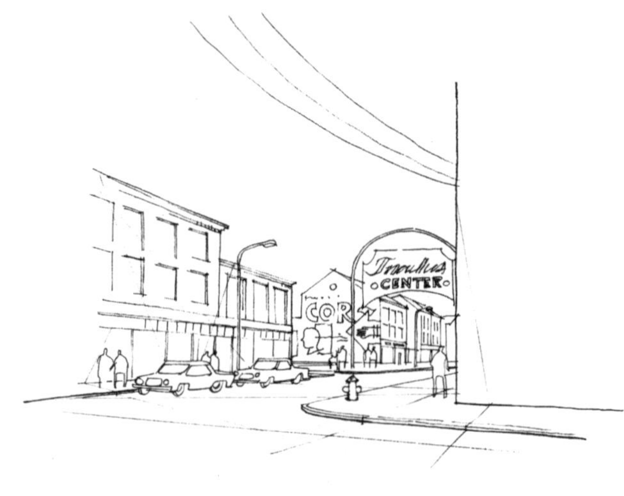

U)

S) Walt Disney examining the model of Main Street, Disneyland, 1955

T) Sebastiano Serlio: "Comic scene," from his *Quinto libro di Architettura*, 1551

U) Venturi, Scott Brown & Associates: view of South Street, Philadelphia, then earmarked as site for an urban freeway, from the "Philadelphia Crosstown Community Study", 1968

V) Views of neighborhood streets in Boston's west end before their demolition as part of urban renewal, spread from Herbert Gans, *The Urban Villagers*, 1962

grudgingly abandoning the rhetoric of abstract form.[31] At the time of Herbert Gans's *The Urban Villagers* and Jane Jacobs's *The Death and Life of Great American Cities*, this reassessment of traditional modes of life gained a considerable political momentum as a project, in general terms, of the Left.[32] [V] At the same time, the aesthetic charm of early postmodernist work, as well as its antagonism to the "monotony" of low-cost housing and worn-out corporate styles made the movement attractive to the elite. As a result, it ended up being swiftly co-opted by the cultural and political mainstream. "With amazing rapidity, postmodernism became *the* new corporate style, after Philip Johnson's notorious Chippendale top for AT&T instantly convinced patrons of its marketability and prestige value."[33]

In the meantime, the once emancipatory return to pictorial and scenic visualizations of public space have been taken over by urban design review boards, architects, and developers alike. As to postmodernism's earlier complicity with Pop, it was somehow lost underway. In fact, the recent transformation of Las Vegas itself into an archipelago of fragments from the most hilarious *fin-de-siècle*-daydreams of the City Beautiful epitomizes this exorcism of Pop more dramatically than any other chapter of recent urban history.[Y]

City Tableaux: Outline of a typology

Tamed and totally defused in the process of its integration into mainstream aesthetics, the phenomenon once called postmodernism has long lost its critical momentum. But the socio-cultural dynamics of what is subsumed as "Disneyfication" by some and whose roots, in fact, reach much deeper than those of any architectural fashion nevertheless continues to set the tone. It will probably shape the "culture of cities" for a long while.[34]

At least three emblematic types of "City Tableaux" appear now to be universally shared as models: First, the wholesale preservation of historic neighborhoods (Plaka in Athens, the Marais in Paris, or the Old City of Berne). Second, contextual zoning of districts whose historic ambience is considered worthy to be protected by design guidelines, however strict or loose. And third, the creation of "scenic enclaves" in places where ambience is not to be preserved but to be created from scratch: theme parks, including Disneylands and Disneyworlds.[35]

Like other architects of their generation, Venturi and Scott Brown have been involved in all three types of architectural revivalism—but unlike most, the concerns involved in these enterprises have been central to their work from the beginning. The work of the VSBA unfolds between the relative extremes of advocacy planning (in the 1960s and 1970s); and planning for the needs of tourism and mass entertainment (in the 1980s and 1990s)[X]—with numerous projects for academic institutions in between. Their work encompasses, in other words, the entire spectrum of strategies within which populist attitudes have worked and been considered appropriate, including, as a special focus, the more erudite historicism of the traditional American campus.[36] [D] As preservationists, VSBA have fought for the survival of existing neighborhoods and streets, such as South Street, Philadelphia[U] and the Art Déco District in Miami Beach. After 1985, state-of-the-art restorations for Ivy League institutions (The Furness Building at Penn, Memorial Hall at Harvard) became a special focus.

On the other hand, some form of "contextual zoning" has been implicit in most of their housing schemes, beginning with Guild House, the project that, together with Mother's House, made them famous (1960–63). It is also a key idea behind the Sainsbury Wing, in London, and the San Diego Museum of Contemporary

30) Rowe and Koetter 1978 (see note 29), pp. 34ff. Among the "activity" influenced by the townscape movement, the authors include Jane Jacobs and the "allegedly scientific notational systems of Kevin Lynch," as well as "Pop-inspired appraisals of the Strip at Las Vegas and enthusiasm for the phenomenon of Disney World" (36f.). The theoretical precedents and premises of Venturi's and Scott Brown's urbanistic aesthetics have in the meantime been studied by Martino Stierli, cf. Stierli 2007 (see note 19).

31) See von Moos 1999 (see note 1), pp. 15ff. and passim for more details.

32) See in this context Andreas Huyssen, "Postmoderne – eine amerikanische Internationale?," in Huyssen and Klaus G. Scherpe (eds.), *Postmoderne. Zeichen eines kulturellen Wandels* (Reinbek b. Hamburg: Rowohlt, 1986), pp. 13–44.

33) Mary McLeod, "Architecture and Politics in the Reagan Era: From Postmodernism to Deconstructivism," *assemblage* 8 (1989), pp. 23–59, here p. 29.

34) See von Moos 2004 (see note 5), for my own speculations on the subject as well as for bibliographical references.

35) M. Christine Boyer, "Cities for Sale: Merchandizing History at South Street Seaport," in Michael Sorkin (ed.), *Variations on a Theme Park: The New American City and the End of Public Space* (New York: The Noonday Press, 1992), pp. 181–204. The concept of the "tableau" is also central in Boyer's more recent book, cf. Boyer 1994 (see note 29), especially pp. 46ff. ("The City of Spectacle") as well as pp. 59ff. ("The Politics of Representational Forms"). Cf. also the previous note. On the politics and design of Disneyland, see Sorkin's essay in the same book ("See You in Disneyland," pp. 205–32) as well as Beth Dunlop, *Building a Dream: The Art of Disney Architecture* (New York: Harry N. Abrams, 1996); with an introduction by Vincent Scully.

36) See the chapter "Scenes of Learning," in von Moos 1999 (see note 1), pp. 25–34.

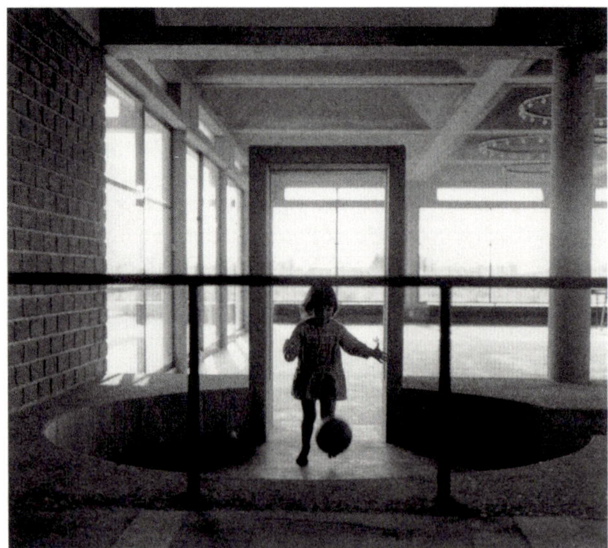

W)

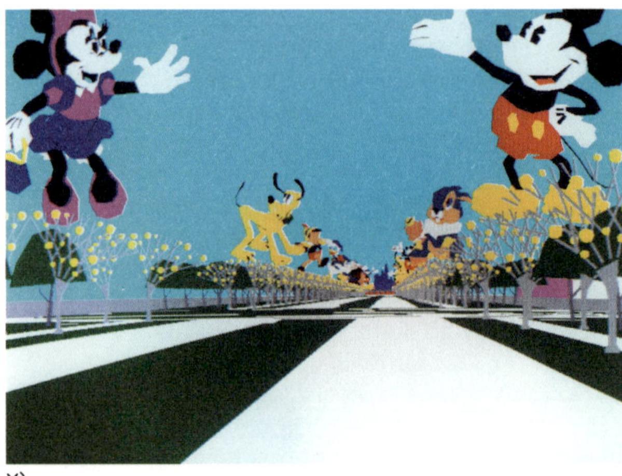

X)

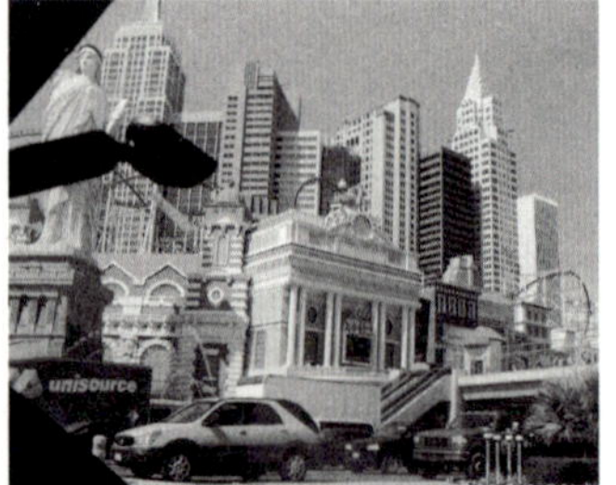

Y)

W) Aldo van Eyck: Burgerweeshuis (municipal orphanage) with playing child, Amsterdam, 1958

X) Venturi, Scott Brown & Associates: Access avenue to the Magic Kingdom at Paris Disneyland, unexecuted proposal, ca. 1989

Y) Las Vegas, "New York Casino," completed ca. 2002

Art exteriors [H) I)] — museum complexes that explicitly respond to design guidelines derived from context, adopting existing rooflines as well as motives and materials already in use in the buildings next door and/or nearby. As to the category of "scenic enclaves," VSBA have made proposals in the form of murals that depict urban monuments, or in the form of public spaces furnished with miniature reproductions (models, in fact) of topical buildings in the respective locations (Copley Square, Boston; Western Plaza, Washington, D.C., or finally, Welcome Park in Philadelphia. [37)]

*

When Umberto Eco spoke about the American trend towards the "crèche-ification of the bourgeois universe," he did not have these projects in mind. [38)] Although he might have (granted that most of them were not built at the time he wrote), for that such "scenic enclaves" should attract and entertain children *as well* as adults has been a stated claim of the work of VSBA. [39)] In some of those environments, architecture is miniaturized to the scale of the toy. In others, the opposite strategy is used; at Franklin Court, fragments (a hedge, trellis, garden benches) are inflated so that the visitors become themselves miniaturized as they stroll about the dream landscape of the ghost garden. [J)] The Big Apple proposed for Times Square, New York, an explicit tribute to Oldenburg's monuments, is emblematic in this respect. [40)]

The themes as such, de-familiarizing the everyday by ways of shrinking and/or blowing up, are inherent in the structure of what we refer to as "folk art"—down to the emblematic roadside sign representing a donut or a hamburger. At the same time, as Disney knew well, they are the stuff of which fairy tales are made. Gulliver is as much a condition of the crèche-city as are the seven dwarfs. Nor are the "crèche" and the playground new themes in architecture. To retreat from an adult stage of evolution to a juvenile stage "as the starting point of a new line" is a key theme in modernity. Evolution theory speaks of paedomorphosis in this context. [41)] So-called "primitivism" in modern art is the one variety of this phenomenon that has long been canonized by high culture. Aldo van Eyck, the "humanist rebel" within the European avant-garde, is a case in point. Due to van Eyck's 734 playgrounds in Amsterdam (1947–55), the CIAM (Congrès internationaux d'architecture moderne) can be said to have begun to re-orient its definition of public space with the needs of playing children in mind. [42)] Van Eyck saw childhood as "a symbol upon which cities could again rest, a symbol from which society could regenerate." [43)] His ideas appear to have been of considerable interest to Venturi and Scott Brown. [44)] Needless to insist that the nature of the proposed and actually enacted projects is conceptually different from those discussed here. [W)] So is van Eyck's ideological project altogether. Not surprisingly, he liked at the same time to refer to Boccioni's motto "We are the primitives of a new sensibility" and to polemicize against his somewhat younger Philadelphia colleagues and what he saw as a paternalistic attitude towards mass taste. He loathed Las Vegas.

But was he aware that his own endeavors of placing the child at the core of a contemporary definition of public space ran exactly parallel in time to the founding of Disneyland (inaugurated 1955)? This coincidence and its roots in what one may call the anthropology of the contemporary city probably casts more light on both phenomena (and even on Las Vegas) than many people are ready to admit.

37) See von Moos 1987 (see note 1), pp. 88f. (Copley Square competition, 1966); p. 113 (Scranton mural project, 1976); pp. 116ff. (Western Plaza Project, Washington, D.C., 1977); and pp. 138f. (Welcome Park, Philadelphia, 1982).

38) Cf. Eco 1986 (see note 2), p. 10.

39) Among the many projects by VSBA that include miniature reproductions of buildings or architectural blow-ups there are many which explicitly refer to the world of toys, such as the underground exhibit of Franklin Court, Philadelphia (1972–76) or the Scranton mural project (1976). In their comments on the "Edison project," a program for prototypical schools (unpublished), the architects write: "We think that, just as little children like to play with doll houses, so older children will like to be in a doll's town, so to speak..." By implication, the comment applies to all their urban design projects that work with these techniques.

40) See von Moos 1987 (see note 1), pp. 134–37.

41) See Arthur Koestler, *Janus: A Summing Up* (London: Hutchinson, 1978), as referred-to by Thomas A. P. van Leeuwen, *The Skyward Trend of Thought: Five Essays on the Metaphysics of the American Skyscraper* (The Hague: AHA Books, 1986), p. 63.

42) See Alexander Tzonis and Liane Fefaivre, *Aldo van Eyck: Humanist Rebel* (Rotterdam: 010 Publishers, 1999), pp. 13–78.

43) Aldo van Eyck, *The Child, the City and the Artist* (Amsterdam: SUN, 2008), p. 19.

44) Although but recently published, the book referred to in the previous note was written in 1962 in connection with van Eyck's teaching at the University of Pennsylvania, Philadelphia. In *Complexity and Contradiction in Architecture*, van Eyck serves as an important theoretical reference for Venturi's concept of "ambiguity," In fact, Scott Brown had met van Eyck in 1960, when they both taught at Penn. Either she or Robert Venturi may have been among the recipients of "The Child, the City and the Artist" in its typescript form (cf. Francis Strauven, *Aldo van Eyck: The Shape of Relativity* [Amsterdam: Architectura & Natura, 1998], p. 474).

Photo credits

© Venturi, Scott Brown & Associates, Philadelphia: pp. 5, 12 top (photo: Denise Scott Brown), 14 top, 14 bottom, 18 bottom, 24 top, 24 bottom (photo: Denise Scott Brown), 28 bottom, 30 top and center, 35–159, 162–168, 178 top, 180 bottom left, 182 left, 184 bottom, 186 bottom right, 188 bottom left

Roy Lichtenstein © 2008, ProLitteris, Zurich: p. 176 top left

Mark Cohn (photo): p. 180 top left

Violette Cornelius (photo): p. 188 top

Timothy Hursley (photo): p. 178 bottom left, 178 bottom right

Metro-Goldwyn-Mayer Inc.: p. 18 top,

© Edward Ruscha, 1965: pp. 26 center and bottom, 28 top

© Stephen Shore, 1975: p. 26 top

Stanislaus von Moos (photo): pp. 180 top right, 188 bottom right

Matt Wargo (photo): p. 176 top right

Donald Appleyard, John Myer, Kevin Lynch: *The View from the Road,* MIT Press, Cambridge, MA, 1964: p. 30 bottom

Architectural Design, May 1969, © Archigram: p. 20 bottom

Architectural Forum, March 1968 (photo: Denise Scott Brown): p. 12 bottom

The Architectural Review, December 1950: p. 22 top

Peter Blake: *God's Own Junkyard,* Holt, Rinehart and Winston, New York, Chicago and San Francisco, 1964: pp. 22 bottom, 184 top

Herbert Gans: *The Urban Villagers*, Free Press of Glencoe, New York, 1962: p. 186 bottom left

Alan Gowans: *Styles and Types of North American Architecture*, Icon Editions, New York, 1992: p. 178 center

Erich Mendelsohn: *Amerika. Bilderbuch eines Architekten*, Verlag Rudolf Mosse, Berlin, 1926: p. 20 top

Robert Venturi, Denise Scott Brown and Steven Izenour: *Learning from Las Vegas,* MIT Press, Cambridge, MA, and London, 1972: p. 16 top

Robert Venturi, Denise Scott Brown and Steven Izenour: *Learning from Las Vegas,* MIT Press, Cambridge, MA, and London, 1977: p. 16 bottom

Captions

Note on attribution: All photographs were taken by the students and instructors of the "Learning from Las Vegas Research Studio," but an exact attribution is no longer possible in most cases.

The instructors of the research studio were Robert Venturi, Denise Scott Brown, and Steven Izenour. The students of the studio were Ralph Carlson, Tony Farmer, Ron Filson, Glen Hodges, Peter Hoyt, Charles Korn, John Kranz, Peter Schlaifer, Peter Schmitt, Dan Scully, Doug Southworth, Martha Wagner, and Tony Zunino.

Page 5
Mock-ups of casino signs, Young Electric Sign Company offices, Las Vegas, 1968

Page 35
Robert Venturi with mock-ups of casino signs, Young Electric Sign Company offices, Las Vegas, 1968

Page 36
Sketches of signs, 1968

Page 37
Robert Venturi with mock-up of the Frontier Hotel and Casino, Las Vegas, 1968

Page 38
Neon sign graveyard, Las Vegas, 1971

Page 39
Neon sign graveyard, Las Vegas, 1968

Page 41
Robert Venturi at the neon sign graveyard, Las Vegas, 1968

Page 43
Parking lot on the Strip, Las Vegas, ca. 1968

Page 44
Parking lot, Las Vegas, 1971

Page 45
Asphalt landscape with parking lot, 1969

Page 47
Preparations for the film *Las Vegas Deadpan,* Las Vegas, 1968

Pages 48–52
Sequence, upper Strip, driving north, Las Vegas, 1968

Page 55
"Gulf" gas station, Las Vegas, 1971

Page 56
"Liquor Drive-in," Los Angeles, 1968

Page 57
Gaslite Motel, Las Vegas, 1968

Page 59
"The Big Duck," shop in the shape of a duck on the highway on Long Island, Flanders, New York, ca. 1970

Page 60
"Big Donut Drive-in," Los Angeles, ca. 1970

Page 61
"Tail Pup," takeaway restaurant, Los Angeles, ca. 1970

Page 62
Advertisement signs on the highway, Las Vegas, 1968

Page 63
Billboard, Las Vegas, 1968

Page 64
"Tanya" Billboard on the Strip, Las Vegas, 1968

Page 67
Thunderbird Hotel and Casino, entrance, Las Vegas, 1968

Page 68
La Concha Motel, Las Vegas, 1968

Page 69
Flamingo Hotel and Casino sign, Las Vegas, 1968

Page 70
Riviera Hotel and Casino sign, Las Vegas, 1968

Page 71
Caesars Palace Hotel and Casino fountain, Las Vegas, 1968

Page 73
Students of the "Learning from Las Vegas Research Studio" filming on Fremont Street, Las Vegas, 1968

Page 74
Students of the "Learning from Las Vegas Research Studio" filming on Fremont Street, Las Vegas, 1968

Page 75
Landscape leaving Las Vegas, ca. 1965
Photo: Denise Scott Brown

Page 77
Landscape leaving Las Vegas, ca. 1965
Photo: Denise Scott Brown

Pages 79–82
American suburbia, Houston, ca. 1968

Page 84
Las Vegas Strip, 1971

Page 85 top
Las Vegas Strip silhouettes, 1966
Photo: Denise Scott Brown

Page 85 bottom
Las Vegas Strip silhouettes, 1966
Photo: Denise Scott Brown

Page 86
Casino entrance, Fremont Street, Las Vegas, 1968

Page 87
Golden Nugget, Fremont Street, Las Vegas, 1968